Romania, Culture, and Nationalism:
A Tribute to Radu Florescu

Romania, Culture, and Nationalism:

A Tribute to Radu Florescu

edited by Anthony R. DeLuca and Paul D. Quinlan

EAST EUROPEAN MONOGRAPHS
Distributed by Columbia University Press, New York
1998

EAST EUROPEAN MONOGRAPHS, NO. DXIX

Table of Contents

Preface

This spring, after forty-five years of teaching history at Boston College, Dr. Radu Florescu will officially retire as a full-time faculty member. Radu became a member of the History Department at Boston College in 1953 and over the years since has become one of the world's foremost authors on Romania and an untiring and compassionate champion of the country of his birth and that of his ancestors. His ability to bring us together into a larger Florescu academic family has led many of us to convene for academic symposia, social engagements, and family gatherings, all enriched by his presence and that of Nicole and their children in various corners of Europe and North America. On each occasion the genteel ambience of a Florescu gathering or the intimacy of a Florescu dinner has contributed to a greater appreciation of the intellectual and cultural exchange we have come to value so highly in our profession.

In many of our lives Radu has emerged as more than just a teacher. He has also been a mentor to us all. Some of us have had the pleasure of getting to know him better by writing our doctoral thesis under his supervision and working closely with him as a colleague and friend in the years following graduation. For many of us he was a dominant influence in our own professional careers, in part by inspiring us to devote our professional careers to the study of his beloved homeland. It is with this in mind that a number of his former students and close colleagues decided to put together a Festschrift in his honor.

Born in Bucharest into an old boyar family, Radu counts among his eminent ancestors Romanian heads of state, generals, diplomats, and academicians. With the outbreak of World War II in 1939 he was forced to interrupt his education and left his homeland to join his parents in London, where his father was serving as a Romanian diplomat. Little did he know at that time that he would not see Romania again for over a quarter of a century.

In 1947 Radu graduated from Oxford University. Not being able to return to his homeland, which was under the control of the Red Army and the Romanian communists, several years later he came to the United States, a country he was already familiar with having lived in Washington for a while in the 1930s when his father was, in essence, the head of the Romanian Embassy. In the 1950s he studied at the University of Texas and eventually received his doctorate from Indiana University.

During those difficult years as an emigre from Romania, Radu never lost his love and faith in the Romanian people and the country of his birth. In an article about him in the *Boston College Magazine* he is quoted as saying: "My vantage point upon Romania is that of a patriot, a lifelong student of my former country's history, and a descendant of a family with ancient roots inextricably linked to the nation's past. This symbolic relationship helps explain the passion I feel for the land of my ancestors."

In 1989 Radu's decades long dream finally came true as Ceauşescu's notorious dictatorship was overthrown and the way was open for Romania to become part of the European community of democratic-minded nations. Since then Radu has continued to do all he can to help and to publicize Romania within the United States. In keeping with the Florescu family tradition of service to Romania, the Romanian government appointed Radu Honorary Romanian Consul for New England. In his new capacity he has applied himself with the same grace, cosmopolitan outlook, energy and enthusiasm that inspired his scholarship and his teaching. In so doing he has set a standard as scholar, teacher, colleague, and friend to which all of us can proudly aspire.

It is with heartfelt thanks that we honor him for all that he has done for us and wish him a most appreciative *la revedere*!

Anthony R. DeLuca
Paul D. Quinlan

Introduction

Professor Radu R Florescu was born October 23, 1925 in Bucharest, the first of three children born to a Romanian diplomat. Florescu, descending from a old boyar family with deep roots in Romanian history, was educated in his early years by tutors in Bucharest and at their family country home in wine vineyards on the banks of the Argeş river. As a son of a diplomat, his schooling extended to Washington D.C., Berlin, London and Oxford where he finished his secondary education at St. Edwards school.

With a British Council Scholarship, Florescu was admitted in 1943 to Christ Church, Oxford. He specialized in 'Modern Greats' — later called P.P.E. (Politics, Philosophy, and Economics) — and would count among his tutors Sir Roy Harrod, A.J.P. Taylor, and The Earl of Longford. [He also attended lectures given by Hugh Trevor-Roper, who a quarter century later would review one of Florescu's Dracula books.] In 1948, Florescu won the Gladstone Memorial Historical Prize and finished his B.Litt under the supervision of Hugh Seton-Watson and Sir William Deakin, Winston Churchill's biographer.

To be sure, his love of all things Romanian had already taken shape as a diplomat's son; in Washington, for instance, he would proudly dress up on national day in traditional Romanian peasant outfits. But Florescu's academic orientation toward his homeland took form at Oxford, only a few years after he boarded one of the last West-bound Orient Express trains weeks before the outbreak of WW II. At his surprise 70th birthday party in Boston, he told friends that his pursuit of Romanian studies grew from that unexpected brutal rupture fifty years earlier.

9

Florescu's first professional teaching experience in the Americas was at a boys school, Bishops College, in Quebec province in Canada. He returned to Oxford where he met his French wife-to-be, Nicole; they were married December 2, 1950 at St. Gregory's and St. Augustine's in Oxford. With Nicole, Florescu boarded a steamship to Texas where he continued his doctoral work under Professor Thad Weed Riker, America's foremost authority on Romania, at the University of Texas. With Riker's sudden passing, the couple — now with a son, Nicky — moved to the University of Indiana, at that time one of the leading centers for East European studies in the United States. Florescu's doctoral thesis, *The Struggle Against Russia in the Romanian Principalities* was later published in 1961 and is still today considered a seminal piece of scholarship. A second edition was published by the Center for Romanian Studies in Iaşi in 1997 and it will be translated and published in Romanian in the near future.

To be sure, Florescu's formidable scholarly output focused heavily on the 19th century with academic papers on Stratford Canning and British diplomacy in the Balkans, the 1848 revolutions, and Alexandru Ioan Cuza and the reform of the Romanian military. But in almost 70 articles, he cut a wide swath across much of Romanian history, folklore, and politics. He delivered papers on Captain John Smith in Transylvania, the effect of the American War for Independence on the Romanians, Mircea Eliade, and on what he termed "Ceauşchism," to name but a few.

Florescu's quest for U.S. citizenship got a welcome boost from then-Texas Senator Lyndon B. Johnson and former House Speaker Sam Rayburn who introduced a special bill in the Congress. U.S. citizenship did not finally clear until 1961, but when it was approved by Congress the news made the front-page of newspapers in Boston. Nicole received her U.S. citizenship some years later, but also retained her French nationality.

From the Hoosier state, Florescu moved to Boston which would become his academic home until his retirement from Boston College in 1998. He began teaching at Boston College's School of Education before, as an Assistant Professor, he shifted over to the Arts and Sciences Faculty. In 1962, Florescu won a Senior fellowship at St. Antony's College, Oxford, where he took his family of three (Nick, John, and Radu) for a one year appointment. His fourth child, Alexandra, was born a year later in Boston.

Alongside his academic growth, Florescu's activities were far-ranging but always within an East European orbit. He hosted an East European Film Festival in New England, promoted the study of Albanian ethnicity, advised Senator Kennedy and the U.S. State Department on Romanian affairs; authored innumerable academic and journalistic pieces on Romanian history and politics; founded the Oxford Society of New England, as well as co-founded the Romanian Academic Society and the Society for Romanian Studies, created the East European Research Center (EERC) of New England, organized the Enescu Centenary at which Yehudi Menuhin performed privately, and parlayed his trophy-winning skill as a ping-pong player to serve as the faculty advisor to the Boston College Ping-Pong team.

Like his father, he played a quasi-diplomatic role between the U.S. and Romania. At Cohasset, our family home near Boston, an unending flow of academics, painters, authors, composers, and diplomats dropped in. One, Professor Constantine Giurescu, included a description of American (or, more precisely, Florescu) home life in a best-seller he would later write about his travels in America. But as the Ceauşescu regime toughened, the flow of Romanians slacked off even while other East European events carried on full steam.

In 1967, Florescu won the first of two Fulbright fellowships. For the first time since before the war, Florescu returned to Romania — spending his first night, ironically enough, in the Transylvanian town of Lugoj (where Bela Lugosi was born) — to begin research on Prince Alexander Ion Cuza. Soon after settling in Bucharest, he received a tip from his Boston College colleague, Ray McNally, to explore specific geographical and historical references contained in Bram Stoker's novel *Dracula*. His Fulbright mission was instantly rerouted, leading Florescu (and a number of Romanian associates) into a five year long pursuit — assisted by an IREX, another Fulbright, and American Philisophical Society grants — of the historical Dracula. Curiously, the first news of Florescu's research can be traced to President Nixon's historic 1969 visit to Romania. Florescu, who was advising the White House media on Romanian affairs, was himself unexpectedly questioned about his doings in Bucharest. *Readers Digest* quickly reported of "an American scholar on the trail of the real Dracula;" the story was splashed around the world by The Associated Press.

In Search of Dracula, the first of seven books by Florescu and McNally on the historical Dracula, was an immediate best-seller. The book drew the widest number of readers ever to Romanian history and catapulted the professors on the national and international media scene. *Time* magazine reported that the book sparked "a minor literary phenomena" and Johnny Carson's house band played spooky tunes as Florescu strolled on the NBC stage — though Carson did grant three minutes of serious discussion on the Romanian prince. *In Search of Dracula* was released in paperback and translated in eleven languages; in the process, the publicity churned up a massive underworld of Dracula buffs that would never leave Professor Florescu or his family alone. Nicole, however, manage to dampen a few of the fans' enthusiasm for late night home calls.

The collapse of the Ceauşescu regime dramatically reopened bridges and started an eastbound family pilgrimage, this time made up of the first generation Florescus. In these events, Florescu seized an opening to intensify and broaden his diplomatic and cultural activities. A few weeks after the emergence of the new government, Florescu returned to Bucharest to read an open letter from Senator Kennedy to the Romanian people on national television. Once back in the States, Florescu momentarily toyed with the idea of pursuing an open ambassadorship to Bucharest. Radu Jr. shipped off his French wife and son in 1991 to start an advertising business. In 1993, John chose to get married to his Idahoan wife in the same monastery where Radu's parents were John's grandparents married more than fifty years earlier. Alexandra moved to Prague shortly thereafter with her American-born Czech husband William Lobkowicz.

Florescu's scholarship continued unabated and moved beyond the grip of Dracula research. In 1976, he wrote *In Search of Frankenstein*, a book exploring the origins of Mary Shelley's gothic novel. The book formed the basis of an ABC network special hosted by Sir David Frost. Digging into other celebrated myths, Florescu presented academic papers on Gilles de Rais and the Pied Piper of Hamelin, among others. But he was most proud of his many doctoral students who pursued Romanian studies and took their knowledge to schools and universities as far away as India. For a younger generation, he also organized summer studies for gifted Romanian teenagers at a school for talented youths near Boston.

In 1996, the Romanian government asked Florescu to serve as Honorary Consul for Romania in New England. A small office on Boston's waterfront became the high-tech (the only consulate web page in Boston) headquarters for students, artists and scholars. Boston College honored Florescu with an Professor Emeritus of History Chair in 1996/97 and Harvard's Dunster House invited Florescu to serve as a Visiting Fellow in 1997. Prior to his retirement, Florescu donated his considerable collection of Romanian books to Boston College's Bapst library.

As his teaching obligations at Boston College slackened, Florescu's interest and presence in Romania intensified. With bases in Boston, Bucharest, and occasionally Cannes, where both his parents had passed away, he carried Romania's banner on a number of fronts. In 1997, he joined other experts at the White House in a vain effort to convince the Clinton Administration to include Romania in the first wave of NATO nations. He worked vigorously on the 1998 visit of President Constantinescu to the United Nations, and a month later, to the White House.

On the academic front, his interests turned back to family roots; he delivered papers on the diplomatic role his father — Romania's last Minister to London — played in the inter-war period. He also continued his research and writings on an earlier ancestor, General Ion Florescu, who was the founder of the modern Romanian army and who had served briefly as Prime Minister in the mid-19th century.

Like many things seen in retrospect, it seems unsurprising now that Florescu should have devoted his life to Romanian studies. His life circumstances made such a calling irresistable; in so doing, he comfortably takes position as the family's first professional historian and, one might rightly say, one of the most distinguished scholars of Romanian history.

John M. Florescu

Romania, Culture, and Nationalism:

A Tribute to Radu Florescu

Vlad Dracula and Pope Pius II:
The Prince and the Pope
From the Vatican Secret Archives[1]

Raymond T. McNally[2]
Boston College

This article is designed to analyze the views of the late fifteenth century Pope Pius II and his contemporary legate Nicholas Modrusa concerning Vlad Dracula and other Romanians during the late fifteenth century. The focus is upon an unpublished late fifteenth century manuscript located in the Vatican Secret Archives (Archivio Segretto Vaticano) and Photostated in Rome by the author of this article.[3] Annotations to the manuscript of Nicholas Modrusa, written later in another handwriting, wrongly attributed the work to Nicholas Segundinus, erroneously referring to Nic-

---

[1]An earlier version of this paper was read at the meeting of The Society for Romanian Studies held on November 16, 1994 at the Romanian Cultural Center in New York City.

[2]The author has known Prof. Florescu as a colleague and friend for over forty years. Their collaboration resulted in several jointly-authored books including the best selling *In Search of Dracula* and *Dracula, Prince of Many Faces*, both of which are still in print. At the Dracula Centennial Conference held in Los Angeles in 1997, their work *In Search of Dracula* was voted the best non-fiction book on Dracula, and they both received a special award for excellence in history. Dr. McNally is President of the Lord Ruthven Assembly of the International Association for the Fantastic and on July 3, 1996 he was admitted into the Order of the Knights of the Holy Sepulchre of Jerusalem and knighted for his research on the historical Dracula by order of the Orthodox Patriarch of Jerusalem.

colo Sagundino, the scholar of Greek and Latin who lived during the pontificate of Pius II and died in 1473. This doubly mistaken attribution subsequently led to confusion as to the real authorship of the document. However, evidence is now clear that the manuscript was written by Nicholas of Modrusa, the Italian papal diplomat, former papal legate to Hungary, and later Bishop of the Croatian See of Modrus from which he derived his pen name Nicholas of Modrusa. The manuscript consists of four books of history written in imitation of the four books of Leonardo Bruni and penned probably between 1473 and 1480, the last years in the life of Nicholas of Modrusa. After Modrusa's death in 1480, his personal library and manuscripts passed on into the Library of Pope Sixtus IV, where they have remained to our day.

The Modrusa manuscript is entitled De Bellis Gothorum (Concerning the Gothic Wars); its author was born in Cattaro, Italy some time before the year 1427. He studied in Venice under the celebrated scholar Paolo della Pergola, who taught there from 1434 to 1455. Nicholas soon rose in the ranks of the priesthood and papal curia, so that he was sent to Bosnia during the critical years of 1460 and 1461 to negotiate with the renegade heretical Hussite King Stephen of Bosnia. In 1463, Nicholas spent time in Gran Varadino in the company of the noted scholar and diplomat John Vitez, future bishop of Oradea and primate of Hungary; there Nicholas frequented John Vitez's rich library. During that same year, Pope Pius II sent Nicholas to Hungary as his papal delegate to the court of King Matthias Corvinus, as Nicolae Iorga has noted.[4] It was during this 1463-64 papal mission that Nicholas personally met the historical Romanian Prince Vlad Dracula, who had been captured by King Matthias in 1462 and was living in Hungary at that time. Nicholas later undertook a second diplomatic mission to Hungary. Then after the death of Pope Pius II in 1464, the subsequent Pope Paul II employed Nicholas as a bishop in the public offices of the Papal States until 1471. After the death of Paul II in 1471, Nicholas served as governor of Cesena under Pope Sixtus IV. He returned to Rome in January, 1473. He was then appointed as bishop to the See of Modrus in modern-day Croatia, where he wrote his history for seven years. He lived there until his death in 1480.

---

[3]The term Archivio Segretto Vaticano refers simply to the archives of the private and diplomatic papers of the popes. The author wishes to thank the authorities of the Vatican Library for permission to study and microfilm the manuscript of Nicholas Modrusa, now located in the Pope Sixtus IV collection.

[4]Iorga, Nicolae, *Geschichte des Osmanischen Reiches*, Vol. II, pp. 119-121.

In 1937, the notable Vatican archivist and scholar Monseignor Giovanni Mercati published a small portion of this late fifteenth century manuscript by Nicholas Modrusa.[5] Much of what Nicholas Modrusa had written in his diplomatic reports had been transmitted directly to the pope, who had included large portions of the Modrusa reports in his own Commentaries, which Pope Pius II wrote mainly at night as a kind of diary. Modrusa later repeated parts of his reports in this manuscript, the four volume history referred to above, now located in the Sixtus IV Collection of the Vatican Secret Archives. Although the Modrusa manuscript is very important for the study of Romanian history, no critical edition of it exists in any language, and the entire text has never been published in any form.

In his manuscript, Modrusa refers to the town of Thomis (today Constanţa) and the historical fact that the Roman poet Ovid spent his exile years there.[6] Modrusa also mentions that Ovid was fearful of the terrible onslaughts of the Getha, even though they were 500 miles eastward away from his place of exile. Modrusa cites how the ancient geographer Strabo demonstrated that the Dacians too, who inhabit the upper banks of the Danube, are Gethea, by arguing that they have the same customs and language as the Gethae.

Furthermore, concerning the ancient Roman province of Dacia, Modrusa states that the lower part, which consists of all the territory encompassed by the Ister (the Danube River) and the Boristen (the Borysthenes in Greek refers to the Dniepr River) as far as the banks of the sea, is possessed by the Vlacchi. So Modrusa held that the Vlachs occupied the entire territory bounded by the Danube and the Dniepr River all the way to the Black Sea. According to him, these Vlachs were once Romans, either exiles or soldiers, so named from their leader Flaccus. Now, by the change of a letter, they are called Vlacchi, a word by which not only that people but also all neighboring peoples today name Italians. What is important in that text is not Modrusa's evidently fanciful derivation of the word Vlach from the Roman conqueror of the Getae, Flaccus, but the fact that this statement proves that educated Europeans from the late fifteenth century, such as Nicholas Modrusa and Pope Pius II, considered the Vlachs to be a Latin-speaking people.

---

[5]Mercati, G. ed., "Notizie varii sopra Niccolo Modrussiense" *Opere Minore*, volume 4, Vatican City, 1937.

[6]During his decade of exile, Ovid claims to have learned the Getic and Sarmatic languages so well that he apparently even wrote a panegyric dedicated to Augustus Caesar in Getic verse, as he explains in *Ex Pont.*, IV, xii, pp. 19-23, but unfortunately for students of philology, that poem is lost.

Modrusa specifically cites that the Vlacchi offer this argument especially to account for their origins, that, although they speak the language of the Mysians, which is Illyrian, yet from the cradle they speak in a vernacular language which is Latin, which is by no means obsolete. Hence, though the Vlachs could speak another language, their native language was a kind of colloquial Latin. Furthermore, Modrusa states that the Vlachs preferred to communicate in the formal Roman language, as he writes that upon meeting with people whom they do not know, when they seek out a shared language, they ask whether the others know how to speak the Roman language. This same view is also set down in detail by Pope Pius II in Book Eleven of his *Commentaries*, which reads as if it came, more or less, directly from Modrusa's earlier diplomatic reports to the Pope, which it probably did.

Modrusa follows this with specific comments about the historical Vlad Dracula and states that this ruler of the Vlachs was a man named Draculus, whom he had met in Buda. It is interesting to note that Modrusa calls him by the Dracula name and not by any nickname such as Kasigli voevoda (the Impaling Prince), a negative appellation given him by his mortal enemies the Ottoman Turks and later unfortunately, in my opinion, repeated by some Romanian chroniclers, namely Țepeș (The Impaler). I think that it is high time that Romanian historians abandon that ignominious nickname from the Turks and call him by the name Vlad Dracula which is the way he signed his name in two surviving Transylvanian manuscripts. In addition, Dracula (or variations on that name) is the way he is known in Latin, Byzantine, German, and Russian sources. Fortunately during the post-Ceaușescu era most enlightened Romanian historians now call him Dracula and not the Impaler.

Modrusa follows with what is, as far as we know, the only eyewitness literary description of the historical Dracula still in existence. As Modrusa writes, he was not very tall but very stocky and strong, with a cold and terrible appearance, a strong aquiline nose, swollen nostrils, a thin and reddish face in which the very long eyelashes framed large, wide-open green eyes. The bushy eyebrows made the eyes appear threatening. The swollen temples increased the bulk of his head. A bull's neck connected to his head from which black curly locks hung on his wide-shouldered person.[7] The description appears to be

---

[7]Mercati, G. ed. "Notizie varii sopra Niccolo Modrussiense" *Opere Minore*, volume 4, Vatican City, 1937, pp. 247-249.

relatively authentic and fits not only with the famous Vlad Dracula portrait at Ambras Castle but also with a newly discovered full-length painting of Vlad Dracula at Forchtenstein Castle, an Esteshazy estate currently in Austria near Wiener-Neustadt. That important painting has the words on it in Latin: Dracula, the Prince and Voevod of Transalpine Wallachia, the most Fearsome Foe of the Turks.[8]

Furthermore, the fifteenth century manuscript by Kritoboulos from the Greek island of Imbros (now owned by Turkey) corroborates many of the facts cited in the Modrusa text.[9] Only one copy of the Kritoboulos manuscript exists in the entire world; it is now located in the Private Palace Library of the former Sultans at Topkapi Palace in Istanbul, where I studied it. In it there are references to the revolt of the Drakouli in 1462 and the uprising of the Getae meaning Wallachians; Kritoboulos sometimes uses the word Drakoulis in Greek as a singular nominative, and the term Drakouli as a Greek plural. This would fit in with the fact that members of that family were all referred to as Draculi (Drăculeşti in Romanian). The terms Dracoules and Drakoulios also appear in the text in the nominative singular respectively and Drakoulin in the accusative singular. Typically like other chroniclers, Kritoboulos sometimes confuses the father Vlad Dracul with his son Vlad Dracula. By the late 19th century, German scholar of the classics Karl Muehller, who published a highly defective edition of the Kritoboulos manuscript in 1870 and another defective edition in 1883, erroneously asserted that the word Drakouli is indeclinable (see p. 53 of the 1871 edition). That word is, in fact, declinable, since Modrusa himself does so in this very manuscript. Furthermore, Muehller foolishly attempted to correct the Kritoboulos text to conform to his own idiosyncratic notions about classical Greek writing, instead of leaving the text in its original Byzantine style! Another famous Byzantine historian Chalkokondyles called Vlad Dracula Drakoules and referred to his brother Radu as the other Drakoules, and another Byzantine historian, Dukas, used the term Draglios.

Returning to the Modrusa Latin manuscript, after describing Dracula's physical appearance Modrusa goes on to detail some of Dracula's cruelties and sees these atrocities reflected in Dracula's frightening

---

[8]The author of this current article has submitted a research article, written jointly with Mr. Benjamin LeBlanc, concerning this painting for exclusive publication in the Romanian review, *Magazin Istoric*.

[9]McNally, R. "The Fifteenth Century Manuscript of Kritoboulos of Imbros as an Historical Source for the History of Dracula," *East European Quarterly*, Vol. XXI, no. 1, March, 1987, pp. 1-13.

physiognomy. But Pope Pius II, evidently basing himself on the same description as found in the Modrusa text, came to a very different conclusion and considered Dracula to look outwardly as one of noble, grand stature. But then the reader must recall that Pope Pius II, though he knew about Vlad's atrocities, favored Dracula, because that Romanian prince was one of the last crusaders, like the Albanian leader Scanderbeg, who vigorously opposed and fought the Ottoman Turks.

The main foreign policy of Pope Pius II was to bolster what he called European Civilization against the Moslem Turkish invaders coming up through the Balkans. In fact, some experts consider that Pope Pius II invented the modern concept of European Civilization. The famous first battle of *Kossova polie* (The Field of the Blackbirds) in 1389 had proved to be only the initial salvo that was to lead to an eventual end to Serbian independence and open the European Christian road to the oncoming Turks. The situation of the papacy, and especially the severe internal crisis that faced that institution, is important to an understanding of the historical importance of Vlad Dracula. The Great Western Schism had resulted in forty years of fighting among three rival factions, each claiming to have a legitimate pope. Finally Martin V had emerged relatively victorious in 1417 and lasted until 1431, the year that Vlad Dracula was born in Transylvania. Martin's successor, Eugenius IV (1431-47), a Venetian and former Augustinian monk was only sixteen years of age when he took over the papacy, and local problems plagued his entire papal reign. Outstanding theologians such as Nicholas of Cusa were arguing that the supreme authority of the Roman Catholic Church should rest with the church councils and not with the pope; it was, as one historian put it, the last sunset glow of medieval constitutionalism. The Duke of Milan from the Visconti family invaded the papal states twice; the second attack forced Pope Eugenius to flee to Pisa and then to Florence, where the famous Cosimo de Medici protected him for nine years, until Eugenius was able to return to Rome. Nicholas V (1447-1455), who became pope one year before Dracula's first short reign in 1448, was a true Renaissance pope primarily interested in art and literature, as well as the rebuilding of the city of Rome. Pope Calixtus III (1455-58) from an old Spanish family of jurists, the Borgias, was pope during the early years of Dracula's reign. Calixtus raised two nephews to become cardinals, including Rodrigo, the future and later infamous Borgia pope Alexander VI, the father of Cesare and Lucretzia Borgia.

Some of these popes had hoped that the Duke of Burgundy, Philip the Good (1419-67) would become a full-time lasting crusader.

Philip had come to the Burgundian throne when his father, Duke John, had been murdered on the bridge of Monteran-font-Yonne and was committed to restoring Burgundian greatness and the old ideal of knighthood. Since his father John had once been taken captive by the Turks at the battle of Nicopolis and released only after the payment of a large ransom, his son Philip evidently had personal motives for revenge against the Turks. In fact, Duke Philip even issued a foolhardy challenge to fight the sultan himself in hand-to-hand combat.

In 1444, Philip the Good of Burgundy dispatched part of his fleet under the command of Walerand de Wavrin to try to stop the fleet of Sultan Murad II from crossing from Asia Minor into Europe. It was a failure, but the narrative of the expedition of 1444, written by the uncle of Walerand de Wavrin, Jean de Wavrin, remains one of the most detailed historical sources for information about the Romanian involvement in the campaign of 1444. The campaign culminated in the disastrous battle of Varna, where Vlad Dracula's elder brother Mircea led a contingent of Romanian soldiers against the Turks in clear violation of Vlad Dracul's peace treaty with the sultan. We know that Vlad Dracul had been obliged to leave both his sons, Vlad Dracula and his younger brother Radu, as hostages with the sultan as a kind of insurance policy that Dracul would no longer war against the Turks. Later Vlad Dracul complained to the citizens of Sibiu that they should not doubt his loyalty to the Christian cause, since he had not even spared the lives of his sons in the struggle. For, in going to war against the Turks, Vlad Dracul knew that he had risked the lives of his own sons still held hostage by the Turks. Fortunately for Dracula and Radu, the sultan Murad II decided not to kill the boys in retribution but to continue to use them as pawns in the game of diplomacy. In fact, in 1448 the sultan placed Dracula on the Wallachian throne, where he lasted only two months, due to intrigues.

Less than five years after Dracula's first short reign of 1448, early in the year 1453 an extremely ominous event took place, namely the final fall of Constantinople to the Ottoman Turks, part of a long line of victories by the Turks from the battle of Mantzikert in 1047 onwards. In early July of 1453, when Frederick III, the Holy Roman Emperor and King of Germany, heard of the tragic news of the fall of Constantinople, he had his secretary, Aeneas Sylvius Piccolomini, the future Pope Pius II, write on July 12th to the then Pope Nicholas V:

> But what is this execrable news which is borne to us concerning Constantinople? My hand trembles, even as I write; my soul is horrified, yet neither is it able to restrain its indigna-

tion, nor express its misery. Alas, wretched Christianity...
Alas, how many names of great authors have now perished!
It is a second death for Homer and Plato. Aeneas Sylvius Piccolomini, with his deep love of antiquity, was lamenting that
just as Troy, that famous bastion of Greek civilization in Asia
Minor had fallen to the mainland Greeks, so for a second
time Greek civilization was extinguished in Asia Minor, only
this time not by fellow Greeks from the mainland but by
Moslem Turks.

According to Aeneas Sylvius, Pope Nicholas V achieved some
fame for many of his undertakings, but his reign was forever stained by
the fall of Constantinople.

It is historically correct that Pope Nicholas V had not been a great
promoter of crusades against the Turks. He took the conservative position that without a real working unification of the two churches, Catholic and Orthodox, there would be no substantial western help for
their eastern brothers. Only after the fall of Constantinople did Pope
Nicholas belatedly issue a papal bull on September 30, 1453, in which
he denounced Sultan Mehmet II as the great red dragon with seven
heads crowned by seven diadems with ten horns as described by St.
John in the *Apocalypse*. Pope Nicholas even offered a plenary indul-
gence to all who would take part in a crusade against the infidel Turks
for six months by the date of February 1, 1454. There were, of course,
few takers from the West. Crusading was no longer popular.

The main Christian hope centered on John Hunyadi, the famous
White Knight of Christendom. At the siege of Belgrade in 1456, the
final Turkish assault began on the eve of July 21st. Roughly 60,000
Christian troops faced some 100,00 Turkish soldiers. The noted orator,
John of Capistrano, later canonized by the Roman Church, preached a
Holy War. Surprisingly, the relatively small army of crusaders won on
July 22nd. When the news of the Christian victory reached Rome on
August 6th, the then Pope Calixtus pronounced it the happiest day in
his life. But the eventual price of victory was high; John Hunaydi died
of the plague on August 11, 1456, at Belgrade, and Europe stood in
dire need of a new champion crusader. Vlad Dracula, the ruler of a
small country in southeastern Europe, rose to fill the gap, at least in
mind of Aeneas Sylvius [NICHOLAS I] who was elected pope on August 19, 1458,
two years after the death of Hunyadi.[10]

---

[10]See Florescu, R. and Raymond McNally, *Dracula, Prince of Many Faces* (Little
Brown, 1989).

The main reign of Vlad Dracula from 1456 to 1462 was destined to coincide roughly with the short and tumultuous pontificate of Pope Pius II, Aeneas Sylvius Piccolomini, from 1458 to 1464. Born in the Tuscan town of Corsignano in 1405, Aeneas was a self-made man. He was the descendant of an illustrious Sienese family that had fallen on hard times. After attending the University of Siena, he worked in the diplomatic service of Frederick of Hapsburg, who had Aeneas crowned Poet Laureate. Aeneas gained a reputation of leading a Renaissance libertine life as a youth and was famed for having penned what many considered to be salacious poetry. He had also later functioned as private secretary to Cardinal Capranica at the Church Council of Basle. He had more than thirty years of experience in public affairs before being elected pope. He hoped to halt the Turkish advance upon Europe through the Balkans and eventually turn back that tide.

Besides Vlad Dracula, there was only one notable crusader left, Scanderbeg of Albania. In September of 1457, Scanderbeg annihilated a Turkish army under the command of Isa Bey in the mountains of Albania. But during the spring of 1458 the Turkish army led by Mahmud Pasha marched into Serbia and launched a new series of attacks in the heart of the Balkans. By the year 1458, the Turks captured Athens, and by the end of the year, the Turks held all of Serbia and turned it into a *pashalik*. In that same year Matthias Corvinus, Dracula's contemporary, became King of Hungary, and Pope Pius II hoped to interest the Hungarian King in crusading.

Pope Pius II formally launched a new crusade against the Turks at the council of Mantua in 1459. The Venetians alone were capable of supplying a fleet, but they proved unwilling to do so. Even the seemingly ever-eager Philip the Good, Duke of Burgunday, withdrew his support, evidently under pressure from King Louis XI, The Spider King of France. Philip came up with a list of excuses for failing to respond to the Pope's call to arms: he was having trouble with his son who wanted to rule and his own health was bad, etc. Instead of fighting, Philip argued for an early version of a containment policy, i.e., let the Turks have what they have taken but try not to let them march any further. This containment policy failed, as the Turks responded by capturing Mistra and Thebes in 1460 and Trebizond in 1461.

When news of Dracula's initial victories against the Turks in 1462 reached the ears of Pope Pius II, he was lavish in his praise of the bravery of that Romanian ruler. But time was running out for both the pope and Dracula. In 1462 the Hungarian King accused Dracula of treason and produced some obviously fake letters for proof of his treachery. Even then most scholars considered the documents to be poor forgeries probably concocted by some of Dracula's Saxon foes at the court of Matthias Corvinus. Pius II himself did not believe in the accusations made against Vlad Dracula and correctly intuited that King Matthias had trumped up the charges in order to avoid supporting Dracula's campaign financially as the Pope had ordered. Nonetheless, Dracula was captured by Corvinus's minions at Castle King's Rock (the ruins of which I specifically located with the help of the young, gifted Romanian scholar Ştefan Andreescu on the road outside Braşov) in 1462.[11]

Just before his death at Ancona in 1464 when the pope was trying to encourage another crusade against the Turks, he gave 40,000 gold coins to the Venetian leader Christoforo Moro to transmit to the Hungarian King Matthias Corvinus in order to finance a new crusade against the Turks. In the meantime, Dracula's imprisonment and subsequent house arrest had been dropped, and he was even allowed to reside in a house in Pest across the Danube River from Buda. (Later Dracula would marry into the Hungarian royal family of Matthias Corvinus and attempt to regain his Wallachian throne in 1476.)

On August 11, 1464, Pope Pius II died; his hopes of crushing the Moslem Turkish onslaught were shattered. Scanderbeg died four years later, and by 1476 Dracula himself would follow the pope and the Albanian freedom-fighter into the grave.

It is ironic that today Prince Dracula is famous all over the world, whereas few people recall anything at all about Pope Pius II. It was the Irish author Bram Stoker (1847-1912) who resurrected the historical Dracula as a fictional vampire. In novels and on stage and screen, Dracula has achieved a special kind of fame denied to the pope, for, as far as we know, no author of fiction has ever attempted to resurrect Pope Pius II as a vampire, in order to bestow on him a bit of human immortality apparently exclusively reserved for the historical Dracula.

---

[11]Ştefan Andreescu and Raymond McNally, "Exactly Where was Dracula Captured in 1462?" *East European Quarterly,* XXIII, no. 3, September, 1989, pp. 269-281.

Vlad III Dracula
and his Relations with
the Boyars and the Church

Kurt W. Treptow
Center for Romanian Studies, Iaşi

The true story of Vlad III Dracula has been shrouded in myth.[1] Outside of Romania, much of it, of course, is tied to vampire myths and the famous novel by Bram Stoker. Within Romania, other myths obscure the history of the famous fifteenth century Wallachian prince Vlad III Dracula.[2] Communist historiography created the image of Dracula as a class hero who struggled to curb the abuses of the evil boyars. This thesis has been repeated so often that it is usually taken for granted. Precisely for this reason the relationship between Vlad and his boyars must be reconsidered.

Vlad III Dracula has often been presented not only as a crusader against the expansion of the Ottoman Turks in Southeastern Europe, but

---

[1]This article is dedicated to Professor Radu R. Florescu, one of the first scholars to undertake a serious and thorough study of the history of Vlad III Dracula.

[2]While Vlad is often referred to in Romania as Vlad Ţepeş, or the Impaler, this name is first attested to in the mid-sixteenth century. I prefer to use Vlad III Dracula because he signed several documents using the name Dracula and is also referred to in texts of the time by this name. The name means "son of Dracul," after his father, Vlad II Dracul, who was referred to as such after Emperor Sigismund of Luxemburg made him a member of the Order of the Dragon, a medieval crusading order.

also against the increasing power of the rich boyars in his country. The thesis, developed by Barbu T. Câmpina, that Vlad defeated the armies of Sultan Mehmed II in the summer of 1462 and only lost his throne later that year as a result of a revolt by the great boyars who joined Radu cel Frumos against the Prince who had impinged upon their feudal privileges throughout the preceding six years,[3] has been accepted and further elaborated in many other recent works.[4] It is, nevertheless, a question which merits further discussion.

Literary sources from the fifteenth century provide us with some information concerning the relations between the Romanian prince and his boyars. For example, the Byzantine chronicler Laonic Chalkondyles wrote:

> To strengthen his power, he killed, in a short time, twenty-thousand men, women, and children; he surrounded himself with a number of distinguished and devoted soldiers and servants to whom he gave the money, wealth, and social positions of those he had killed, so that, in a short time, he brought about a radical change, and this man completely altered the organization of Dacia [Wallachia].[5]

The German stories about Dracula provide even more specific information:

> he asked his boyars to come to his house for a feast. When the feast was over, Dracula went to the oldest of them and asked how many princes he thought the country had had? And then he asked the others, one by one, the same question. They all said what they knew; one answered fifty, another thirty, but none of them answered that there had been seven of them, so he had them all impaled. There were five hundred of them altogether.[6]

---

[3]See Barbu T. Câmpina, "Complotul boierilor și răscoala din Țara Românească din iulie-noiembrie, 1462," pp. 599-624 in *Studii și referate privind istoria României*, pt. I-a (București, 1954). This idea was originally suggested by Gh. Ghibănescu at the end of "Vlad Țepeș (studiu critic)" in *Arhiva, organul societății științifice și literare din Iași*, vol. VIII, no. 7-8, pp. 373-417 and vol. VIII, no. 9-10, pp. 497-520 (1897). Câmpina's version is heavily dosed in Marxist-Leninist ideology.

[4]See, for example, Nicolae Stoicescu, *Vlad Țepeș, Prince of Wallachia* (Bucharest, 1978).

[5]Laonic Chalcocondil, *Expuneri istorice*, ed. Vasile Grecu, (București, 1959), p. 283 (Bk. IX). An English translation of the section of Chalkondyles' chronicle concerning Vlad III Dracula can be found in Kurt W. Treptow, ed., *Dracula, Essays on the Life and Times of Vlad Țepeș* (New York, 1991), Appendix V, pp. 323-333.

Native chronicles also tell of Vlad's efforts to assert his authority vis-à-vis the boyars:

> He did something to the citizens of Târgoviște because he found that the boyars of Târgoviște had buried his brother (Mircea) alive. As he wanted to know the truth he looked for his brother in the ground and found him buried face down.

> So when it was Easter and all the citizens were at the feast and while the young were dancing, he unexpectedly captured all of them. All those who were old he had impaled around the city, while those who were young, together with their wives and children, all dressed up for Easter, he had taken to Poienari where they worked to build the fortress there until their clothes fell off and they all remained naked. For this reason he was named Țepeș (the Impaler).[7]

This evidence points to the fact that Vlad III Dracula sought to strengthen the central authority of the state to preserve his position and enhance his power, a policy that explains Chalkondyles' account according to which:

> he sent for some of his boyars, one by one, whom he thought might be treasonous and plot to overthrow him, and he had them mutilated and impaled, together with their wives, children, and servants...[8]

---

[6]See P.P. Panaitescu, "The German Stories about Vlad Țepeș," pp. 185-196 in Treptow, *Dracula: Essays...*, p. 191. Ștefan Andreescu argues that in the story Vlad answers 7 because this is the number of Princes he would have considered as being legitimate in the line of succession from the founding of Wallachia: Basarab I, Nicolae Alexandru, Vladislav I, Radu I, Mircea cel Bătrân, Vlad Dracul, and himself. This is stretching the evidence too far for Dracula would not have had any reason to consider, for example, Mihail I, who had been Mircea's designated successor as being illegitimate (see Ștefan Andreescu, *Vlad Țepeș (Dracula): Între legendă și adevăr istoric*, (București, 1976), p. 81).

[7]*Istoria Țării Românești, 1290-1690: Letopisețul Cantacuzinesc*, eds. Constantin Grecescu and Dan Simionescu, (București, 1960), p. 205. For other variants see ibid., p. 4 and Căpitanul Constantin Filipescu (Radu Popescu), *Istoriile domnilor Țării Românești cuprinzând Istoria Munteană de la început până la 1688*, ed. Nicolae Iorga, (București, 1902), pp. 15-16. This certainly does not refer to all the citizens of Târgoviște but a group who Vlad suspected of having betrayed his father during the Hungarian invasion led by John Hunyadi in 1447. Ștefan Andreescu convincingly argues that this occurred on Sunday, 17 April 1457 (see Andreescu, *Vlad Țepeș (Dracula)*, p. 83). We know from documentary sources that Vlad was in Târgoviște on 16 April 1457, and, as this was the first Easter of his reign, it is likely that he would have taken revenge on his father's opponents early on. This episode is also recounted by the Saxon chronicler Johann Filstich (1684-1743), *Tentamen Historiae Vallachicae / Încercare de istorie românească*, ed. Adolf Armbruster, trans. Radu Constantinescu, (București, 1979), p. 103.

Vlad himself alluded to such a program in a letter to the officials of Braşov on 10 September 1456, shortly after coming to the Wallachian throne for the second time:

> You can judge for yourselves that when a man or a prince is strong and powerful he can make peace as he wants to; but when he is weak, a stronger one will come and do what he wants to him.[9]

While these sources give us some indications about the relationship between Vlad III Dracula and his boyars, they, by themselves, are inadequate to draw any conclusions. Literary works, in general, are filled with exaggerations. Chalkondyles, for example, presents his account of Vlad's domestic policy merely as an introduction to the main part of his story — the war with the Turks in 1462. The Byzantine chronicler had never been to Wallachia and cannot be considered as a reliable source concerning domestic matters. He also had an interest in portraying Vlad as a formidable enemy to merit the personal attention of the Ottoman Sultan. Likewise, the German Stories were themselves written to justify Matthias Corvinus' imprisonment of Dracula in 1462. They were also extremely biased in light of Vlad's conflicts with the German cities of Transylvania. Thus, only by using the available documents in conjunction with these literary sources can we gain an understanding of the true nature of Vlad III Dracula's relations with the boyars.

Unfortunately, only four internal documents from the reign of Vlad III Dracula still exist that list the members of the *sfatul domnesc*. Nevertheless, an examination of these documents does provide us with some evidence about his relations with the boyars. First of all, these documents support the literary evidence which claims that Dracula's domestic policies were directed toward consolidating his authority. Only two members of the *sfatul domnesc* on 16 April 1457 remained on the *sfatul domnesc* on 10 February 1461: Voico Dobriţa, who appears to have been the most influential boyar at Vlad's court, and Iova *vistier*.[10] The significance of this is illustrated by the fact that the composi-

---

[8]Chalcocondil, *Expuneri istorice*, p. 283.

[9]Nicolae Iorga, *Scrisori de boieri, Scrisori de Domni*, 2nd ed., (Vălenii-de-Munte, 1925), pp. 164-165. An English translation of this letter can be found in Treptow, *Dracula, Essays...*, Appendix IV.B, pp. 313-314.

[10]Docs. 115 and 120 in *Documenta Romaniae Historica. B. Ţara Românească, vol. I (1247-1500)*, eds. P.P. Panaitescu and Damaschin Mioc, (Bucureşti, 1966), pp. 198-200, 205-206.

tion of the *sfatul domnesc* of other fifteenth century Wallachian princes does not indicate any comparable trends over a similar period of time. Thus, Dracula's attempts to exert his authority over the *sfatul domnesc* were unique in fifteenth century Wallachian politics, thereby supporting the literary evidence.

A careful examination of the internal documents also tells us that the changes in the *sfatul domnesc* were the result of a carefully planned policy, gradually introduced throughout the reign of the Wallachian prince. Of the twelve boyars on Vlad II's *sfatul domnesc* on 16 April 1457, at least three — Manea Udriște, Stan al lui Negre, and Cazan al lui Sahac[11] — also served in the *sfatul domnesc* of his predecessor, Vladislav II. This is not at all surprising as the same situation is encountered whenever there was a change of princes during the fifteenth century — with one notable exception — even when the transition occurred as part of a military conflict. The *sfatul domnesc* from 5 March 1458, comprised of nine names, includes 4 new ones (in bold). That of 20 September 1459, comprised of 11 names, includes 3 changes (in bold). The final list from 10 February 1461 includes 4 new names (in bold) among the members of the *sfatul domnesc*:[12]

MEMBERS OF THE *SEATUL DOMNESC* DURING THE REIGN OF VLAD III DRACULA, 1456-1462

16 April 1457	5 March 1458	20 Sept. 1459	10 Feb. 1461
Manea Udriște	*jupan* Dragomir Șacal	*jupan* Dragomir Șacal	*jupan* Voico Dobrița
Codrea *vornic*	*jupan* Voico Dobrița	*jupan* Voico Dobrița	*jupan* Galeș vornic
Dragomir Șacal	*jupan* Stan al lui Negre *vornic*	*jupan* Stan vornic	*jupan* Stepan Turcul

[11]The best work on the structure and function of the *sfatul domnesc* is Nicolae Stoicescu, *Sfatul domnesc și marii dregători din Țara Românească și Moldova, sec. XIV-XVII*, (București, 1968). The standard reference book for the high officials serving on the *sfatul domnesc* in Wallachia and Moldavia is Nicolae Stoicescu, *Dicționar al marilor dregători din Țara Românească și Moldova*, (București, 1971).

[12]Docs. 115, 117, 118, and 120 in *Documenta Romaniae Historica, B*, vol. 1, pp. 198-206.

Voico Dobrița	Iova *vistier*	*jupan* Stepan Turcul	*jupan* Cazan *logofăt*
Stan al lui Negre	Buda *stolnic*	*jupan* Oprea	**Buriu** *spătar*
jupan Duca	Gherghina *comis*	*jupan* ?	Iova *vistier*
Cazan al lui Sahac	Stoica *paharnic*	Bratul de la Milcov	Oprița (Oprea) *paharnic*
Oprea *logofăt*	Pătru *stratornic*	Moldovean *spătar*	**Linart** *stolnic*
Moldovean spătar	**Cazan** *logofăt*	Iova *vistier*	Gherghina *comis*
Buda *stolnic*	xxx	??? *spătar*	Radul *stratornic*
Milea *paharnic*	xxx	Tocsaba *stolnic*	xxx
Iova *comis*	xxx	Stoica *paharnic*	xxx
xxx	xxx	Gherghina *comis*	xxx

It is interesting to note the presence of Radul *stratornic*, a member of Vladislav II's court,[13] in the final list. It must also be mentioned that the absence of a particular boyar from a list may only mean that for any number of reasons he could not be present when a specific document was issued. This could, for example, explain the absence of Oprea from the list of 1458, although he reappears on the two subsequent lists and continues to be a loyal supporter of Dracula even after his overthrow in 1462.[14]

---

[13]Docs. 112 and 113 in *Documenta Romaniae Historica, B*, vol. 1, pp. 195-197.

[14]See the letter of Basarab Laiotă to Brașov dated 9 May 1476, Doc. CCLXXVIII in Ioan Bogdan, *Documente privitoare la relațiile Țării Românești cu Brașovul și Țara Ungurească*, (București, 1905), p. 333, complaining that they lend support to his enemies Oprea *logofăt* and Voico al Tatului. Oprea *logofăt* is also mentioned in a letter of Radu cel Frumos to Brașov, pardoning certain boyars who fled after the war of 1462, but not Oprea (see Doc. LXXXI in *ibid.*, pp. 104-106; and Doc. 77 in Grigore Tocilescu, *534 documente istorice slavo-române*, (București, 1931), pp. 73-74).

Evidence of Vlad's efforts to eliminate his opponents from the *sfatul domnesc* is also found in a letter from 23 April 1459 referring to a boyar *Koldra* who had 3,000 gold florins worth of property in Braşov. This may refer to Codrea, who is no longer found among the members of the *sfatul domnesc* after 16 April 1457. Codrea was either killed by Dracula[15] or died in exile. Likewise, a letter from King Matthias Corvinus of Hungary to Braşov, dated 4 July 1458, ordered the councilors of the city to turn over all the wealth of Mihail *logofăt*, a member of the *sfatul domnesc* during the reign of Vladislav II, who had been killed by Dracula.[16]

Thus, these documents make it clear that Vlad III Dracula conducted a policy aimed at strengthening his authority, but at the same time they indicate that his efforts in this direction were not as sudden or drastic as described in the literary sources. They also contradict the theory put forth by some historians that 1459 marks the turning point when Vlad succeeded in consolidating his authority over the boyars;[17] indicating instead that it was a policy gradually implemented throughout his reign.

A deed issued by Prince Mircea Ciobanul on 1 April 1551 sheds further light on Vlad's relations with the boyars. It refers to a revolt led by a boyar, Albu cel Mare, against Dracula (here for the first time referred to as Ţepeş) a century before:

> In the time of Vlad voievod Ţepeş there was a boyar called Albu cel Mare, who took the above mentioned villages (Glodul and Hinţea) by force and devastated the holy monastery (Govora)...
>
> In the days of Vlad voievod Ţepeş, this boyar, Albu cel Mare, tried to take the throne from him, but Vlad voievod went with his army against him and killed him together with his whole family. When Vlad voievod saw the holy monastery devastated, he granted these villages, Glodul and Hinţea, to it."[18]

---

[15]This is the conclusion of Ştefan Andreescu, *Vlad Ţepeş (Dracula)*, p. 83, but the circumstances of Codrea's removal from the *sfatul domnesc* and his death are unknown, therefore any such conclusion is pure speculation. For the original document see Hurmuzaki, *Documente*, vol. XV/1, p. 52.

[16]Doc. 3128 in Gustav Gündisch, *Urkundenbuch zur Geschichte der Deutschen in Siebenbürgen*, vol. VI, (1458-1473), (Bukarest, 1981), pp. 18-19.

[17]See, for example, Ştefan Andreescu, *Vlad Ţepeş (Dracula)*, pp. 84-85; and Radu Florescu and Raymond T. McNally, *Dracula: A Biography of Vlad the Impaler, 1431-1476*, p. 61.

While this document may indicate an organized resistance on the part of some of the great boyars against Dracula's centralization policy, it may just as well merely indicate a continuation of the conflict between the two families. This conflict had its origins in the days of Prince Alexandru Aldea, who, together with his leading boyar Albu, opposed Vlad Dracul's attempts to take the throne.[19] It is also possible that the document refers to Vlad Dracul instead of his son.[20] Given these circumstances, it cannot be relied upon as a source of evidence about Vlad III Dracula's relations with the boyars.

Therefore, the available evidence tells us that Vlad did in fact gradually implement a policy aimed at increasing the central authority of the prince. The evidence, however, to indicate an open conflict between the Prince and the boyars is quite limited. Indeed, most of his opponents were in exile in Transylvania as reflected in the Prince's letters to Braşov and Sibiu. For example, in an undated letter to Braşov, Vlad complains:

> And again I say to your graces as my good friends: there is to be found in your midst Mihail logofăt and Pardo, my enemies. I have forgiven all the others, but these I have not forgiven, and as I have not forgiven them, so you should banish them if you are friends of my majesty.[21]

There also exists a letter to Braşov dated 4 June 1460 in which Dracula asks the councilors of Braşov to turn over his enemies to Voico Dobriţa, one of his leading boyars, or if they would not come with him, to expel them from the city in his presence. The text indicates that this request was in accord with an agreement negotiated by Vlad's emissary, Cârstian.[22]

---

[18]"Doc. 3, Mircea Ciobanul, Prince of Wallachia, confirms to the monastery of Govora the villages of Glodul and Hinţea," in *Documente privind istoria României, veacul XVI, B. Ţara Românească, vol. III (1551-1570)*, (Bucureşti, 1952), pp. 3-5.

[19]Ştefan Andreescu argues that Albu cel Mare was in fact the son of Albu Taxabă, the most influential boyar at the court of Prince Alexandru Aldea, who attacked the Monastery of Govora in revenge for Vlad Dracul's depriving his family of Glodul and Hinţea (see Ştefan Andreescu, *Vlad Ţepeş (Dracula)*, p. 82). Yet it seems quite possible that Albu cel Mare refers to the same Albu who was the leading boyar at Aldea's court and a fierce opponent of Vlad Dracul, and that the events described in the document from the mid-16th century occurred during the reign of Vlad Dracul, they being confused over one hundred years later with the reign of Vlad III Dracula.

[20]As Vlad Dracul is credited with founding the Monastery of Govora, he may also have donated the above-mentioned villages to it.

The situation faced by Dracula was not unusual. Almost every Prince of Wallachia during the fifteenth century faced a similar situation.[23] Even when relations between the two were good, the Saxon cities preferred to maintain some political leverage over their larger neighbor to the south; therefore, they regularly harbored pretenders to the throne or their supporters, regardless of who was the actual prince. There is no indication in the documents that the problem faced by Dracula was substantially greater than that faced by other rulers of Wallachia during this period. Yet, for a variety of political reasons and his unusual zeal for dispensing with his enemies, he responded to this threat with far greater violence than most others.

A review of the internal documents from Vlad's reign also shows that they preserve all of the formulae common to such land grants in the fifteenth century, including the traditional exemption clauses from feudal dues. For example, in the *hrisov* (deed) issued by the Prince on 20 September 1459, through which he granted to Andrei and his sons lands in Poiana of Stev and in Ponor, we find the following clauses:

> And if one of them will die, the land will remain with the others, without any taxes...

> All of this is to be their land and to be inherited by their children, grandchildren, and great-grand-children, without any taxes such as for sheep, pigs, water, and wine, or any special services, such as cutting hay, trees, etc., that is to say all great and small services. And no one should dare cause any trouble for them, no clerk or tax collector, and none of the boyars or

---

[21]Doc. LXVII in Ioan Bogdan, *Documente privitoare la relațiile Țării Românești cu Brașovul și Țara Ungurească în secolul XV și XVI*, pp. 90-91. Bogdan dates this document between 1456 and 1458. As is known, from the letter of Matthias Corvinus cited earlier, Mihail *logofăt* was killed by Dracula prior to July, 1458. We are able to date this letter more precisely thanks to another document in which Mihail Szilagyi orders Brașov and Sibiu to receive Mihail *logofăt* and other refugees from Wallachia and Moldavia, together with their families, and to shelter them and protect them from harm (see Annexa II in Gündisch, "Cu privire la relațiile lui Vlad Țepeș cu Transilvania," pp. 692-695. Szilagyi's letter is dated 28 March 1458, therefore, this letter from Dracula most likely dates from the period April-June, 1458; Pardo is unknown, not being mentioned in other sources. This document is also found in Gr. Tocilescu, *534 documente istorice slavo-române*, Doc. 70, pp. 67-68.

[22]Doc. CCLXII in Bogdan, *Documente privitoare la relațiile Țării Românești cu Brașovul și Țara Ungurească*, pp. 320-321.

[23]For example, see the letter of Basarab Laiotă to Brașov dated 9 May 1476, Doc. CCLXXVIII in Bogdan, *Documente privitoare la relațiile Țării Românești cu Brașovul și Țara Ungurească*, p. 333, complaining that they lend support to his enemies Oprea *logofăt* and Voico al Tatului.

servants of my realm, because whoever dares to harm them will be severely punished.[24]

Thus, it can be said with certainty that while Vlad attempted to increase his own authority, he had no intention of doing so by imposing upon the traditional feudal prerogatives of the boyars. Instead, he sought to strengthen his own faction amongst the nobility by promoting the interests of his relatives and friends. This was a normal policy for his time although he pursued it with more vigor than others. Thus, it is not possible to see Dracula as some sort of class hero or even to assert that he tried to impinge upon the social status of the boyars. It is clear that he had no such intention.

There is no evidence to indicate that Vlad's boyars helped his brother Radu cel Frumos to attain the throne. It is only in the summer of 1464 that one of Vlad's boyars, Voico Dobriţa, is reconciled with the new prince and again joins the *sfatul domnesc*.[25] The loyalty of Dracula's boyars is also confirmed by letters of Radu cel Frumos to Braşov and Sibiu, complaining that they were harboring boyars, loyal to his brother, who had taken refuge there.[26] Likewise, some of the boyars loyal to Vlad during his second reign can also be identified among his supporters in 1476 as he prepared to take the throne for a third time. Thus, we find Basarab Laiotă, in a letter dated 9 May 1476, complaining to Braşov that they were supporting his enemies, especially Oprea *logofăt*, a member of Vlad's *sfatul domnesc*, 1456-1462.[27] There is also a letter from Cârstian, *pârcălab* of Târgovişte, announcing the victory of Dracula over Basarab Laiotă in 1476 to the citizens of Braşov.[28] This is the same Cârstian referred to in the letter of Vlad to Braşov, dated 4 June 1460, mentioned earlier.

---

[24]Doc. 118 in *Documenta Romaniae Historica, B*, vol. I, pp. 203-204.

[25]Doc. 124 in *Documenta Romaniae Historica, B*, vol. I, pp. 209-213, dated 10 July 1464.

[26]See Doc. LXXXI in Bogdan, *Documente privitoare la relaţiile Ţării Româneşti cu Braşovul şi Ţara Ungurească*, pp. 104-106; and Doc. 4 in S. Dragomir, *Documente nouă privitoare la relaţiile Ţării Româneşti cu Sibiul*, (Bucureşti, 1935), p. 13.

[27]Doc. CCLXXVIII in Bogdan, *Documente privitoare la relaţiile Ţării Româneşti cu Braşovul şi Ţara Ungurească*, p. 333. The document also mentions Voico al lui Tatu who is not identified in the existent documents from Dracula's second reign, but whose father Tatu Sârbul was among the loyal supporters of Vlad father, Vlad Dracul. See Nicolae Stoicescu, *Dicţionar al marilor dregători din Ţara Românească şi Moldova (sec. XIV-XVII)*, (Bucureşti, 1971), pp. 25, 28. There is also a similar letter dated 28 February 1476 in which Basarab Laiotă calls on Braşov to expel his enemies, see Doc. CI in Bogdan, *Documente privitoare la relaţiile Ţării Româneşti cu Braşovul şi Ţara Ungurească*, pp. 126-127.

Therefore, the little information that the documents provide about Vlad III Dracula's relations with the boyars clearly contradicts the accepted image. Although Vlad tried to strengthen his authority, this cannot be construed as an attack on the privileges of the boyars. After all, the prince and the boyars had essentially the same interest, consolidating and strengthening the power of the state which protected their status and privileges. *Thus, it is better to view Vlad III Dracula's policy as being one aimed at strengthening and securing the positions of his family and friends — typical behavior for his times — instead of being one directed against the boyars as a social class.* Dracula's boyars on the whole appear to have been remarkably loyal to him, even during the great Ottoman invasion in the summer of 1462.

While there are few documents that shed light on Vlad III Dracula's relations with the Church, certain aspects need to be pointed out for the Church, as an institution, was an important support for the state, providing it both legitimacy and strength. As in other countries, it also was an important part of the feudal socio-economic system. Unlike his relations with the boyars, Vlad's ties with the church have neither been a source of investigation or dispute.

He is credited with building a church in Târgşor, and possibly founding the Monastery of Comana.[29] Likewise, he granted tax exemptions to the monasteries of Cozia and Tismana,[30] and may have expanded the important monastery at Snagov.[31] It is also known that, like other fifteenth century princes in the Romanian lands, he made donations to monasteries on Mount Athos, the spiritual center of

---

[28]Doc. CCCXII in Bogdan, *Documente privitoare la relaţiile Ţării Româneşti cu Braşovul şi Ţara Ungurească*, pp. 357-358. The same Cârstian is also referred to in a letter of Dracula to Sibiu dated 4 August 1475, see Doc. CCLXV in Bogdan, *op.cit.*,,pp. 322-323.

[29]Radu Florescu and Raymond T. McNally have explained the building of the Church of St. Nicholas at Târgşor in 1461 as being done in atonement for the murders of his predecessor Vladislav II in 1456 and Dan the Pretender in 1460 (see Radu Florescu and Raymond T. McNally, *Dracula: A Biography of Vlad the Impaler*, p. 65), but it seems unlikely that Vlad would have been overcome by such sentiments. In fact, he may have built it there in celebration of his victories over his opponents, Vladislav II and Dan III, both of whom are known to have perished at Târgşor.

In 1922, the Romanian historian Constantin C. Giurescu found a votive inscription in Slavonic in the village of Strejnicu in the county of Prahova attesting to the foundation of the church at Târgşor in 1461 by Vlad III Dracula see Constantin C. Giurescu, "O biserică a lui Vlad Ţepeş la Târgşor," in *Buletin Com. Mon. Ist.*, XVII (1924), pp. 74-75. See also B. Theodorescu and I. Barnea, "Cultura în cuprinsul Mitropoliei Ungrovlahiei," pp. 827-888 în *Biserica Ortodoxă Romînă: Buletinul oficial al Patriarhiei romîne*, LXXVII:7-10 (iulie-octombrie, 1959), p. 863.

Orthodoxy.[32] Thus, on the whole, his relations with the church appear to have been without incident.

Nevertheless, an important change in the structure of the Church hierarchy took place in the mid-fifteenth century. The evidence we have for this comes from the reigns of Vlad III Dracula and his brother Radu cel Frumos. It is clear that after the fall of Constantinople to the Ottomans in 1453, the Metropolitan of the Wallachian Church is no longer appointed by the Patriarch, but is selected from among the native clergy. Exactly how this was done is unclear from existent documents.

It seems that from this time, at least until the reorganization of the Church at the beginning of the sixteenth century,[33] the *Stareţ* of the Monastery of Cozia, which had been founded by Mircea cel Bătrân, was selected as the head of the Wallachian Orthodox Church. This conclusion is based on the following evidence: A *hrisov* issued by Vlad on 16 April 1457 (6965) at Târgovişte confirms to the Monastery of Cozia the village of Troianeşti, on both sides of the Olt River, which the monastery and its abbot Iosif bought from Drăgoi, son of Drăgoi, for 50 florins. The deed exempts the monastery from taxes and services

---

[30]"Doc. 115, 16 April 1457 (6965), Târgovişte, Vlad Ţepeş voievod întăreşte m-rii Cozia satul Troianeşti, pe ambele maluri ale Oltului, scutindu-l de slujbe şi dăjdii," pp. 198-200 and "Doc. 117, 5 March 1458 (6966), M-rea Tismana, Vlad Ţepeş voievod întăreşte m-rii Tismana toate satele ei, pe care le-a avut în timpul tatălui său, Vlad Dracul, scutindu-le de slujbe şi munci domneşti," in *Documenta Romaniae Historica B. Ţara Românească*, vol. I, pp. 201-202.

[31]The chronicle of Cantacuzino states that Vlad founded the Monastery at Snagov (see *Istoria Ţării Româneşti, 1290-1690: Letopiseţul Cantacuzinesc*, pp. 4, 205), but its existence is already attested to during the reign of Mircea cel Bătrân (see *Documenta Romaniae Historica B. Ţara Românească*, vol. I, pp. 34-35. Thus, it may be that Dracula rebuilt or strengthened this important stronghold. It is also interesting to note that Snagov is traditionally accepted as Vlad's burial place, although no grave has ever been found. On efforts to locate Dracula's tomb at Snagov see Dinu V. Rosetti, *Săpăturile arheologice de la Snagov* (Bucureşti, 1925), vol. I, pp. 44-45.

[32]See "Doc. 116, 12 June 1457, Vlad Ţepeş voievod acordă privilegii m-rii Rusicon de la Athos," p. 201 and "Doc. 119, (1 September 1460-31 August 1461), Vlad Ţepeş voievod dăruieşte m-rii Filoteu de la Athos un obroc anual de 4000 aspri," in *Documenta Romaniae Historica B. Ţara Românească*, vol. I, p. 205.

[33]This practice undoubtedly ended after the Church reforms proposed by St. Nifon to Prince Radu cel Mare (1495-1508) to move the Metropolitanate from Curtea de Argeş to Târgovişte and to create two bishoprics, one at Râmnic and the other at Buzău, were implemented (1517). See Niculae Şerbănescu, "Mitropoliţii Ungrovlahiei," pp. 722-826 in *Biserica Ortodoxă Romînă: Buletinul oficial al Patriarhiei romîne*, LXXVII:7-10 (iulie-octombrie, 1959), p. 744.

normally due to the Prince on this land.[34] The same Iosif will become Metropolitan, and is mentioned as such as a participant in the *sfatul domnesc* when Radu cel Frumos issued a deed confirming lands to the Monastery of Snagov on 28 October 1464. Iosif is the first Metropolitan mentioned in documentary sources since Eftimie in 1412. He is also found as abbot at the Monastery of Cozia in a document issued by Vladislav II on 7 August 1451.[35] Thus, we may conclude that he was probably the first native Metropolitan and may have been named to the position either by Vlad III Dracula or by Radu cel Frumos since he became Metropolitan sometime between 16 April 1457 and 28 October 1464. He reigned perhaps until 1477 when Macarie is Metropolitan. Macarie, likewise, had been abbot at Cozia, as shown in a document dated 15 July 1475. His successor, Ilarion, is mentioned as abbot at Cozia on 9 January 1478. Ilarion became Metropolitan sometime before 17 April 1488 when Visarion is listed as Abbot at Cozia.[36]

If we assume that the Fall of Constantinople brought about the change in practice of naming the Metropolitan, as appears likely,[37] then we can infer that Iosif was the first native clergyman named to the highest post in the Wallachian Orthodox Church as we have documentary evidence that shows him as Abbot at Cozia before this time. Thus, the practice of naming the head of the most important monastery in the country as Metropolitan began with the reign of Vlad III Dracula or Radu cel Frumos, between 1457 and 1464.

It seems likely that this change in the traditional practice of the Church occurred during the reign of Dracula who undertook a deter-

---

[34]"Doc. 115, 16 April (6965) 1457, Vlad Țepeș voievod întărește m-rii Cozia satul Troianești, pe ambele maluri ale Oltului, scutindu-l de slujbe și dăjdii," in *Documenta Romaniae Historica, B.Țara Românească*, vol. I, pp. 198-200.

[35]"Doc. 106, 7 August 1451 (6959), Târgoviște, Vladislav al II-lea voievod scutește căruțele m-rii Cozia de orice fel de vamă, la târguri, la vaduri sau pe drumurile munților," in *Documenta Romaniae Historica B. Țara Românească*, vol. I, pp. 186-187.

[36]Niculae Șerbănescu, "Mitropoliții Ungrovlahiei," pp. 722-826 in *Biserica Ortodoxă Romînă: Buletinul oficial al Patriarhiei romîne*, LXXVII: 7-10 (iulie-octombrie, 1959), pp. 741-745.

[37]Another possible moment for this radical change in Church practice would be as a reaction against the Council of Florence, which proclaimed the union of the Orthodox and Catholic churches in 1439. The Union provoked outrage in many Orthodox countries, and the inhabitants of Constantinople are said to have shouted *"Better Islam than the Pope,"* when the union dictum was read (see L.S. Stavrianos, *The Balkans since 1453*, (New York, 1958), p. 56). It seems unlikely, however, that either Vlad Dracul or his successor Vladislav II would have taken such an extreme measure given the delicate nature of their relation with Catholic Hungary and political ties to Constantinople.

mined policy to strengthen the Prince's control over the institutions of the state and to increase its autonomy; the church would also be viewed in this light. Radu cel Frumos, who had just come to the throne thanks to Ottoman power, would more likely have accepted a Metropolitan named by the Patriarch at Constantinople if the practice of naming the Abbot of Cozia had not begun during Vlad's reign. Thus, Dracula can, perhaps, be credited with strengthening the autonomy of the church which he would see as equivalent to strengthening state autonomy, a policy clearly reflected throughout his reign, as we have seen from our discussion of his relations with the boyars.

Dora d'Istria (1828-1888) through American Eyes

Cornelia Bodea
Romanian Academy, Bucharest

In the study of the socio–cultural and political life of women in the 19th century, Dora d'Istria holds a significant position. Within the European gallery of prominent 'femmes de lettres,' this writer was considered in her time on a par with Madame de Staël, George Sand, Daniel Stern (viz. Countess d'Agoult), sometimes even on a higher intellectual and political level. As noted by the American weekly magazine *The Revolution* in 1870, "no woman is more widely esteemed in Europe than the Princess Dora d'Istria, and biographies of her have been written in all the languages of the Old World."

I will quote a few examples of enthusiastic admiration: "woman of native genius as well as refined feelings" (*The Athenaeum*, London, 1861); "a woman of genius of a peculiar and powerful character," "a new Corinne," "a noble and gifted woman" (Frederika Bremer, 1863); "eine geistreiche und gelehrte Gräfin" (I.O. Kohl, 1868); "une grande cosmopolite, qui s'inquiète des destinées des peuples et chante sans cesse la liberté" (Le Marquis de Villemer/Charles Yriarte, 1870); "veramente un genio" (A. de Gubernatis, 1869), "un capolavore vivante" (idem, 1870); "a liberal thinker," "a woman of splendid abilities," "a strong women's rights woman" (Laura Curtis Bullard, *The Revolution*, Feb. 1871); "Questa donna straordinaria il piu cosmopolita" (Oscar Greco, 1875); "Il piu cosmopolita degli scrittori e dei pensatori moderni" (Paolo Mantegazza, Florence, 1887); "A high sounding name in the United States" (*The World*, New York, 1881).

Who was she? Her biographers are numerous. Yet almost all of them repeated mainly the information which was provided by her own autobiographical notes or confessions.

She was born in Bucharest in 1828, an offspring of a ruling family, Ghica, which gave a dozen princes to Moldavia and Wallachia from the 17th to the 19th century. Her real name was Helena Ghica. Her father, Mihail D. Ghica, was a leading dignitary, an art collector, and a donor. He founded the Romanian Museum of Antiquities in Bucharest in 1834. Her mother was interested in literary and educational projects.

From early youth, Helena received a thoroughly polyglot education at home. After 1841, she pursued her studies in Western Europe — Dresden, Berlin, Vienna, Venice — under strong liberal influence. As she herself pointed out, she "beheld national agitation from one end of Europe to the other," and "heard the sonorous voice of liberty resounding like the trumpet of the archangel, as far as the banks of the ancient Ister (read: *the Danube*)."[1] Given her national, democratic sensibilities, there were times when her beliefs contradicted the conservative views of her own family. She understood better than them how difficult it was to impede the revolutionary process.

The Revolutions of 1848 proved to be a fleeting glimmer of hope, succeeded by darkness, when liberalism went into temporary eclipse. The cause of liberty was lost everywhere: with the Romanians as well as with other peoples in Europe whose aim had been national emancipation, national unification, and getting rid of foreign control.

Helena Ghica returned home to Bucharest at the end of 1848, full of hatred against foreign (viz. tsarist) oppressors. Yet, ironically, married a Russian officer in the occupation army which put an end to the revolution in both Principalities of Moldavia and Wallachia. Count Alexander Koltzoff–Massalsky's surname was associated with the legendary Rurik dynasty. Helena Ghica-Massalsky resided in Russia for six uncomfortable years. The liberalism which she experienced in Western Europe proved totally incompatible with the despotism of Tsar Nicho-

---

[1]Dora d'Istria, *La Suisse Allemande et l'ascension du Moench*, II, Paris, 1856, p. 32: *Récit de la Roumaine Daina.* Idem, *Switzerland the Pioneer of the Revolution or La Suisse Allemande.* Translated from French by H(ume) G(reenfeld), II, London, 1858, p. 250: *Story of Diana the Roumain.*

las I and the conservative views of the Russian aristocracy. Political and social circumstances therefore forced her to leave Russia in early 1855 during the Crimean War. Not only did she flee Russia, but also her native country, then under Austrian military occupation, which followed the Russian occupation.

She returned to Western Europe considering herself a political exile. She remained there for the rest of her life. She died at Florence in 1888.

Thus the year 1855 represented the decisive turning point in countess Ghica-Massalsky's career. The pen name — Dora d'Istria — which she adopted that very year, reflected a national sentiment and also provided an emotional link to her native-land: "an ardent patriotism that must accompany me through life, and descend with me to the tomb" (These are words from her message: "To my Rumanian Brethren," published as a Preface to her book *La Suisse Allemande*, Paris, 1856).[2]

The name Dora d'Istria comes from "dor de Istria," which means "missing the land on the Ister;" in other words "longing for the land on the Danube"/"missing Romania!" From 1855 to 1859 especially, the liberal princess became irresistibly attracted to the Romanian national movement. She took an active part in the struggle, which was triggered by the Crimean War and the ensuing diplomatic peace negotiations, in order to obtain the unification of Moldavia and Wallachia. The main task of the national promoters was to urge the signatories of the Paris Peace Treaty (1856), and of the subsequent Convention Settlement (1858), to include favorable terms regarding the status of the Principalities. Dora devoted herself by her writings, her diplomatic skill and her knowledge to Romania's national cause. A long list of articles and essays dedicated to Romanians and Romania offered evidence of that "passionate love of country which transcends all passions. Liberty and happiness for my native country: such are the foremost aspirations which shall henceforth be the objects of my existence." These were her very words. Dora d'Istria's writings can be compared to those of the male supporters of the national cause — the forty-eighters like V. Alecsandri, M. Kogălniceanu, C. Bolliac, the Brătianus, the Golescus and so many others. She demonstrated the same capacity in wielding the pen, as in mastering the lesson of history, literature, folklore, and current politics. A thinker, a sound intellect: creative, original, vigorous.

---

[2]In the French edition, 1856: "*A mes frères les Roumains*", p. VI. In the English Translation: *To my Rumanian Brethren*, p. XIX

The debut was marked by *La vie monastique en Orient* (Brussels, 1855), followed by *La Suisse Allemande* (Paris, 4 vols., 1856). More significant for the historical destiny of the Danubian Principalities during those crucial years was the fact that *Il Diritto* of Turin offered its columns to her historical surveys. A first series of ten issues was devoted to *Gli Eroi della Rumenia. Profili storici*. The selection of the topics and the titles chosen for those heroes are indicative by themselves, such as: *Radu Negru ovvero la Democrazia primitiva* (*Early Wallachian Democracy under the Rule of Radu Negru*); *Giovanni I Bassaraba ovvero la Battaglia della Valle della Morte* (*Prince Basarab I and the Battle of Death's Valley*); *La Dinastia degli Asan ovvero la lotta contra gli imperatori di Bisanzio* (*The Assen Dynasty and their Struggle against Byzantium*); *Mircea il Vecchio. l. La Battaglia di Kossovo, 2. La ritirata del Sultan Bajazet* (*Mircea the Old. 1. The Battle of Kosovo, 2. The Retreat of Sultan Bajazet*); *Giovanni Uniade. Le Vittorie di Vasag e di Nisa* (*John Huniady and his Victories*); *Vlad il Diavolo e la Battaglia di Varna* (*Vlad Dracul and the Battle of Varna*); *Stefano il Grande. 1. Il Toro Moldavo, 2. La Battaglia di Racova, 3. Il Monasterio di Niamzo* (*Stephen the Great. 1. The Moldavian Aurochs, 2. The Battle of Racova, 3. The Neamtz Monastery*).

In the same periodical she raised the vital question of the status of Moldavia and Wallachia (i.e. *Osservazione sull'Organisazione dei Principati Danubiani*), supporting their unification in compliance with the Romanian National Platform. In other issues she revealed the truth behind the opposition of Austria to Romanian unification (*Propaganda Austro-Romana nei Principati Danubiani*). Several other issues of the same Italian journal discussed the question raised by the possibility of a foreign ruler for Moldo-Wallachia (*Un Principe straniero nella Moldo-Wallachia*).

The message of all those essays — as their author pointed out — was to show how a small people surrounded by great and powerful states was able to defend its independence and at the same time protect Western Europe from the Ottoman threat. Accordingly, those western states formerly protected by the Romanian people, were now simply to pay back a long forgotten debt.

It is worth pointing out that Dora d'Istria, like all those Romanians and philo-Romanians who championed the national cause, supported the view that the territory of the future nation should correspond to that of ancient Dacia. The perspective of an integral political unification proved to be a common denominator. In order to highlight long-range dynamic forces contributing to the national awakening and subsequently to the political ideal of a modern unitary

Romania, Dora used folklore and literary sources to press her point – e.g.: "Chants et récits populaires" in *La libre Recherche* (Bruxelles, March 1857); "La Nationalité roumaine d'après les chants populaires" in the *Revue des Deux Mondes* (Paris, March, 1859); "Le feste rumene" in the *Mondo illustrato* (Torino, 1861), etc. Also, in a comprehensive two volume study on women in a vaguely defined East (*Les femmes en Orient*, 1859-1860), the chapters devoted to Romanian women covered the whole Romanian ethnic territory. References to Transylvanian women appear to dominate her information. Bucharest is described as "the genuine metropolis of the Romanian lands." In this way her struggle contributed effectively to cast more light on the Romanian historical realities.

In the year 1859, the main objective was realized with the election of Alexander I. Cuza in both Principalities. The first modern Romanian national state became a *fait accompli*. One of Dora d'Istria's targets was achieved... (Perhaps one might acknowledge in passing that her enthusiasm for that Prince was practically blurred by her secret hope of seeing a member of her own princely family propelled to the fore front of the United Principalities,[3] which did not come true).

Yet, even though Dora's efforts did not turn to the advantage of her family, her publications supported her fame as a writer defending democratic principles and the liberation of oppressed peoples. She distinguished herself by means of her erudition, her refined literary skill and cosmopolitan spirit. Though continuing to be involved in Romanian political issues, her main interests turned elsewhere: towards Greece (the country of the learned instructor of her youth, G.G. Papadopoulos), and the other Balkan provinces. There she spent more than a year of research and writing. Then returning to Italy, her adopted country, the scope of her writings widened. Now she encouraged all peoples in their struggle for the achievement of their national emancipation. The year 1861 witnessed her cooperation with Garibaldi with similar conspiratorial projects in mind for the peoples of the Balkans and those under Habsburg control, aiming at "*emancipazione delle nazionalita oppresse, al anneinamento del despotismo e della superstizion.*"[4] Letters exchanged between Dora d'Istria and Garibaldi attest to the

---

[3]Letter addressed to Tullo Massarani, dated 16 Aug. 1875, on Alexandre I. Cuza (Cf. T. Massarani, *Una nobila vita: Carteggio inedito*, I, Firenze, 1909, p. 213 sq. Also P. Ciureanu, "Dora d'Istria" in *Revue des Etudes Roumaines*, II, 1952, pp. 99-104.

[4]Dora d'Istria, *Gli eroi della Rumenia. Profili storici*. Con Prefazione di Paolo Mantegazza. Firenze, 1887, pp. 11-12.

persistence of such intentions even in 1866. Using folklore and historical traditions as vehicles for national awakening to promote the struggle of the Serbs, the Albanians and the Greeks, she chose the *Revue des
Deux Mondes* to publish: "La nationalité serbe d'après les chants populaires" (Jan. 1866); "La nationalité albanaise d'après les chants populaires" (March, 1866); "La nationalité bulgare d'après les chants
populaires" (Jul. 1867); "La nationalité hellénique d'après les chants
populaires" (Aug. 1867). The revolt in Crete 1866/67 provoked her
public reaction in favor of the insurgents and earned the title of *megas
politis* for her — Great Greek Citizenship — solemnly granted to her by
the Legislative Chamber of Athens, an honor thus far formally conferred only on Lord Byron. Yet, if her "Lettre à la Chambre Législative
d'Athènes" (June 1867) enjoyed publicity in all of the main periodicals
of Europe, her "Réponse au Comité épiro-thessalo-macédonien des
Dames" (Answer to the Committee of the Epiro-Thessalo-Macedonian
Women) was even more resounding. It crossed the Atlantic to the New
World. The *New York Tribune* reproduced the text at the end of October
1867.

In America, the condition of women was more intensely debated.
Two years later, the echo produced by that "Answer" was still evoked. I
cite Dora's interesting commentary of the 10th of December 1869 to a
Viennese poetess and old friend of her, Baroness Josephine von
Knorr:[5]

> You'll do fine if you'll convey to Dr. Pollak a copy of my let-
> ter. In this manner he will enjoy finding out — as he is inter-
> ested in the matter — that this letter, already translated in
> most languages of our Continent, crossed the Ocean, and
> enjoyed within the New World a quite different success from
> that of the Old World. Given the keen interest which they
> manifest for progress, the Americans immediately under-
> stood that the release of so many million women, captive in
> the jails of Islam, was truly a humane and evangelical
> achievement.

Within the United States, which are so little centralized, where a
newspaper from the South does not echo a newspaper from the North,
where Philadelphia insists on having its own opinion, as New York

---

[5]Biblioteca Academiei Române (BAR) Msse. S10/CCLXXXIX. Published by I.
Karadja, "Deux lettres de Dora d'Istria," *Revue du Sud Est Européen*, 1928, nr. 1-3, pp.
34-38. — As for the Addressee, see *Österreichisches Biographisches Lexikon 1815-1950*, vol.
IV, Wien–Köln–Graz, 1969, p. 2.

does, the press was unanimous in reproducing and praising the letter and its author. The popular *The New Tribune* of the "Imperial City," edited by the first-rate publicist of both Americas, Horace Greeley (one single issue reaches 120,000 copies) inserted immediately after the "Telegrams" — as an exceptional honor — "The Letter of the Celebrated Dora d'Istria" (vol. XXVII, 2 Oct.). One might therefore apply to this letter Victor Hugo's:

> ...and Young America
>
> lap to him from the seaboard.

It is indeed no wonder that in 1867 Dora d'Istria was praised and admired in America as a true celebrity. Suffice it to learn that seven years earlier (1860), Anna C. Johnson, the American author of *The Cottages of the Alps* dedicated her book "To Madam Dora d'Istria in testimony of the friendship of the author." Miss Johnson gave her American readers a first sketch of the Romanian princess's life, works, and conventions. It struck the American author as a curious coincidence "that a lady should have come from the far East, and another from the far West, to meet in the little republic with the same object, the same opinions, and the same enthusiastic love of liberty, one being born subject of a despot and the other of a free government.[6]

Three years later the Swedish writer Frederika Bremer, who enjoyed a large popularity in the United States, contributed with additional enthusiastic appreciations to Dora's fame in the New World. Referring to the latter's "great work" *La Suisse Allemande* (1856) Frederika pointed out:

> I have seldom read a work of this class with greater pleasure or more true enjoyment. The spirit which pervaded it was so strong-minded, there was such a warm feeling for the ideal of social life, so clear an insight into the endeavors and condition of the people of the free States, as opposed to those where despotism prevails, so noble and so daring were the scenes she portrayed, and the language in which she expressed herself. She is a woman of genius, of a peculiar and powerful character.[7]

---

[6]Anna C. Johnson, *The Cottages of the Alps*. By the author of *Peasant Life in Germany*, New York, Charles Scribner, 1860, pp. V-XI.

[7]Frederika Bremer, *Greece and the Greeks. The Narrative of a Winter Residence and Summer Travel in Greece and its Islands*. Translated by Mary Howit. London, 1863, I, p. 268.

Frederika Bremer's enthusiasm reached superlative level when discussing Dora d'Istria's *Les Femmes en Orient*, published in Zürich in
1860:[8]

> *Les Femmes en Orient*, the Countess Dora d'Istria's work, says
> Frederika, was one of the best read most celebrated books in
> the circles of the cultivated French reading world. I had been
> able to meet with it even in Athens. The union of masculine
> judgement and precision with feminine insight and feeling,
> the affluence of poetical beauty derived from the popular
> songs and life of races hitherto but little known, the number
> of interesting anecdotes and facts, as well as the clear view of
> her object, which the authoress never loses sight of, combine
> to make this work as unusually entertaining as it is instruc-
> tive. The authoress proves herself to be a perfect artist, and
> her learning and many-sided knowledge are produced merely
> as a foundation for the living descriptions in which she so
> greatly excels.[9]

A synthesis of the Romanian princess's moral, literary, and ide-
ative features by the popular Swedish author runs as follows:

> A noble and gifted woman, in whom a man's head and a
> woman's heart are united with singular harmony. Her ideals
> of individual and social life are not altogether the same as
> mine, are not sufficient for me, but she is still young, and
> with her bias in mind and her gifts, I know no height on the
> path of human development to which she may not attain.[10]

This is a recognition which responded to each stage of her writing career. The portrayal sketched by Frederika Bremer in 1863 is
reflected in the princess's following works. The first to succeed was *Des
Femmes par Une Femme* (On Women by a Woman);[11] a genuine master-
piece which contributed to the author's celebrity. Published in 1865,
Des femmes par Une Femme represents the counterpart or the extension
of *Les Femmes en Orient* (1860). In both works history alternates with
current occurrences, travel descriptions with folklore, the present with
the past. Additional information is derived from a broad and diverse
reading. All in all, both represent an impressive, colorful, dramatic pic-

---

[8]Dora d'Istria, *Les femmes en Orient*, 2 vols. Zürich, Meyer and Zeller, 1860.

[9]F. Bremer, *op. cit.*, p. 269.

[10]*Ibidem*.

[11]Dora d'Istria, *Des femmes par Une Femme*. Paris, Bruxelles, 1865, 2 vols. — Nou-
velle édition 1869.

ture of a woman's life and society in the East, West, South, and North of Europe, as well as beyond it.

The 1860 two volume book examined the condition of womanhood in the *Eastern Peninsula* (*La Péninsule Orientale*) which is tantamount to Southeastern Europe. It discusses Romanian, Bulgarian, Dalmatian, Montenegrin, Turkish, Albanian, and Greek women. As was natural, priority was given to the Romanian women. The London book reviewer in *The Athenaeum* (Aug.3, 1861) underscored "the passionate attachment shown by the author towards the nation that gave her birth."[12] However, given the fact that Ghika's ethnic background was Albanian, Albanian women also enjoyed special attention. Greeks in their turn were no less represented. Volume two, as indicated by its subtitle *La Russie*, covered the condition of women within the vast Russian Empire, including Russian, Siberian, and Cossack women; and successively the Polish, Latvian, Georgian, Armenian, Kurd, Fino-Mongolian, Mongol, Nogai etc.

The 1865 comprehensive two volumes, *Des Femmes par Une Femme*, encompass in the first part "The Latin Society," which means the French, Italian, Spanish, and Portuguese women. Here stress is placed on French women. Volume two presents "The Germanic Society," viz.: German, Saxon, Prussian, Austrian, Scandinavian, Anglo-Saxon, Swiss, Belgian, and Dutch women. Two final chapters deal with the Jewish, and respectively the Hindu (Gitanos) women within the Latin and Germanic societies. Additional attention is given to Anglo-Saxon women in the New World.[13] In the latter case information was obtained mainly from R.W. Griswold's *The Female Poets of America* (Philadelphia, 1849, 2nd edit. 1853), John J. Hard's *Female Writers of America*, and Adolphe Kolatschek's *Die Stellung des Frauen in America* (Wien, 1864).

Des Femmes par Une Femme brought Dora d'Istria's fame to a climax. The French, German, Belgian, Italian, and Greek press admired her plea for equal social, civil and political rights for women the world over. Thus, the merits of the "celebrated Dora d'Istria" (as mentioned in the *New York Tribune*, Oct. 1867) proved to be far from a mere courtesy.

The year 1868 inaugurated Dora's own contributions in the American press. The starting point was set in *Le Messager Franco-Amer-*

---

[12] *The Athenaeum, Journal of Literature, Science, and the Fine Arts*, London, 1861, nr. 1762, Aug. 3, pp. 147-148.

[13] *Ibidem*, II, pp. 229-231.

icain from New York, with "Une visite au Musée de Felice Schiavoni," the Italian artist who taught her painting and painted her portraits as well. Unfortunately, this periodical is hard to find, even in the United States, particularly the issues which included Dora's articles, such as "La guerre et les Femmes" (28 Dec. 1870); "Les Femmes fortes" (9 March, 1871). It is again regrettable that a projected translation of *Des Femmes par Une Femme* started "by a distinguished American woman writer" in *L'Indépendance hellénique* of Athens was discontinued after two issues (March 22, and April 1, 1873).[14]

By way of contrast in other American periodicals contributions by or on Dora d'Istria are available. Here are some titles: "A Russian Princess on Woman's Rights" published in *The Revolution*, Feb. 1, 1871; "The Orthodox Greek Church," a well documented essay, included in *The International Review* (N.Y., I, 1874, July). In the same journal, in July 1875, a study on "French Literature under the First Empire" was followed by "French Literature of the Reformation" (Nov. 1876). At Philadelphia, *The Penn Monthly* published "The Condition of Women among the Southern Slav"" (Jan. 1878); "The Poetry of the Turkish Peoples: I. Iran and Turan, II. The Peoples Poetry of the Turks, — War and Love" was included in the issue of September 1878, and continued with "The Erudite Poetry of the Turks. — Mysticism" in October. The final part, IV "The Turkomans. — War and Love in their Popular Poetry" appeared in Dec. 1878.

Besides personal contributions published by major American magazines, Dora d'Istria also enjoyed additional praise from her editors due to her winning personality, her literary skill, and her deep convictions expressed in her writing. However, there were a few exceptions. In 1871 for instance, after an exchange of opinions with Laura Curtis Bullard, the editor of *The Revolution*, referring to Dora's Russian name as "the Princess Koltzoff-Massalsky (Dora d'Istria)," described her as "A Russian Princess..." This strange salutation was due to Dora's underestimation of the American code of laws for women, when considering that:

> the women of despotic Russia are better cared for by laws of their country, than those of republican America; and this results from the fact that Russia has been ruled so often by

---

[14]Cf. O. Greco, *Bibliografia femminile italiana del XIX secolo*. Venezia, 1875, p. 62: "Una distinta signora americana da Washington ha incominciato la Traduzione inglese di questa opera col titolo *Womanhood of all Nations — Indépendance hellénique* del 22 marzo e 1 aprile 1873."

Empresses, and they have naturally made laws favorable to their sex.[15]

In the preceding issue of *The Revolution*, Dora defended her views: "Even after the changes introduced by Nicholas I, they (the women) were not excluded from the throne." And added:

> These arrangements are greatly superior to the law the French call 'Loi Salique' — a law whose very name recalls its barbarous origin, and which is a tissue of contradictions...[16]

This small incident did not prevent the American feminist editor to continue praising Dora's "able plea for equal rights, social, civil, and political for women the world over." However she could not abstain from insinuating:

> The Princess Helene intends visiting America soon; she not only reads, but speaks English well, and added to this advantage her well trained mind and keen powers of observation, will, no doubt, enable her to get clearer notions of our social life, and our political peculiarities than has fallen to the experience of most foreigners who have visited our country.[17]

It took Dora a good span of time to convince herself to visit America. The fact that she felt hurt at being considered a Russian princess caused her to sign her essays published in American magazines as "Dora d'Istria Princess Ghika" and not Princess/Countess Koltzoff-Massalsky...

As mentioned above, contacts continued nevertheless. In a letter dated June 2, 1872, Dora d'Istria thanked the grand poet of America, Henry W. Longfellow, for having sent her his picture:

> I'll be happy to treasure this souvenir coming from the celebrated poet of whom America is so rightly proud, and who thanks to the elevation of his feelings and to the nobility of the inspirations has been so popular, both in the Old World as well as in the New one.[18]

Another prominent American with whom she corresponded was the famous inventor Thomas A. Edison. A reply addressed to him on

---

[15]*The Revolution*, New York, March 9, 1871: "Distinguished Women in Florence. The Princess Koltzoff Massalsky (Dora d'Istria)."

[16]*Ibidem,* Feb. 13, 1871: "A Russian Princess on Women's Rights."

[17]See above, nr. 15.

[18]*Annex I* (Dora d'Istria to Henry W. Longfellow).

the 25th of January 1873, from Florence, reveals an earlier starting point.[19]

In a letter addressed to a cousin on the 4th of December 1874 Dora was gratified by the fact that "la puissante Société Américaine des Sciences Sociales" (to wit: The Social Science Association) elected her as a corresponding member and proposed that she write for them on the education of Italian women.[20] "This came to me before having finished the essay on the French literature in the 19th century" — the one which was published by *The International Review*.[21]

Among the few other recorded testimonies of her relations with distinguished Americans on culture, society, and politics, the visit she received in 1878 in Florence from the outstanding suffragist and reformer Julia Ward Howe (1819-1910) is worth mentioning. This was to be their sole meeting. It was only later, when Julia Ward Howe published her *Reminiscences* in 1899, that the confusion which hovered over that visit became obvious. In 1878, the American visitor had mistaken Princess Dora d'Istria for "Princess Belgioioso" the Italian patriot and "femme de lettres" who lived from 1808 to 1871! Strange enough, the enthusiastic American crusader in the movement for peace, the author of the 1870 resounding *Appeal to Womanhood throughout the World* — calling for a general Congress of women to promote the alliance of different nationalities, the amicable settlement of international questions, and the general promotion of peace — seemed to be unaware of Dora d'Istria's article welcoming that *Appeal* and its authors as well. This was published in February 1871 in the *Nuova Antologia* under the title of "La guerra. Un appello alle donne dei due mondi di Giulia Ward Howe!"

Here is Julia Ward Howe's incorrect recording:[22]

> ...Soon after my arrival in Florence (1878) I was asked to speak on suffrage at the Circolo Filologico, one of the favorite halls of the city. The attendance was very large. I made my argument in French...

> A morning visit to the Princess Belgioioso (sic!) may deserve a passing mention. This lady was originally Princess Ghika,

---

[19]*Annex II* (Dora d'Istria to Thomas A. Edison).

[20]*Annex III* (Dora d'Istria to Maria D. Ghica).

[21]*International Review*, vol. II, July 1875: "French Literature under the First Empire," pp. 513-539; Nov.-Dec. 1876: "French Literature of the Restoration," pp. 800-809.

[22]Julia (Ward) Howe, *Reminiscences 1819-1899*, New York, 1899, pp. 422-423.

of a noble Roumanian family. She had married a Russian — Count Murherstsky (sic!). I never knew the origin of the Italian title. My dear friend, Mrs. Ednah D. Cheney, went with me to the princess's villa, which was some distance from the city proper. Although the winter had begun she received us in a room without fire. She was wrapped in furs from head to foot while we shivered with cold. She appeared to be about sixty years of age, and showed no traces of the beauty which I had seen in a portrait of her taken in her youth. She spoke English fluently, but with idioms derived from other languages, in some of which I should have understood her more easily than in my own.

In the same year 1878 a lengthy eulogistic sketch, signed by Grace A. Ellis, appeared in the *Scribner's Monthly* of New York:[23]

In Europe, the author pointed out, this lady is everywhere known, beloved by many personal friends, and admired by all who have read her works. Her thought is profound and liberal, her views are broad and humane. As an authoress, philanthropist, traveler, artist, and one of the strongest advocates of freedom and liberty for the oppressed of both sexes, and of her suffering sisters especially, she is an honor to the time and to womanhood. The women of the old world have found in her a powerful sympathy, yet rational, champion; just in her arguments in their behalf, able in her statement of her needs, and thoroughly interested in their elevation and improvement..."

With regard to the princess's high quality works, Grace A. Ellis repeated Deschanel's opinion, the critic of the *Journal des Débats*, that "each of her works suffices for that of a man."

Grace A. Ellis, the author of the sketch, was a Bostonian by birth.[24] Her maiden name was Little. In 1869 she became the wife of J.L. Ellis, a talented young lawyer who died a year after their marriage. It was under the name of Ellis that she developed a busy ten year activity as a writer. In 1879 she married J.P. Oliver, a physician of Boston. Subsequently she signed herself Grace A. Oliver. With her obvious talents, she was always ready to support every good cause in which she believed. She was a kindly, public spirited woman, a reputation which

---

[23] *Scribner's Monthly. An Illustrated Magazine for the People,* New York, 1878, vol. XVII, nr. 2, Dec.

[24] Cf. *Woman of the Century. Leading American Women in All Walks of Life.* Edited by Frances E. Willard and Mary A. Livermore. New York, 1893, Under "Oliver Mrs. Grace Atkinson."

explains the enthusiasm with which she supported Dora d'Istria's visit to the United States.

On the 15th of April 1879, the *Boston Daily Advertiser* published a congratulatory lengthy review on the "Writing of the Princess Dora d'Istria — that "indefatigable authoress, Princess Helena Ghika who has a world-wide reputation under her *nom de plume* Dora d'Istria." The article was sent to her in Florence by Longfellow[25] and it arrived within a fortnight as it is to be deduced from Dora's thank-you note dated April 30, 1879. Who could have been the author of the *Boston Daily Advertiser*'s article? Certainly not the poet, according to Dora's own opinion. ("Longfellow m'a bien envoyé l'article du journal de Boston, mais je ne crois pas qu'il en soit l'auteur").[26] But she felt particularly flattered by the kindness of its author:

> I have always granted a special importance to the wide American Republic and I was always in sympathy with it, and the kindness of the celebrated personalities who, like you, personify its genius would be the sweetest reward for my modest works that cover my life!

"While living in the midst of the most ancient civilizations of the Old World — Dora went on — my thoughts indulge incessantly overseas towards those societies whose terrific development amaze our Orient, which, hélas, had lost even the souvenir of the time when one could say: *Ex Oriente lux!* — (This is translated from Dora's letter to Longfellow).[27]

If Grace A. Oliver could not be suspected of contributing to the above article in the *Boston Daily Advertiser*, the large echo of her sketch in the *Scribner's Monthly* cannot be denied. Kate Sanborn (1839-1917), a pioneer in the field of lecturing on feminism and literary matters, recalled in her *Memories and Anecdotes*, published in 1915, that after reading *Scribner's Monthly* she ventured to ask the Princess to send her the material for a lecture. To this request Dora responded generously, sending books, many sketches of her career, full bibliographical lists, pictures of her etc. etc. Kate Sanborn's lecture was delivered in New

---

[25]*Annex IV* (Dora d'Istria to Henry W. Longfellow).

[26]N. Iorga, "Lettres de Dora d'Istria," *Revue Historique du Sud Est Européen*, 1932, pp. 134-209. Cf. pp. 173, 174. — N.B.: Dora d'Istria's letters addressed, between Aug. 1877 and July 1887, to Hugo Meltzel, Co-editor of *Kolozsvár. Journal de Littérature comparée*, at (Cluj) Kolozsvár are to be found at the BAR, MSSE. Bucharest, Coresp. inv. 207019-207097.

[27]*Annex IV* (Grace A. Oliver to H. W. Longfellow).

York on the 26th February 1879. "The audience was greatly interested," as she acknowledged. Dora d'Istria "was as new to them as to me, and all she had donated was handed round to an eager crowd."[28] In the New Yorker newspapers the lecture was lavishly and enthusiastically reported.[29]

According to Kate Sanborn's *Memories*, in about six months she read in the newspapers that Dora d'Istria was taking "a long trip to America to meet Mrs. Oliver, Edison, Longfellow, and myself" (to wit: Kate herself). — This might be an idealized version, but anyhow the facts were correct.

As matters stood, on the 11th of July 1880, Grace A. Oliver, though personally a stranger to the celebrated Longfellow, thought it timely to inform him about "the expected arrival of the Princess." Unaware of the fact that he got to know her *via* correspondence, Grace Oliver tried to introduce "the Princess Koltzoff Massalsky" to him, telling him that she was better known to the European public as Countess Dora d'Istria, and that for many years they often corresponded, and that she also wrote a sketch of Dora: "I know that you must be overrun with celebrities in virtue of your own position... But it should certainly confer a great pleasure on her if she could meet the poet whom America delights to name as her first. May I ask you to take the trouble of calling on her if not too inconvenient?..."[30]

Information about her contacts during this sojourn is scarce: no news about possible public appearances or meetings; no evidence about having visited New York. Since she left for Europe embarking from Newport, I can only presume that this was the port which she used when entering the United States. There is no indication about her getting in touch with Thomas Edison either. But, as the latter had become a resident of New York since 1869, he might have come to Boston to see her! The well-known Italian anthropologist, Paolo Mantegazza, one of Dora's old true friends, and the editor of her *Gli eroi della Romenia* (Florence, 1887) noted in his preface to the book that Dora "published in the *Neologos* magazine of Constantinople her American imp" which could be interpreted "The Work in America" (?)[31] Much to my regret, like in the case of the *Messager Franco-Américain*, I

[28]Kate Sanborn, *Memories and Anecdotes*, New York, London, G.P. Putnam's Sons, 1915, p. 177; N. Iorga, "Lettres de Dora d'Istria," pp. 188-189.

[29]N. Iorga, "Lettres de Dora d'Istria," p. 190 (*New York Daily Tribune; The World*).

[30]*Annex V* (Grace A. Oliver to H.W. Longfellow).

[31]Dora d'Istria, *Gli eroi della Rumenia*, "Prefazione" di Paolo Mantegazza, p. 6.

was unable to get either the magazine or identify any quotation of the article.

Dora's farewell letter, addressed to Longfellow, on the 22nd of September 1880, the very eve of her departure for Europe, has only a few references to her American sojourn. "I feel happy, she said, to be able to have with me and read while at sea, the *Ultima Thule*.[32] These fine poems shall be to me an echo of America, which will escort me and bring back for a long time my most cherished dreams and aspirations. Thank you so much for sending me this charming book. I wanted so much to meet again. I thought even to ask you to have dinner with me on Sunday at Newport. But, I was told that this would be a too tiresome long trip for you, and so, for fear of your fatigue, I decided to make this farewell for you in hopes of welcoming you some day in Italy. Visiting Saratoga, the Niagara Falls, and traveling the Hudson River at sunrise, I have thought much of you."[33]

The sole record of her stay in America comes from Kate Sanborn. The New York lecturer had just accepted a position teaching at Smith College (Northampton, Mass.) as professor of English literature. The two women met in Swampscott, near Boston, at a seashore hotel. Miss Sanborn published her *Memories and Anecdotes* 35 years after the visit to Swampscott, and 27 after Dora d'Istria's death. In the book's table of contents, the episode is entitled: "Dora d'Istria. Our Illustrious Visitor." An extensive eulogy of Dora d'Istria, taken mostly from the *Scribner's Monthly* article of Grace A. Ellis,[34] precedes the humorous description of the informal meeting of the two foremost women: the one who was spoken of as "the leading woman humorist of America," and the other who was spoken of as "looking like Venus and speaking like Minerva,"

> I called on her later at a seashore hotel near Boston. She had just finished her lunch, and said she had been enjoying for the first time boiled corn-on-the-cob. She was sitting on the piazza, rather shabbily dressed, her skirt decidedly travel-stained. Traces of the butter used on the corn were visible about her mouth and she was smoking a large and very

[32]H.W. Longfellow, *Ultima Thule*, Boston, Mifflin and Comp. The Riverside Press, Cambridge, 1880, IV-7-61 p.

[33]*Annex VII* (Dora d'Istria to H.W. Longfellow).

[34]Kate Sanborn, *Memories and Anecdotes*, pp. 177-178. See also (Edwin W. Sanborn), *Kate Sanborn, July 11, 1839, July 9, 1917*, Boston, McGrath-Sherrill Press, 1918, pp. 64-65.

strong cigar, a sight not so common at that time in this country. A rocking chair was to her a delightful novelty and she had already bought six large rocking chairs of wickerwork. She was sitting in one, and busily swaying back and forward and said: "Here I do repose myself and I take these chairs home with me and when *de* gentlemen and *de* ladies do come to see me in Florence, I do show them how to repose themselves."

Suddenly she looked at me and began to laugh immoderately. "Oh," she explained, seeing my puzzled expression, "I *deed* think of you as so *deeferent*, I deed think you were very tall and *theen*, with *leetle*, wiggly curls on each side of your face."

She evidently had in mind the typical old maid with gimlet ringlets! So we sat and rocked and laughed, for I was equally surprised to meet a person so 'different' from my romantic ideal. Like the two Irishmen, who chancing to meet were each mistaken in the identity of the other. As one of them put it, "We looked at each other and, faith, it turned our to be *nayther* of us."

Back home in Florence, Princess Dora d'Istria sent to Grace A. Ellis/Oliver and Kate Sanborn "valuable tokens of her regards as souvenirs." However, we may question whether the Princess would have been pleased with this informal, unconventional humorous episode presented in such a lively colloquial style and poor phonetic English, as recorded by Kate Sanborn.

King Carol II and Germany

Paul D. Quinlan
Providence College

After World War I, Romania's foreign policy was firmly anchored to close ties with France, strict adherence to the Paris peace treaties, collective security, and the League of Nations. During much of the interwar period, although Germany and the Soviet Union loomed as potential threats in the distant future, Hungary's clamoring for a revision of the Trianon Treaty vis-à-vis Transylvania was Romania's chief concern. In 1921, Romania formed an alliance with Yugoslavia and Czechoslovakia, called the Little Entente, which was directed against Hungarian revisionism.

Romania's main ally was France. The French backed the setting up of the Little Entente, signed treaties of friendship with Entente members in the 1920s, including Romania, and provided military and financial assistance. The goal of France and the Entente was not only to maintain the status quo in Eastern Europe but also to establish a *cordon sanitaire* against future threats from a revitalized Germany and Soviet Union. Unfortunately for Romania, after Hitler took over in 1933 and Germany became aggressive, the whole French backed system began to crumble. France had neither the resources nor the will to stand up to Hitler. Without the support of a large power, attempts by the Balkan states to join together for their own security proved equally futile.

Although Carol did not have an extensive background in foreign affairs prior to coming to power in 1930, he would prove himself to be an astute diplomat. Like his political ideas, his ideas about international

58

developments generally reflected popular thinking. Typical of many aristocrats, at first Carol viewed Hitler as a petty agitator from the cafes of Vienna who could not make it as an artist. He did not think much of the Nazis either. In a letter to his cousin Prince Friedrich (Friedel) of Hohenzollern-Sigmaringen shortly before the July 1932 Reichstag elections, he inquired about the situation in Germany. "How will the elections turn out? Will the Nazis win a majority? And then what?"[1] Upon being told the news of Hitler's appointment as chancellor he threw his hands in the air in bewilderment.[2] Several months later in another letter to Friedel he again expressed his concern about the Nazis, but at the same time saw some positive results as well.

The news from Germany is confusing. I must say that the anti-Semitic movement has created a very bad impression all over Europe. On the other hand, the anti-communist measures have been favorably received. Everyone is glad that Germany has a strong government once more.[3]

In time, Carol came to admire and envy Hitler's rebuilding of Germany, which he hoped to do in Romania as well. But Carol's basic view of man as a plebeian rabble-rouser from the sidewalks of Vienna never changed.

Carol's policy toward Germany involved not only foreign affairs, but also Germany's interference in Romania's domestic affairs by supporting and helping to finance several right-wing groups, especially the National Christian Party of Octavian Goga and A.C. Cuza. German interest in the Legion of the Archangel Michael under Corneliu Codreanu only seriously began to develop at the beginning of 1937, however. German interference in Romanian internal affairs was a sensitive issue with Carol, and on a number of occasions he vehemently protested to Berlin.[4]

At first Carol hoped to win over the Legion to his side, but in 1936 and 1937 he came to realize that this was impossible. From this time on Carol and the Legion locked horns in a struggle to the finish. From time to time, the Legion even attempted to assassinate the King

---

[1]Letter, Carol to Friedrich, June 29, 1932, Furst Friedrich, 53, 88, (12), Staatsarchiv Sigmaringen, Sigmaringen.

[2]Eugeniu Buhman, *Jurnal* (Unpublished diary in the possession of Radu R. Florescu), p. 235.

[3]Letter, Carol to Friedrich, April 13, 1933, Furst Friedrich, 53, 97. Sigmaringen.

[4]King Carol II, *Însemnări zilnice*, Fond Regele Carol II, dosar III, p. 3, Arhivele Statului.

and members of his government. Carol was especially concerned about their death threats to his notorious Jewish mistress, Elena (Magda) Lupescu, who was high up on their hit list. By the beginning of 1938 Carol was ready to establish his royal dictatorship, partly so he would be in a better position to take vigorous action against Codreanu and the Legion.

Carol's fear of Germany's expansion into Eastern Europe went hand in hand with his fear of the development of the Legion. In March of 1938, at the time of the *Anschluss*, Carol's minister of the interior and right-hand man, Armand Călinescu, an implacable foe of the Legion, urged Carol to take tougher measures against the Legion. Călinescu warned Carol that:

> the events in Austria are no accident, but part of Germany's larger expansion plan... The Danube is a commercial and strategic route between East and West. All of the countries it crosses have come under intense pressure: Austria, Czechoslovakia, and Romania will follow. Their method is threefold: on the ideological level, backing nationalistic, rightwing movements, and applying pressure.
>
> How does Romania stand? For the moment we have the initiative... For Berlin, however, Goga was just a step toward their goal of a Legionary government. The Germans will continue to encourage the Legion and will count on them when the crucial moment arrives, even if we adopt a more pro-German foreign policy. By then it will be too late for us to resist.
>
> What can we do?... Destroy the Legion by arresting Codreanu and the rest of their leaders, begin a massive build up of the armed forces, expand our network of roads, improve agriculture, etc...[5]

Carol was worried, but hesitant to go as far as Călinescu urged at this time. And no doubt he was hearing similar arguments in the boudoir from his mistress who was as anxious as Călinescu to remove Codreanu.

During the summer of 1938, Carol's attention, like that of other European leaders, was increasingly preoccupied with the likelihood of a European war if Germany was not given the Sudetenland. Outwardly, Romania stood by its alliances during the crisis and even made it clear

---

[5] Armand Călinescu, *Însemnări politice 1916-1939* (București: Humanitas, 1990), pp. 383-385.

to the Russians that they would permit the passage of Soviet aircraft over Romanian territory. However, the Romanian government dreaded the prospect of getting dragged into a war with Germany.[6] The mutilation of Czechoslovakia at Munich, Romania's most reliable ally in Eastern Europe, sent shock waves through Bucharest, although Carol, like other heads of state, breathed a sigh of relief that war had been avoided.[7] But as Carol feared, it increasingly appeared that in the future it would be Germany, not France, that would play the dominant role in Southeastern Europe. Consequently, Romania was gradually forced to adopt a more neutral position between the Western Powers and Germany in her foreign policy.

To determine how much Romania could rely on the Western Powers after Munich, in November 1938 Carol visited England and France. From a personal point of view, the trip was a triumph for Carol, but in practical terms it was disappointing. Chamberlain told Carol that although Britain had not assigned Central and Southeastern Europe to Hitler as a sphere of influence, "natural forces seemed... to make it inevitable that Germany should enjoy a preponderant position in the economic field.[8] With the exception of a promise to send a trade mission to Bucharest, three days after he arrived in London Carol left empty-handed. And the same was true in Paris.

On his way back to Romania, Carol agreed to visit Hitler at the Berghof. He hoped through closer economic relations with Germany, Romania could avoid the fate of Austria and Czechoslovakia, as well as curtail German support for the Legion. During the meeting, Carol promised Hitler that he would give greater consideration to Germany's economic wishes.[9]

Perhaps the meeting also led Carol to believe that Germany had no special interest in the Legion.[10] In any case, the day after Carol arrived back in Romania, Călinescu followed the King's orders and had

[6]Dove B. Lungo, *Romania and the Great Powers 1933-1940* (Durham, North Carolina: Duke University Press, 1989), pp. 126-135; Carol II, *Însemnări zilnice*, pp. 107-108, 203-206.

[7]Buhman, *Jurnal*, p. 288.

[8]Great Britain, *Documents on British Foreign Policy 1919-1939* (London: 1949-1954), Third Series, III, p. 232.

[9]Armin Heinen, *Die Legion "Erzengel Michael" in Rumänien. Soziale Bewegung und politische Organization: Ein Beitrag zum Problem des internationalen Faschismus* (Munchen: R. Oldenburg Verlag, 1986), p. 376. See also Lungo, *Romania and the Great Powers*, pp. 142-143.

[10]Ibid., p. 377.

Codreanu and thirteen other Legionaries murdered, supposedly shot while trying to escape while they were being transported from one prison to another. Outwardly, Hitler was furious. He ordered the medals Carol had abundantly passed out to German officials during his trip to be returned and turned the German press loose on the King. But most important for Carol with the murder of Codreanu and most of his top lieutenants dead or in jail the Legion as a mass political movement was irreparably weakened, survived by disheartened, squabbling splinter groups led by second-raters like Horia Sima.

The German reaction to Codreanu's death frightened Carol, making him all the more willing to consent to a far-reaching economic treaty with Germany. In January 1939, the Germans indicated they were ready to begin negotiations. Shortly after Hermann Goering's special trade assistant, Helmuth Wohlthat, was sent to Bucharest. What the Germans wanted, however, was more than Carol had bargained for. They wanted to increase their purchases of soybeans, wheat, and especially oil to the point where Berlin would practically dominate the Romanian economy.[11] Unfortunately for Romania, the British and the French could do better economically trading with other countries, and the Germans, in the short run, were willing to pay the Romanians the best price they could get for their products in order to achieve dominance in the long run. The negotiations were long and arduous as Berlin held the threat of Hungarian and Bulgarian territorial demands over the heads of the Romanians as a Damoclean sword. On March 14 Călinescu wrote in his diary:

> For Germany, economics is the most important consideration, politics is secondary. For us it is the other way around.
> We must protect our frontiers, but we will have to pay.[12]

Then suddenly on March 15, Germany took over the rest of Czechoslovakia. Fearing that Germany might encourage an attack by Hungary on Romania as a ploy for an eventual German takeover, Carol ordered a partial mobilization and sent an SOS to the Western Powers. On March 17, Viorel V. Tilea, the recently appointed Romanian minister to England, rushed to the Foreign Office with his now famous ultimatum scare.[13] Although there never was a German ultimatum to Romania as Tilea claimed — "he acted like an idiot," Carol said — the

---

[11]Gerhard L. Weinberg, *The Foreign Policy of Hitler's Germany: Starting World War II, 1937-1939* (Chicago: University of Chicago Press, 1980), p. 494; Lungo, *Romania and the Great Powers*, pp. 149-150.

[12]Călinescu, *Însemnări politice*, pp. 408-409.

incident manifested the chaos and fear that permeated the Romanian government at the time. Three days later Carol told Călinescu that if "attacked we will defend ourselves. The danger is not imminent, but it cannot be excluded... We do not want to provoke Germany, that would hasten events and neither us nor the West could stop them."[14]

By March 23, Carol, who felt he was close to the top of Hitler's hit list, believed he had no choice but to sign the economic treaty with Germany. Taking advantage of the German invasion of Czechoslovakia, Wohlthat, as one historian wrote, "was able to drive a bargain so favorable to Germany that it practically delivered the riches of Romania's oil and agriculture into the hands of the Third Reich."[15] Ultimately this was true, but at the time of the signing the treaty was only in skeleton form; the details would be worked out later.[16] Romania signed the treaty, as Călinescu said, "in order to gain time and some economic advantages, not to draw Romania politically closer to Germany."[17] Ultimately, however, Carol signed to preserve the country's frontiers and independence.

In spite of the treaty, Carol desired to keep Romania within the orbit of the Western Powers. In the event of war, he wanted to fight on their side.[18] He was convinced that in a future war, barring a communist triumph, England and France would be victorious in the end.[19] Moreover, he feared a triumphant Germany and knew that even as Germany's ally Romania would wind up becoming a satellite of the Reich.[20] Strongly backing Carol's views was Călinescu. Urdărianu, on the other hand, feared a German victory and strongly urged Carol to

---

[13]Carol II, *Însemnări politice*, pp. 219-233 passim. For the Tilea affair see Paul D. Quinlan, "The Tilea Affair: A Further Inquiry," *Balkan Studies* 19, no. 1 (1978), pp. 147-157.

[14]Călinescu, *Însemnări politice*, pp. 411-412.

[15]Weinberg, *Foreign Policy of Hitler's Germany*, p. 536. Lungo, *Romania and the Great Powers*, pp. 159-161; Andreas Hillgruber, *Hitler, König Carol und Marschall Antonescu* (Wiesbaden: Franz Steiner, 1954), pp. 46-47.

[16]Lungo, *Romania and the Great Powers*, pp. 159-161; Andreas Hillgruber, *Hitler, König Carol und Marschall Antonescu* (Wiesbaden: Franz Steiner, 1954), pp. 46-47.

[17]Călinescu, *Însemnări politice*, p. 413.

[18]Ibid., pp. 417-418.

[19]Carol II, *Însemnări zilnice*, pp. 212-273 passim; U.S. Department of State, *Documents on German Foreign Policy 1918-1945* (Washington: 1949-1969), Series D, II, p. 574.

[20]Călinescu, *Însemnări politice*, p. 415.

adopt a policy of benevolent neutrality towards the Reich, at times even becoming violent.

Carol's immediate concern, however, was the present. Anxious about the willingness and ability of England and France to come to Romania's aid against Germany, Carol felt he had no choice but to follow a policy of neutrality. Part of this policy entailed staying out of any future conflict as long as possible as in World War I, along with trying to secure guarantees for Romania's frontiers. Thanks to the German invasion of Czechoslovakia followed by Tilea's exaggerated story of an ultimatum, on April 13 England abandoned her traditional policy of splendid isolationism toward the Balkans and, along with France, pledged to come to Romania's aid in case of a German or a Hungarian attack.[21] The pledge by England and France delighted Carol. At the same time, he hoped to round this off with a German guarantee of Romania's frontiers, but without success.[22] Carol also still hoped for economic assistance from England. Toward the end of April, the trade mission Chamberlain had promised in the previous November arrived under the leadership of Sir Frederick Leith-Ross of the Foreign Office. In the end, Romania received 5 million pounds in credit guarantees and a British promise to purchase 200,000 tons of wheat.[23] But it was far less than Carol had hoped for. "It's a pity the Germans can't be trusted," an angry Carol noted in his diary, "because otherwise I would send to hell all these so-called dear friends who are only interested in their own interests and are incapable of giving anything."[24]

With the German takeover of Czechoslovakia, a major supplier of armaments for Romania, along with the dwindling supply of weapons from France, Romania was forced to rely chiefly on Germany for armaments. Carol knew better than anyone the severe shortcomings of his army. He constantly railed against his Joint Chiefs of Staff for their lack of leadership, intelligence, and esprit de corps, and against the army for its shortage of officers and instructors, its shabby medical service, its uniform problems, and its March mobilization, which he called "a mess." In spite of it all, little seemed to change. The army's chief problem was its shortage of armaments, which everyone was hoarding or

---

[21]Great Britain, 5 *Parliamentary Debates* (Commons), V (1939), p. 346.

[22]Călinescu, *Însemnări politice*, p. 415.

[23]Sir Frederick Leith-Ross, *Money Talks: Fifty Years of International Finance* (London: Hutchins & Co., 1968), p. 265; Gunther to Secretary of State, May 13, 1939, State Department Telegram, No. 107, 871.24/170, National Archives, Washington.

[24]Carol II, *Însemnări zilnice*, p. 268.

demanding cash up front for in the spring and summer of 1939. The shortage made it necessary for Romania to follow a policy of avoiding a war unless attacked. At the end of 1938, only ten out of thirty-seven divisions could be fully equipped.[25] Against Hungary the Romanian army could hold its own, but against the Germans they stood little chance. Moreover, the Romanian army had a dismally low reputation abroad, another reason why the British and the French were reluctant to supply Romania with weapons.

By the middle of April, the March crisis had died down enough for Carol to order a demobilization. However, an atmosphere of pessimism still pervaded the royal palace. "Our situation is bad," Călinescu wrote. "More and more I have the feeling we will not escape the next war."[26]

Like the other capitals of Europe during that last summer of peace, Bucharest was a whirlwind of diplomatic jockeying. Above all, Carol was determined to keep Romania neutral as long as possible if war broke out, but he knew sooner or later Romania would become involved. Suddenly on August 21, word was received of an imminent signing of a German-Soviet Nonaggression Pact, which would make Romania's situation even more complicated and ominous. Now Romania would have to protect three of its frontiers, which was militarily impossible. Upon hearing the news, Carol claimed that he was not "overly surprised" and had suspected that there was "a concubinage" between Germany and those "semi-barbaric bandits." Urdăreanu was more pessimistic than ever and felt the country and the dynasty were lost unless they joined the Axis camp. Although the Romanians did not know for certain if the pact contained more than what was officially announced, they feared that Hitler and Stalin had worked out a deal over territory in Eastern Europe that probably included Bessarabia.[27] Călinescu considered "the situation to be very serious."[28] "Everything is black! Black! Completely black!" Carol jotted down in his diary. Somewhat of a comforting thought for Carol, however, was his feeling that "Poland would be attacked first, because the Germans want their

---

[25]Lungo, *Romania and the Great Powers*, p. 140.

[26]Călinescu, *Însemnări zilnice*, p. 417.

[27]Grigore Gafencu, *Prelude to the Russian Campaign: From the Moscow Pact to the Opening of Hostilities in Russia.* trans. E. Fletcher Allen (London: Frederick Muller, 1945) pp. 253-254; Jay Pierrepont Moffat, *Correspondence, August-September, 1939*, 4:43, Houghton Library, Harvard University.

[28]Gafencu, *Russian Campaign*, p. 253.

territory. I hope this will happen as it will make our situation better."[29] Two days after the pact was announced Bucharest informed Warsaw that in a Polish-German conflict Romania would remain neutral. The following day, Grigore Gafencu, Romania's foreign minister, assured the German minister to Romania that "Romania was determined to remain neutral in any conflict between Germany and Poland even if France and Britain were to come in."[30]

There was virtually nothing Carol could do to prevent a war. He supported King Leopold of Belgium's appeal for peace by the smaller states of Europe, but he felt little would come of it. He had even less faith in Roosevelt's last minute appeal for peace.

Then, on September 1 the world held its breath as Hitler unleashed his *Wehrmacht* on Poland. For the first several days of September Bucharest was almost in a state of panic. Would Romania be next? Hungary was also mobilizing. On September 3, Romanian troops were ordered to the frontiers and a partial mobilization was declared. Carol hurriedly left the downtown palace for Cotroceni, claiming the former "needs some repairs." On September 6, after meeting with his Crown Council, Carol officially announced Romania's neutrality. All of the members of the Council supported neutrality, which Carol found "extraordinary." "I am glad it's over, my nerves couldn't take it any more."

What was Lupescu's role in all of this? She probably had some indirect influence via the boudoir and Carol kept her informed of events, knowing that she was not well-acquainted with foreign affairs, which was also true of Urdăreanu. Nevertheless, Carol relied mainly on his ministers, especially on Călinescu and Gafencu, not on Lupescu. Like Carol, she detested Hitler and occasionally her animosity erupted into fits of rage.

Instead of holding out for six months against the Germans as Western military experts had hoped, Poland barely lasted three weeks. Carol too was surprised, believing from Romanian intelligence and his own personal observations that both sides were fairly evenly matched. Then on September 17, the Red Army invaded Poland from the east, providing the coup de grâce to what was left of Poland. Although Romania had a formal alliance with Poland providing for military assistance against a Russian attack, given Poland's and Romania's military situations there was nothing Carol could do. What especially alarmed

---

[29] Carol II, *Însemnări zilnice*, pp. 364-365.
[30] *German Foreign Policy*, VII, p. 363.

Carol was a similar fate for Romania. "The Russian advance changes the situation," Călinescu noted. "The German danger is further off. Now the Russian danger is primary."[31]

From this time on Carol's main concern was the Soviet Union. Throughout the fall and winter of 1939-1940 there were growing indications that the Soviets would resort to force to get Bessarabia back. Bucharest tried to get the British and the French to extend their guarantee to cover a Russian attack, but given their own shaky military situation the two Western Powers turned the Romanians down.[32] In spite of the swift collapse of Poland, Carol, like most Romanians, was still confident of an eventual Western victory; Bucharest newspapers continued to publish pro-French editorials.[33] What especially troubled the average Romanian was that Sir Reginald Hoare, the British ambassador to Romania, reported to the Foreign Office what would "happen to them in the meantime."[34]

Hoping to integrate himself with Hitler, in March and April 1939 Carol began releasing Legionary small fry from jail providing they swear allegiance to him.[35] Carol's juggling act also continued to try to pacify the Reich economically. As a result of the March Treaty, Germany and Romania joined together in the cultivation and processing of agricultural products, especially foodstuffs, oilseeds, and textile plants, and new industries were established for this purpose. Mixed German-Romanian firms were also formed to exploit Romania's mineral and petroleum resources. Although in the long run the treaty reduced Romania to an economic fiefdom of Germany, in the short term Romania achieved some advantages. Carol was correct in his belief that England and France would eventually win the war, but unfortunately for him it took too long for him to be saved. If it had been different, historians might have viewed his signing the economic treaty with Germany as a masterstroke.

---

[31] Gafencu, *Russian Campaign*, p. 254.

[32] Paul D. Quinlan, *Clash Over Romania: British and American Policies toward Romania, 1938-1947* (Los Angeles: American Romanian Academy of Arts and Sciences, 1977), pp. 54-57.

[33] Gerald J. Bobango, *Religion and Politics: Bishop Valerian Trifa and His Times* (Boulder, Colorado: East European Monographs, 1981), p. 155.

[34] Hoare to Foreign Office, February 16, 1940, F.O.371/24983 R2505/195/37, Public Record Office, London.

[35] Heinen, *Legion Erzengel Michael*, pp. 419-420.

But then came Germany's massive invasion of France and the Low Countries on May 10, 1940, and Carol's diplomatic juggling game began to rapidly crumble. The news of the German attack, which Carol received while he stood on the reviewing stand watching the annual Independence Day Parade, "hit like a bombshell" Carol's private secretary, Eugeniu Buhman, recorded in his diary. The dinner that followed was somber and lifeless; Carol barely talked. Everyone was tense.

Over the next several weeks, with the news of the endless German victories, Carol became more despondent. By the end of May it was clear to Carol that France had lost and that England, if she should survive, could provide no help to Romania. On May 27, Carol signed an oil agreement with Germany that he had been dragging his feet on since the winter. Two days later he announced at a Crown Council meeting that he decided to join the Axis camp — he had little choice.[36] In essence it boiled down to going with the Soviets or with Hitler, and the Germans appeared to be the lesser of the two evils, especially since they had no direct territorial claim against Romania, while the Soviets appeared bent on getting Bessarabia back. Moreover, there appeared to be no room for kings in the communist system.

For Carol, the time for dealing with problems through fancy footwork was over. On June 26, the Russians handed the Romanians a twenty-four hour ultimatum to surrender Bessarabia, to which the Germans had already consented. To keep Transylvania from being taken over by the Hungarians, or worse, have the rest of the country invaded by the Soviets or the Germans, Carol threw himself at Hitler's mercy. What choice did he have? At the end of June and the beginning of July, the Romanian government informed Berlin that it wanted an alliance with Germany and it requested that a military mission be sent to Romania. At the same time, Bucharest renounced the English and French guarantees, dropped out of the League of Nations, and hastily introduced more anti-Semitic legislation.

But it was too late for Carol. At the end of August, Hitler forced Romania to surrender roughly two-fifths of Transylvania to Hungary. Since June, one-third of Romania had been lost without a single shot being fired. A scapegoat was needed, and the obvious choice was Carol. Several days later Carol was forced to abdicate and fled the country amid a hail of Legionaries' bullets.

---

[36]Gafencu, *Russian Campaign*, pp. 282-285

As can be seen, until the summer of 1940 Carol's policy toward Germany was complicated and equivocal, which was precisely the way Carol designed it. But Carol was playing a deadly game. For such a delicate policy of tightrope walking to succeed Carol had to use all the wit and finesse he had. Carol proved himself to be a shrewd diplomat and that he failed in the end was essentially due to factors beyond his control. Hence, it is no wonder that historians for decades afterward have been confused and misled by Carol's tactics. Today, however, with the availability of Carol's own diary, along with other recently open archival material, the pieces of Carol's diplomatic juggling can finally be put together. Carol was no friend of Hitler and his Third Reich, knowing full well that if they were victorious, Romania would ultimately wind up being a satellite of Germany. Until the fall of France, he was confident that, in the end, the Western Powers would be victorious. He was right. Unfortunately, his timing was off.

Efficient and Rapid:
The Letters of Major Walter Ross of OSS to his Commanding Officer, Lieutenant Commander Edward Green, During the Evacuation of Allied Airmen from Romania, August 30-September 2, 1944

Ernest H. Latham, Jr.

"Worthy of the highest commendation is the efficient and rapid manner with which the actual return of our interned airmen in Roumania was effected. All personnel connected with this operation are to be informed of the appreciation of the AAF in the recovery of these airmen."

Cable of General Hap Arnold to commanding officer OSS
Bari, September 4, 1944.[1]

The evening of August 23, 1944, King Michael broadcast to Romania the generally welcomed news that Marshal Antonescu's government had been replaced, the country had abandoned the Axis alliance and would reestablish diplomatic relations with the Allies. The shortwave service of the BBC immediately carried the news around the world, including to the Allied headquarters for the Mediterranean Theater of Operations in

Caserta, Italy, and the U.S. 15th Air Force with its headquarters across the peninsula in Bari. Nowhere, however, was the rejoicing at this turn of events greater than among the nearly 1300 Allied prisoners of war in Romania, many of whom had access to a shortwave radio and thus learned the news immediately.

The initial euphoria among the Allies, whether in Italy or Romania, quickly dissolved when confronted by the problems involved in rescuing the POWs, now free, but some 550 miles behind enemy lines. A major fear was that the Germans might recover and take command of the situation with the same skills they had shown a year before in Italy. In fact, by 1944 Germany had been weakened by the additional year of defeats and retreat and probably did not have sufficient forces in the area to turn events in its favor; and thus the fear of such a recovery was probably unrealistic. Nevertheless, during the attempt to reestablish its position, Germany might sweep up all the POWs and transport them deep into the Reich. There was, however, the more immediate danger that the unarmed ex-prisoners might find themselves caught between the lines of a rapidly advancing Soviet army bent on revenge against its erstwhile enemy and a determined German army by then embittered and resentful at what it considered betrayal by its erstwhile ally. Neither as the unarmed enemies of the Germans nor as the unarmed allies of the Soviets, did prospects for the POWs look promising.

Another major problem for the rescue effort was the difficulty in planning the operation with no clear idea of the scale necessary for the effort. No one among the Allies knew how many ex-POWs would be involved or their ability to travel. Representatives of the International Committee of the Red Cross (ICRC) and the American interests section of the Swiss legation in Bucharest had kept the American authorities well informed concerning the welfare and whereabouts of some 110 POWs captured by the Romanians and eventually interned at

[1]Cable XVAF ABLE 128 from commanding general U. S. 15th Air Force to commanding officer, OSS Bari, 4 September 1944. U.S. National Archives and Records Administration, Record Group 226, Entry 190, Box 118 (such citations of documents in the National Archives will henceforth be abbreviated, e.g. NARA RG-226 E-190 B-118. It will be immediately clear to the reader that this paper could not have been written without the cooperation of the National Archives and its many helpful and patient archivists. I am particularly grateful to Ms. Mia Waller, Mr. John Taylor, and Dr. Larry McDonald, whose expertise in OSS records spared me many hours of fruitless searching. I must also mention my great good fortune in first being introduced to the National Archives a number of years ago by Dr. Greg Bradsher, whose kindly interest in my subsequent research has been an unfailing encouragement.

Timişul de Jos following the low-level bombing raid on Ploieşti on August 1, 1943, the famous Operation Tidal Wave.

Smarting from the staggering losses sustained in that ill-fated disaster, the Americans suspended for nine months all bombing of Romania until April 4, 1944. By that time Allied air force units were established in Bari, Foggia, and elsewhere on the Puglian plain along the east coast of Italy. With stations much closer to their Romanian targets than the airfields in North Africa that had been the point of origin for Operation Tidal Wave, the bombers now had more time over their targets and also, most important, enjoyed the protection of fighter escorts. The bombing resumed in earnest on April 4, 1944. The Americans by day attacked an expanded target list while the British bombed by night. Simultaneously, of course, the number of allied POWs rose as well. Indeed, at the hands of the ever capable German and Romanian anti-aircraft and fighter units the number escalated sharply, increasing by a factor of twelve in less than five months.[2]

As the war moved deeper into Romania, communication with the outside world diminished for both the Swiss of the ICRC and the legation as well as for the Romanian government. Although the American government knew all too well how many Americans were missing in action as a result of the raids, there was no way of knowing how many of these were dead somewhere in the Balkans or of those still alive how many were hiding or imprisoned in Romania, Bulgaria, or Yugoslavia. The risks associated with bailing out of disabled, frequently flaming aircraft left no doubt that many of those still alive would be severely wounded or badly burned.

The obvious place to turn for information and operational help was the Office of Strategic Services (OSS), which had been founded on June 13, 1942, by Colonel William "Wild Bill" Donovan, a New York lawyer, an army reservist, and a personal acquaintance of President Roosevelt. A permanent empire-builder, Donovan had convinced the president that to fight a global war America needed a globally oriented strategic intelligence organization. Such an organization would focus its efforts on the gaps between the political and economic information collected within the foreign affairs community and the order-of-battle technological and cryptographic intelligence collected by the military

---

[2] A survey of the circumstances and treatment of American POWs in Romania may be found in the present writer's "All Thankful: Reports by Neutral Observers of American Prisoners of War Held in Romania 1943-1944," *Romanian Civilization*, Vol. V (Spring 1996), No. 1: pp. 5-28. See also the cover photograph and caption accompanying this issue.

and naval services. It is only a short hop between collecting information and acting on it, a hop Donovan willingly made as opportunities presented themselves.[3]

Neither the State Department nor the War Department welcomed this ambitious newcomer onto the scene. The OSS, resembling its chief, was largely composed of personnel serving for the duration of the war with only limited prior military or diplomatic experience on which to build. In some areas the misgivings and hostilities of the professional soldiers and diplomats were sufficient to block the OSS's activities almost completely. Against the Japanese in the Pacific Theater of Operations, for example, General MacArthur's disdain for the OSS's efforts was reflected throughout his command; and intelligence functions there remained largely in the hands of the military and naval professionals with the exception of Burma where the OSS's penetration operations carried on an almost private war deep behind the Japanese lines.[4]

In the North African, Mediterranean, and European theaters of operation, however, the OSS was welcomed, albeit cautiously. Although confidence in the OSS grew in the course of the war, it never reached a level of complete trust and respect. Nevertheless, the OSS soldiered on in its own style, focusing its efforts on America's major European enemies, Germany and Italy. Neither Romania nor the Balkans in general was a priority target for investigation or operations. The Ploieşti raid of August 1, 1943, was almost the first military action America undertook in the Balkans; and it remained the only major one until the resumption of the bombing in the last year of the war. America and the OSS were content to leave the peninsula to the British, who had jealously guarded, traditional interests,[5] and to the Soviets, who were increasingly perceived as the war's strategy unfolded to be the prime Allied presence in the Balkans.

---

[3]Anthony Cave Brown, *The Last Hero: Wild Bill Donovan* (New York: Vintage Books, A Division of Random House, 1984). Pages 670-673 deal with Romania in August and September 1944. General Donovan's colorful career has been increasingly a subject of scholarly interest especially since the declassification of the OSS records. A complete and reliable biography which utilizes the now available and declassified OSS records is still to be published. Brown's biography, which suffers from errors, inaccuracies, and a hagiographic approach, can only be used with caution.

[4]Lawrence H. McDonald, "The OSS and Its Records," *The Secrets War: The Office of Strategic Services in World War II*, ed. George C. Chalou (Washington, DC: National Archives and Record Administration, 1992) provides an excellent overall survey of OSS history and institutional problems as well as a description of the organization and contents of the OSS record group (RG 226) at the National Archives.

The above is not to imply that the OSS was totally indifferent to Romania and the Balkans. As information and intelligence targets of opportunity presented themselves, they were exploited. The OSS's stations in Cairo and, in Romania's case, especially in Istanbul, accumulated travellers' reports, open source publications and whatever else might be useful. In the OSS's Research and Analysis Division in addition to the usual reports on specific events and subjects, ten of the widely circulated Number Intelligence Reports had been published about Romania by the summer of 1944. These were a mere fraction, however, of the reports devoted to the major members of the Axis Pact. Predictably, the Romanian reports described the country as a source and causeway for supplying Germany with foodstuffs and petroleum products.

The invasion of the Italian peninsula and the establishment of the Allied headquarters at Caserta and the Allied air fields in and around Bari and Foggia opened up opportunities for the Americans to become more active in the Balkans. Simultaneously, the adamant British opposition to American operations in the Balkans softened. By the summer of 1944 the OSS had joined the British services in supporting anti-German partisans in Yugoslavia and Greece, and American OSS officers in liaison positions operated in both countries, albeit in numbers far below those of their British colleagues. There was, however, no American operation then underway in Romania.[6]

A large OSS unit had established itself as the 2699th Regiment in Bari close to the operational headquarters of the 15th Air Force. Although primarily active in Italy, the regiment included a Company B, under Lieutenant Commander (LCDR) Edward J. Greene, which was concerned with the Balkans and Romania. Propelled by the OSS's need to covertly infiltrate agents into German occupied areas and hopes of recovering these agents as well as downed aviators, well or wounded, the 15th Air Force had been developing the necessary skills for covert

---

[5]Minutes of a meeting held with members of the OSS group in Bari on 28 August 1944 report: "General Donovan pointed out that the British have tried to keep us out of the Balkans and that we will have to have our own planes." NARA RG-226 E-190 B-118.

[6]Although handicapped by classification considerations, the two volume *War Report of the OSS*, finally released in 1976 (New York: Walker and Company: Washington, DC: Carrollton Press, Inc.) with an introduction by Kermit Roosevelt, remains an important source for the context of operations. Volume 2, *The Overseas Targets*, contains several subchapters directly relevant to this article: "Middle East," pp. 47-49; "Bases in Italy," pp. 85-89; "Istanbul", pp. 269-272; and "Bucharest", pp. 331-332.

operations, such as low-level parachute drops, short strip landing and take-offs, and night navigation.[7] Although at the time of King Michael's address to the nation there was no American intelligence officer present in Romania, the OSS had been planning in August 1944 to send in a small team to investigate possibilities for rescuing downed Allied aviators and any POWs who could escape from the prison compounds and link-up with an OSS representative.[8]

It was, however, not through OSS channels that the break-through for the POWs rescue came but from the initiative of one of the POWs himself, Lieutenant Colonel James A. Gunn III of San Antonio Texas.[9] Colonel Gunn had been the commander of the 454th Bomber Group with the 15th Air Force flying out of the San-Giovanni airfield in Cerignola, Italy. Barely a week before the Romanian coup, on August 17th, he was shot down on a bombing mission against Ploieşti and captured near the village of Cornu, a suburb of Câmpina, some twenty miles northeast of Ploieşti. Initially confined in Ploieşti, after two days Gunn was moved to Bucharest where he joined some 400 other Allied officer prisoners of war in a converted schoolhouse on the south side of the city. It was here he heard news of the fall of Marshal Antonescu. The following morning Gunn searched for some means of communicating by radio or wire directly with the Allies in order to describe the Romanian situation and request the evacuation of the Allied personnel. The Germans had by then, however, commenced

---

[7]24 July 1944 Lieutenant General Ira Eaker ordered the 15th Air Force to establish a special unit, the Air Crew Rescue Unit (ACRU #1) to undertake such rescues in the Balkans. Wesley F. Craven and James L. Cate, eds., *The Army Air Forces in World War II*, Vol. 3, *Europe: Argument to V-E Day January 1944 to May 1945* (Chicago: The University of Chicago Press, 1951), pp. 522-523.

[8]A memorandum 25 August 1944 from Lt. B.N. Deranian, Chief SO, to LCDR E.J. Green, Commanding Officer of Company B, 2677th Regiment, OSS (Provisional) "Subject: Evacuation of American Airmen in Roumania" indicates that a small team of four officers and a radio man were being prepared "to depart within the next two or three days." A memorandum from the Commanding Office of 2677th Regiment OSS (Prov.) to the Director of the OSS 30 August 1944, "Subject: Rumania," indicates this group was "fully equipped, briefed, and scheduled to drop into Rumania on the night of the 28th." NARA RG-226 E-190 B-118.

[9]Gunn retired from the U.S. Air Force in 1967. His account of his efforts on behalf of his fellow POWs was published the previous year as "Escape from Romania" in the *Aerospace Historian*, Vol. XVIII (Autumn 1966), No. 3, pp. 114-120. This article was read into the *Congressional Record* of May 3rd, 1967, and also reprinted in its entirety in William J. Fili's *Of Lice and Men: A True Story of Depersonalization and Survival of a P.O.W.* (Philadelphia: Dorrance & Company, 1973), pp. 114-120.

their attack on the city which restricted most possibilities for communicating with the outside world.

Finally, on August 24th Gunn located the Romanian Minister of National Defense, Lieutenant General Racoviţă,[10] in his temporary headquarters in a forest outside Bucharest. Gunn requested that the Allied personnel be evacuated from Bucharest because of the German attacks. General Racoviţă agreed to this, and it was done the following day. Gunn also asked to borrow a plane to fly to Italy to organize the evacuation, offering in return to arrange American bombing support against the Germans, who were operating out of the Băneasa airfield. This offer interested the Romanian side but not enough to give him an airplane immediately. On August 27th, however, Gunn was allowed to depart from Ploieşti as a passenger in a Savola Marchetti with a Romanian pilot and crew. Shortly after take-off, however, the airplane had to return to the airfield.

As the frustrated Col. Gunn stepped from the plane, he was met by Captain Constantin "Bazu" Cantacuzino[11] of the Royal Romanian Air Force, who offered to fly him to Italy if the American was willing to travel lying down in the fuselage of the single-seat Messerschmidt,

---

[10]General Mihail Racoviţă (March 7, 1889-June 28, 1954) a career cavalry officer. Commissioned in 1908, he served in the First and Second World Wars. As commander of the Romanian 4th Army on July 7, 1944, he was the last Romanian to receive the high German battlefield decoration, the Ritterkreuz. Approached in July 1944 to support an anti-Antonescu, anti-German coup he demurred in view of the size of the German armor then in Romania; nor is his precise role certain when the coup finally did take place on August 23, 1944. At that time General Sănătescu appointed him Minister of National Defence, a post he retained until the cabinet reshuffle of November 4, 1944, when Sănătescu himself assumed the portfolio as Minister of War ad interim.

By this time Racoviţă had fallen under suspicion for alleged anti-Soviet, pro-German sentiments. Arrested by the communist authorities in June 1950 as "an enemy of the state," he was sentenced to hard labor for life and died at Sighet Prison four years later. Dr. Alesandru Duţu, Florica Dobre, *Drama Generalilor Români* (1944-1964) Bucureşti: Editura enciclopedică, 1997, pp. 224-226; Elizabeth W. Hazard, *Cold War Crucible: United State Foreign Policy and the Conflict in Romania 1943-1953*, Boulder, CO: East European Monographs, 1996, pp. 52-53; Mark Axworthy, *Third Axis Fourth Ally: Romanian Armed Forces in the European War, 1941-1945,* London: Arms and Armour Press (A Cassell Imprint), 1995, pp. 65, 156, 158-60, 176-177, 180-181, 208.

[11]Constantin "Bazu" Cantacuzino (1905-1959) in the 1930s a famous Romanian automobile driver and pilot competing in international meets. In 1939 national champion in air acrobatics. During World War II in the Royal Romanian Air Force Gr. 9 he was Romania's leading fighter pilot, credited with more than 60 air victories and holding the probably unique distinction of being an ace three times over: against the Soviet Air Force, the U.S. Army Air Corps, and the German Luftwaffe. Axworthy, *op. cit.*, pp. 310, 320.

an ME-109G. The German fighter was repainted with American insignia, and the radio was removed to make room for the large Texan. Gunn provided Cantacuzino hand-drawn maps and instructed him on the proper altitude and approach to San-Giovanni airfield to avoid the American radar and the anti-aircraft defense.

Despite the obvious risks connected with flying an enemy fighter, whatever the insignia, into an American airfield, the flight was uneventful and they landed safely the evening of August 27th. After a hurried meal, the two men were immediately driven to the 15th Air Force headquarters in Bari, and there they met with representatives of the U.S. Army Air Corps and the OSS to start the planning for an evacuation. As noted above, the OSS already had plans underway to parachute into Romania the following day a small team composed of junior officers and a radio operator. In view of the pressing needs presented by the evacuation and the unexpected intelligence opportunities, this plan was set aside; and planning began for a much larger, more complex mission to be commanded by a higher ranking officer.[12]

The promised raid on the German positions at Băneasa was carried out the next day, August 28th, by the 99th Fighter Group.[13] In Bari the day was spent outfitting the members of the mission, issuing supplies including a more powerful radio, readying the bombers for their unusual mission and planning the details of the evacuation.

At 7:00 a.m. on August 29th Capt. Cantacuzino reported to Bari airfield where he was given a cockpit drill in the American fighter the P-51. Immediately after a trial take-off and landing, escorted by three other P-51s, he flew to Popești, a military airfield some five miles southwest of Bucharest and a comfortable distance from German military activity. Having landed safely there, he radioed an all-clear signal to his fighter escort, which, having climbed to a higher altitude around noon, passed the message back to Bari. That was the signal for two Flying Fortress bombers to take off 10 minutes later for Popești. Cantacuzino was then to see that all Romanian planes were grounded and all anti-aircraft activity suspended between 2:30 p.m. and 4:30 p.m.

---

[12]Top Secret memorandum 30 August 1944, "Subject: Rumania," to Director OSS from LCDR Green, Commanding Officer of Company B, 2677th Regt., OSS (Prov.). Paragraphs 1-4 give an account of the Cantacuzino-Gunn flight and the midnight planning meeting at Bari 27-28 August 1944. NARA RG-226 E-190 B-118.

[13]This operation was not a total success, for inadequate land-air coordination resulted in the loss to American bombing of half a company of the Romanian 4th Parachute Battalion. Axworthy, *op. cit.*, p. 190.

When the two bombers arrived, Canacuzino's orders were to signal all clear and see that the bombers could safely land, off-load the evacuation team and evacuate the first 20 Allied ex-POWs. The evacuation team would then establish immediate radio contact with Bari and proceed to organize the POW evacuation which called for flights of 12 bombers landing at 60 minute intervals in daylight hours each taking off with 20 persons until the mission, initially code named Operation Gunn and then Operation Reunion, was completed. Tucked in among the personnel on the first two bombers that landed that afternoon was a unit of OSS agents under the command of Major Walter Ross from Company B, 2677th Regiment OSS (Provisional), the Balkan operations unit in the Mediterranean Theater.[14]

There was little in Major Ross's background as a businessman to hint at his future intelligence successes. He was born in Oskaloosa, Iowa, November 19, 1903. He had been a student between 1921 and 1923 at Knox College in Galesburg, Illinois. He began a business career in 1923 as an employee of Globe Superior Corporation. He joined Rollins Hosiery Mills three years later, and in 1928 he moved over to General Motors Acceptance Corporation in New York City. He remained with General Motors until 1942, when he joined the army and eventually the OSS. Although there is nothing in the records to indicate that Ross knew General Donovan, it is possible that they had met in New York during the years when both were working there.[15]

In the words of LCDR Green, Ross's commanding officer at Company B, "the primary function of the entire mission was to evacuate the American airmen as soon as possible," but the unique intelligence opportunities that the unexpected developments in Romania offered were too inviting to ignore. The mission's objectives were accordingly increased, and the appropriate, additional personnel were assigned to the team, especially in communications. Among these newly assigned was Colonel George Kraigher, Commanding Officer of the Air Crew Rescue Unit of the 15th Air Force at the specific request

---

[14]It was an assignment that LCDR Green, the Commanding Officer of Company B, very much wanted for himself, but he could hardly be spared. Since Major Ross was of appropriate rank and "most familiar with this type of work and could be spared for a week or ten days," he received the assignment. Memorandum of 30 August 1944, from LCDR Green to the Director of the OSS, "Subject: Rumania," paragraph 5. NARA RG-226 E-190 B-118.

[15]The outline of Major Ross's life and career are taken from his entry in *Who's Who in America 1974-1975* (Chicago: Marquis *Who's Who*, Inc., 1974), Vol. 2, p. 2644 and from his obituary in the *New York Times* (November 21, 1990, p. D-23).

of General Eaker of the 15th Air Force. Ensign Beverly M. Bowie, Lieutenant (junior grade) R.J. Forbes and Photographer's Mate 1st Class Nelson B. Paris were assigned responsibility for after-action reporting on the strategic bombing of Ploieşti with further instructions to learn everything they could about the German situation with regard to petroleum. The three army second lieutenants and a radio sergeant chosen earlier for the August 28th drop because of their knowledge of Romanian and other useful languages and skills, were to remain behind after the evacuation mission and join up with the Bucharest City Team that the OSS was assembling to be part of the American component in the future Allied Control Commission. Their mission, again in Green's words, was "to remain indefinitely as an intelligence unit to provide military, political, and economic intelligence from that area."[16]

On Tuesday, August 29, his cockpit drill satisfactorily completed, Capt. Cantacuzino took off from Bari in an American P-51 and landed safely at Popeşti around noon. At 12:10 p.m. the two flying fortresses took off according to plan with the OSS team. At 3:30 p.m. they landed without incident at Popeşti.

During the next four days Major Ross wrote three informal, impressionistic letters and one note to LCDR Green. They were usually written late in the evening by Ross himself, apparently on a portable typewriter.[17] The first letter was written the day after his arrival:

----

[16]Top Secret memorandum of 30 August 1944 from LCDR Green to Director of the OSS, "Subject: Rumania," paragraphs 5, 7, 8. NARA RG-226 E-190 B-118.

[17]The three letters of August 30, 31 and September 2, 1944, exist in the archives in two forms. The first is the actual manuscript as typed in blue ink by Ross on 8"x11" onionskin paper with his various corrections and type-overs. The second form is a corrected version with numbered paragraphs, probably produced within the headquarters of the 2677th Regt. OSS (Prov.) in multiple copies for circulation within the intelligence community as appropriate. There are no significant differences between the two versions of the August 30th letter, limited differences between the versions of August 31st but major editing and omissions distinguish the two versions of September 2nd. All three of the manuscript letters are classified secret in the same pencilled handwriting at the top of the first page. The corrected versions are likewise classified. The note of September 1, 1944, exists in only one version, unclassified and obviously typed and initialed by Ross himself.

The versions reproduced here are the Ross manuscript versions in all cases. Any changes made in the retyped corrected version are indicated by endnotes. The only changes to the originals are to incorporated Ross's own corrections, usually of typographical errors. Ross's spelling errors and sometimes incorrect, phonetic spelling of Romanian names have been retained. A corrected spelling of such names appears in the endnotes.

Bucharest 30 August 1944[18]
(Secret)
Lt. Cdr. Edward Green
Hq. 2677th Rgt. OSS
APO 534 % PM, New York.

Dear Ed,

Doubtless you have heard of our safe arrival therefore, I will not dwell on it other than to mention that it was without incident worthy of any special mention. The plan worked perfectly and we went down on the Popeşti field at 1530.

There was a fair crowd at the airport, but not huge as our arrival had been kept pretty quiet. Capt. Cantacuzino met us at the field along with other Roumanian officers and a half dozen provisional government people, the most important of whom was Georgiscu,[19] whose exact place in the set up I will explain to you later. The planes according to plan had taxied to a spot as close to a take off position as possible did not even stop the motors while we got off and took off the gear. The Mustangs were buzzing the field all the while and it was quite a sight to see them hovering over and around us. As we circled and came in for the landing we could see the AA batteries with the crews at the guns, so close that their facial expressions were almost discernible. The big B-17's made about the best target they had

---

[18]To the left of the date and above LCDR Green's address is handwritten by someone other than Ross, "Return to Col. Dean."

[19]Valeriu "Rica" Georgescu (code named: Jockey) before the war had been managing director of Standard Oil of New Jersey's Romanian subsidiary, Român-Americană. He had close personal ties to Iuliu Maniu, leader of the National Peasants Party and with him and on his behalf an active relationship with the British intelligence organization, Special Operations Executive. These contacts landed him in prison in 1941, but Marshal Antonescu allowed him to continue such contacts. As a result Georgescu had the rare if not unique honor of being an intelligence officer who rebuilt and maintained a network of agents from inside a prison cell. A member of the Romanian delegation to the armistice talks in Moscow, following which, in disappointment, he threatened to resign as Subsecretary of State for Industry, Commerce, and Mines. He did so on November 3, 1944, on the eve of the second Sănătescu administration. In 1947 Georgescu and his wife left Romania and their two children to visit the United States from which they did not return. They became U.S. citizens in 1952 and were finally, following the direct intervention of President Eisenhower, reunited with their children in the mid-1950s. Georgescu resumed his career with Standard Oil from which he retired in 1964 at the age of 60 and settled in Geneva. Elizabeth Hazard, *Cold War Crucible: United States Foreign Policy and the Conflict in Romania 1943-1953*, (Boulder Colorado: East European Monographs, 1996); and Ivor Porter, *Operation Autonomous: With S.O.E. in Wartime Romania*, (London: Chatto & Windus, 1989). Georgescu figures in both books as a major figure before his departure from Romania in 1948.

ever seen, I guess, and the temptation to cut loose must have been great.

Capt. Cantacuzino had spent most of the time since his arrival with the government representatives so he was delayed in getting any word to the airmen's camp which would let us send any of the men back in the same ships. Consequently they had to move right on off because of the gas situation with their escort.

Nobody wanted us to set up our headquarters on the field for many reasons and since Bucharest was reported quiet it seemed satisfactory to look at other places in the city proper. So, in two closed cars and with a truck to carry the gear we came into Bucharest and gathered for a moment at the office occupied by Georgescu. He wanted us to set up our headquarters right in his building but we insisted upon a private place of our own. A Major Jaeger,[20] who is the second in command of the group of airmen prisoners had met us at the field and driven into town so when the question of a place to set up shop was up for discussion he told of a private residence that had been offered to him for use by any Americans who might come into Bucharest. After looking at it we decided to take it and moved in at once.[21]

---

[20]This is possibly Major William H. Yaeger, Jr., the highest ranking American officer among the American POWs captured on August 1, 1943 during Operation Tidal Wave, the low level bombing mission over Ploieşti. At age 28 and unwounded, he, therefore, became the leader of the American POWs incarcerated at Timişul de Jos. As such he represented the Americans during the periodic visits of the International Committee of the Red Cross and the American interests section of the Swiss legation in Bucharest. According to reports in Richard Britt's memoir and the Dugan-Stewart history, where he appears as Major "Z", Yaeger's leadership was sorely flawed by his hoarding food, intoxication, one suicide attempt and unnecessary fraternization with his Romanian captors. Particularly irksome to his colleagues was one occasion when he went to Bucharest and addressed the local Rotary Club. Upon his return he was given the silent treatment by the other officers. He eventually was driven to billeting in the enlisted men's barracks. In the end the Romanian authorities apparently transferred him to Bucharest where the more senior officers were eventually collected. Thus he was likely "the Texas major call Jager," whom Ivor Porter met on August 24th, 1944, on his way to the National Bank to set up radio communication with the British authorities. However helpful Yaeger may have been to Porter and Ross in August 1944, his earlier conduct in the POW camp was not forgotten, and an officer who had been with him in Timişul de Jos preferred charges against him later after the POWs had been evacuated to Italy. Latham, *op. cit.*, p. 20, footnote 39; James Dugan and Carrol Stewart, *Ploieşti: the Great Ground-Air Battle of 1 August 1943* (New York: Bantam Books, Inc., 1963), pp. 248, 259; Richard W. Britt, *The Princess and the POW* (Comfort, Texas: Gabriel Publishing, 1988), pp. 111, 115, 122, 124-125, 141, 178-179, 237.

It is a large stone structure, completely walled in and in a fairly good residential section of the town. The place was approved by Georgescu as satisfactory from his standpoint and the owner of the house was around to see us established. Most of the furniture had been moved out, but we brought in some beds for a place to sleep. It will serve as a headquarters, billet, and place to mess. The owner turned over a couple of his old servants for our use and today at noon we had a fairly decent meal. We will be able to keep the place indefinitely, as the owner has another place in the forest outside town and prefers Americans to the Russkys if he must and probably will have to let it go for such use.

After getting to the house about dusk we started setting up the radio hoping to make a contact at once. We had the small set working fairly early but getting settled, writing the message, coding etc. made it impossible to get on the air before about two a.m. and the operator could not make contact. Early today the large set was in operation and in contact with the station but they can't seem to hold on to the Bari end long enough to get the message thru. It has been somewhat embarrassing to me because of our assurance to the 15th of being able to get through but we have not been able to do so up to late this evening as this is being written. Col. Kraigher is most unhappy about it, of course and so am I.

Last night was quiet for the most part. We had dinner arranged at a place selected by Lt. Valjaun, a Roumanian officer assigned by the government as our liaison officer during our stay and half the crowd went about nine with the Colonel and I to follow late with the others. Which wasn't good for just as we got to the restaurant a raid alarm was sounded and we had to duck for our basement which is a good shelter, where we ate field rations. No bombs were dropped in the city, however. During the night we could hear some small arms fire and a machine gun once in a while but nothing more.[22]

We are going to try to start the evacuation tomorrow but it will be uncertain in view of the communications situation. We have the men lined up and ready to go so hope nothing will stop us. I plan to send this out on one of them if I am able to do so.

[21]The house was owned by Demeter "Mitu" Bragadiro, the well known owner of a Bucharest brewery and the husband of Alexandra "Tanda" Caradja, daughter of Princess Catherine Caradja, whose friendship with the American POWs has become legendary. Catherine Caradja, *Princess Catherine* (Comfort, Texas: Gabriel Publishing, 1991), pp. 141-143.

Later:

No radio yet to get any messages thru. The large set has broken down twice (transmitter) and it is now out of working order. The message was being transmitted with Bari reporting very poor reception and we were asked to change frequencies. In doing so we lost the station completely and since then have not been able to get thru. We are also trying Cairo. The boys say it is not anything the matter with the radio but simply the atmospheric conditions, range, etc.

We have now dispatched Cantacuzino back to Bari in the P-51 to carry the messages thru and hope to get word to the 15th that way. In any case it isn't much of a feather in our cap. There will be some C-47's coming in a day or two I think and you had better try to get together with Huston to see if he has anything to suggest. It may be you will want to send another set, perhaps a large one of some kind with more range and power. Talk to the 15th about it and see if they have something in case Huston does not.

/s/ Walter
Walter M. Ross
Major AGD
Aug 31 0900

We are just now transmitting our first message thru to Cairo for relay to you.[23]

The second letter, written late in the night of Thursday, August 31st details the events of the first day of the evacuation and provides Ross's first political reporting on the new Romanian government:

31 August 1944
Bucharest[24]

---

[22]It is unclear what exactly Major Ross heard on the night of August 29-30. German resistance within Bucharest ceased completely on August 26th. The following day the German units to the north, encircled in the Băneasa Forest, surrendered although Generals Stahel and Gerstenberg with some 1900 of their men had eluded the encirclement and fled north towards Ploiești only to surrender on August 28th. Combat continued during the night in question around Ploiești, and the last Germans in that zone finally surrendered on August 31st. Even in ideal weather conditions, however, it is unlikely Ross heard small arms or even machine gun fire from Ploiești, some 36 miles distant. Thus it seems the firing he heard was from some nervous sentries in or near Bucharest.

[23]This post scriptum is handwritten by Ross.

[24]Below "Bucharest" is handwritten by someone other than Ross, "Noted: A2 - 15 Air Force 2 Sept 44 0920."

(Secret)
L. Cdr. Edward Green
C. O., Co. B Hq 2677th Rgt OSS (Prov)
APO 534 N.Y.

Dear Ed,

This letter is being pounded out late at night in order to get it on the plane which should be here in the morning and be on the way to Bari about as soon as we can establish radio contact. I have a number of things on my mind and I am going to give them to you about as I think of them. Plane communications also gives me a lot more space for transmittal of any message than I could get by radio.

First the radio — it made it to Cairo this morning and we were able to get off the first message I had set up for you. You should have had it relayed to you from Cairo as we could get that station but could not get Bari. The other set is still not in working order, but we have another set going in a truck which had been put together by some escapees and which is strong as the other one we have. We have not been able to get Bari on it either. So far as I am able to deduce from the radio team, it is a question of distance and interference over the mountains rather than the set itself. We are able to use the small one to get to Cairo so they will have to send for you. I would not trust Bari until we are definitely able to establish contact and be certain it will work.

As you know by now, Cantacuzino flew the Mustang back last evening and took the message telling that we were ready to evacuate this morning. He got thru and back okay so we were all ready today to get the gang of boys off. It was quite a show and accomplished with a lot of trouble and work.

The camp[25] where the boys were located is some 20 kilometers from Popeşti where the planes were scheduled to land. Trucks were very difficult to line up for eight hundred men, even with the government on our side, as they are scarce. However, enough vehicles were there to start the exodus at five a.m. this morning. By 1000 the whole crowd was gathered and that many men plus helpers and natives makes a lot of people.

---

[25]This unidentified camp was not favorably remembered by some of the soon-to-be-liberated Americans. Richard Britt recalled: "...the barracks were filthy and full of lice... we were not about to fight the lice ...and chose to stretch out on the hard ground." Britt, *op. cit.*, pp. 232-233.

The first twelve planes came in right on the dot and we sent up the signals that all was clear to land. It was especially interesting to us for during the morning Russian patrols had been over the city in A-20's and some Mustangs. The boys had already been divided into squads of twenty, each with a leader who would keep them together. After the planes landed and taxied to the side, the boys marched right into the doors single file by squads, one to twelve, 20 at a time. The sixth plane blew a tire on the landing and could not get off so 20 had to stay behind for tomorrow.

At eleven the second twelve came in, landed and loaded so as to take off without incident, except for one plane developing some kind of an oil leak. It could not take off with its original group but took off last of the day after repairs were made. The third twelve got in at twelve, landed, loaded, and got off without a hitch. About this time some Russian planes were over the field and a couple of small scout or patrol planes landed during the time the Fortresses were on the field. However, they didn't get too much attention because of the presence of the big boys.

At one o'clock the two B-17 hospital planes came in. We hadn't known the Fifteenth had Fortress planes set up for stretchers so they had laid them on at once upon receiving word of the patients and arranged for them to come in today, which was a wonderful thing. We had gotten a red cross bus and a couple of ambulances together to pick up the boys at the hospital. I forgot to tell you that on the first planes there had been a couple of doctors with stretchers, etc. They went to the hospital at once with helpers to bring the hospital cases back. On the trip was Joe Morton (AP correspondent)[26] and also our Field Photo guy. They said the human interest thing at the hospital was terrific and I can well believe it. I had been there yesterday and believe me, if the trip had been for no other purpose than to get out the hospital cases alone it would have been worth it a thousand times. Conditions were not terrible, but pretty bad and it was a godsend to get the boys out of the place. Burns, gangrene, amputations, broken bones, etc.

The stretcher cases were loaded into the bomb bays and the others into the remainder of the ship. There were twelve, I believe on stretchers the rest could get in with crutches, etc. As near as I can recall at the moment the total in the last two planes were forty-nine. So the total evacuees for the day was

---

[26]This parenthesis in handwriting, probably not Ross's, is inserted above the paragraph with an arrow pointing to its appropriate location in the text.

749 or right at that figure. There was no sign at any time of the enemy.

Tomorrow the balance of the boys right on hand go out starting as before at 1000. There will be about two hundred more and the immediate job is done after that. In the next ten days or two weeks it is probable that another two hundred will be rounded up. There are a lot holed up in the town and countryside who have not learned of the evacuation but who will string in as they do hear of it. The Germans bombed so heavily last week that a lot who were here moved out to the country and they are stringing back. There were fifteen, for example, who rode the top of a railroad car today all the way from Constanța to be here for the ride home.

I hope to get this on the plane tomorrow for you to receive sometime on the first. You should have gotten a letter from me today the same way thru John Richardson or a Major at the Fifteenth by the name of Pendleton, who I think is the boss of Bob Mooney, the photographer for the Fifteenth who was here today.

The way is clear for Mattei Ghica Cantacuzino[27] to come on. I hope you got the word in time to get him on the planes the first. I cleared it with Col. Kraigher and with Georgiscu. If he did not get on the first, send him as soon as another plane is coming. I understand Col. Kraigher is ordering his B-25 over for his own use in getting back so maybe Mattei can come on that if not tomorrow.[28]

---

[27]Prince Matei Ghica Cantacuzino, an aviator in the Royal Romanian Air Force with close ties to Maniu, Georgescu and thus British intelligence was the designated pilot in the aborted plan to fly Maniu out of Romania in the spring of 1943. In 1944 the prince stole a German plane intending to fly the Romanian diplomat Constantin Vişoianu to Cairo, there to participate in armistice negotiations with the Anglo-American allies. Vişoianu changed his mind and went by train and the prince used the stolen plane to fly himself, other endangered British agents and important intelligence materials out of Romania. For this he was tried in absentia by court martial and condemned to death on July 1, 1944. At the time Ross wrote this letter Ghica is obviously awaiting return transportation to Romania from the Bari area. He did return and continued to be actively involved in exfiltrating efforts under the communists including the successful covert flight with the Liberal editor and politician Mihai "Mişu" Fărcăşanu and his wife. Ghika also fled the country and eventually settled in Caracas. Porter, *op. cit.*, pp. 67, 91-92, 176, 181, 239, 249.

[28]There are two vertical pencil lines in the left margin of this paragraph.

The Russians are here.[29] It is not possible to estimate their strength but they are not in Bucharest in any great force. The war situation is terribly confused from here and even the new government doesn't know the situation more than a day behind the real deal. It is said that the Russians have the situation well in hand, so to speak. Ploieşti was reported by the new government to be in Russian hands this morning altho some fighting is going on in the area.[30]

The Roumanians want the Americans to help them by bombing along the Hungarian border and gave us late yesterday as targets the railroads and bridges in the towns I mentioned in my other communication.[31]

In connection with Hungary, I made a contact tonight with a person who claims to be able to put me in touch with someone who knows the Hungarian situation. It is just remotely possible that in a day or two I might be able to give some dope that would help Howard Chapin. But it will be after this evacuation.

Speaking of the evacuation, Joe Morton[32] says he can't mention our part in it as instructed by you. I think that was okay on the basis of the start, but believe it is all right now. Joe is inclined to give most of the credit to Cantacuzino and rightfully so, altho I told him we had our own plans before Cantacuzino turned up and that it would have been more difficult, to say the least for the Fifteenth to carry out the thing without us. I don't think we will get any credit in the first story as it will

---

[29]This paragraph is bracketed in the left margin.

[30]The relative absence of Soviet troops reflects the fact that it was Romanian forces and Romanian forces alone which drove the Germans out of Romania with the exception of the battle for Ploieşti, where on the afternoon of August 29th units of the Soviet 6th Motorized Infantry Brigade relieved Romanian forces to the east of the city in preparation for the final assault on German positions the next day. (Axworthy, *op. cit.*, p. 190) With regard to Bucharest, Axworthy observes: "... when the Red Army and the Tudor Vladimirescu Division entered Bucharest on 30-31 August they simply ignored the embarrassing fact of its prior liberation and promptly 'liberated' it again." (Ibid., p. 191).

[31]By this time radio contact with headquarters in Italy had been established and this is likely a reference to a message Ross had sent out by radio.

There is a vertical pencil line in the left margin of this paragraph.

[32]In the Ross manuscript version of this text there is a line crossing out everything from "says he can't" through "all right now." Thus in the retyped version, paragraph 15 reads: "speaking of the evacuation, Joe Morton is inclined..." This deletion may reflect either a desire to keep the OSS's role out of the news story or a concern about the implications of censoring a news story.

go to Bari on the plane with this but I can't see now any reason for hiding our light under a bushel.

About the government, the set up is this at present — the King is reputedly said to have had a strong hand in the overthrow of Marshal Antonescu. Antonescu and his accomplices are in custody and well guarded. In the latter group is reported to be the Roumanian Gestapo chiefs Vasiliu and Cristescu, and also the Prefect of Police Elefterescu.[33]

The head of the new government is Gen. Constantin Sănătescu, who is regarded and spoken of as the Prime Minister.[34] Actually, this title is bestowed upon him by the chiefs of the four principal parties who seem to be pretty well together for the purpose of the job at hand.The four party chiefs are:

National Peasant — Iuliu Maniu.[35] He is old, 70, but reputed to be quite a fighter and is regarded as one of the strongest

---

[33]Ross appears here to be subsuming under the term "Gestapo chiefs" all of the leaders of the Romanian police and secret services. In fact, however, these Romanian services, although capable of brutality and injustice, lacked the pervasive cruelty associated with the dreaded, more efficient and thorough German Gestapo.

General Constantin "Piki" Z. Vasiliu was appointed January 3, 1942, Subsecretary of State in the Ministry of the Interior (for Police and Security). When Operation Autonomous had gone awry and Ivor Porter was imprisoned, Vasiliu provided the regular contact between Porter and Marshal Antonescu, to whom Vasiliu was very close. Shortly after Marshal Antonescu's arrest on August 23, 1944, Vasiliu was summoned to the royal palace and also arrested. Subsequently tried for war crimes, he was found guilty and executed by firing squad with Marshal Antonescu on June 1, 1946.

Eugen Cristescu (1895-1950?), head of the Romanian Special Service for Information (secret police) during the war and simultaneously a German agent. Summoned to the royal palace on August 23, 1944, when the Antonescu government was overthrown, and suspecting that something was amiss, Cristescu went to the German authorities in Bucharest to warn them of his suspicions. Subsequently arrested, he accompanied the other leaders from the old government to the Lubianka Prison in Moscow, was returned to Romania for trial, found guilty, and condemned to death, a sentence subsequently commuted to hard labor for life. He is understood to have died in Văcăreşti Prison in 1950.

Colonel Mircea Elefterescu, Chief of the Bucharest Gendarmerie and Prefect of the Capital's Police at the time of the August 23rd coup, a position usually equated to the municipal chief of police. A career military officer, sometime Chief of the Cabinet and close friend of Marshal Antonescu, he was seen by some as an eminence grise of the government. Arrested at the time of the coup, transported to Moscow with the others, returned to Romania for trial in 1946, he was ultimately sentenced to 20 years and died in prison. Porter, *op. cit.*; Cristian Troncota, Eugen Cristescu, *Asul Serviciilor Secrete Româneşti*, (Bucureşti: Editura Roza Vânturilor, 1994); Josif Constantin Drăgan, *Antonescu: Mareşalul României şi Războaiele de Reîntregire* (Cannaregio Venetia, 1986).

There is a pencil bracket in the left margin of this paragraph.

men in the new set up. This is at present the strongest of the four parties but might rapidly disintegrate if Russia is to have complete say so in Roumania, in which case the Communist party would forge to the front.

National Liberal — Constantin Brătianu.[36] This is the money crowd. In the past it has exercised a lot of power but just how it will fit into the new picture remains to be seen.

Communist Party — Lucreţius Pătrăşcanu.[37] This crowd purports to support the new government but claims the privilege of acting more or less on their own. It is reported they have banded together with the Socialists and with a young, aggressive leader (46) the party is one to reckon with.

Socialist Party — Constantin Petrescu.[38] This is really the liberal group in the Socialist party. It isn't alone an important group but might be courted by the others for support and if Socialism should happen in Europe it could develop.

---

[34]General Constantin Sănătescu (1885-1947), career military officer, general staff officer, attache in London (1928-30). Served with distinction in World War I and as major general in World War II. In 1943 he was appointed Chief of the Military Household of King Michael and in 1944 became Marshal of the Palace. He had a major role in the planning and execution of the August 23rd coup. Appointed President of the Council of Ministers August 23, 1944 and continued in that office until December 5, 1944, when he was promoted to lieutenant general and made chief of the general staff.

[35]Iuliu Maniu (1873-1953), intrepid, incorruptible leader of the National Peasants Party. After the union of Transylvania with Romania, a symbol of Romanian democracy. Uncompromising opponent of communism, he was tried in 1947 by the communist government, condemned to life imprisonment, and died in the prison at Sighet. Like Brătianu, Petrescu, and Pătrăşcanu was appointed Minister Secretary of State without portfolio in the post-coup government.

[36]Constantin "Dino" I.C. Brătianu (1866-1950), member of an illustrious family of Romanian politicians. He played an important role in the August coup. As anti-communist leader of the National Liberal Party, was imprisoned in 1950 and died at Sighet two months later.

[37]Lucreţiu Pătrăşcanu (1900-1954), lawyer and leading communist. Educated in France and Germany, member of the Romanian Communist Party since 1921. An intellectual, he served as Minister of Justice in the early communist governments until 1948 when he was accused of pro-Titoist sentiments and imprisoned. There he was tortured, tried, found guilty of high treason in 1954, and executed at Jilava Prison. He was rehabilitated in 1968 under Nicolae Ceauşescu.

[38]Constantin "Titel" Petrescu (1888-1957), lawyer and non-Marxist leader of the right wing of the small Social Democratic Party. Jailed in 1948 for "hostility to the real unity of the working class," i.e. opposing the takeover of his party by the communists, he was released in 1956 and died the following year.

The Minister of Foreign Affairs is Gr. Niculescu-Buzești.[39] He was an intimate collaborator of the late Titulescu and is a pretty bright appearing sort. I was much impressed with his talk and manner and from other sources have gained the information that he will surely have a part in any permanent set up in Roumania.

The Minister of National Economy is Valeriu Georgescu.[40] This chap, like Buzești is young, well liked, and almost certain to have a place in a new government formed on a permanent basis, if formed in the near future.

Others are:

Gen. Racoviță, Minister of War[41]

Gen. Potopeanu, Minister of National Economy and Finance[42]

Gen. Marinescu, Minister of Health[43]

Gen. Boitzianu, Minister of Education[44]

Gen. Aldes, Minister of the Interior[45]

Gen. Eftimiu, Minister of Public Works.[46]

Mr. Negel, Minister of Agriculture.[47]

---

[39]Grigore Niculescu-Buzești (1908-1949), lawyer by training, career diplomat, charge in Riga 1939-41, played important role in extricating Romania from the Axis Pact in 1944. At Maniu's urging fled Romania to continue struggle for democracy in exile. Died in the United States shortly thereafter.

[40]Here Ross seems to have been confused or misinformed. General Gheorghe Potopeanu, not Georgescu, was the Minister of National Economy and ad interim of Finance in the first Sănătescu cabinet, as Ross correctly states in the following paragraph. Valeriu Georgescu joined the cabinet only on September 1st as Subsecretary of State for Industry, Commerce, and Mines.

[41]See note 10 above.

[42]General Gheorghe Potopeanu (1889-1966), general staff officer (1929-1933), military attache in France and Belgium (1935-38), Minister of National Economy under Marshal Antonescu January 1941-January 1943. Appointed to the same ministry by Sănătescu, Potopeanu resigned on October 13th, 1944, to answer charges that he was a war criminal. These charges were dismissed in 1945, but in 1948 he was rearrested, found guilty for "crimes against peace" and sentenced to 5 years imprisonment. Released in 1953, he was again arrested in 1957 on charges of spying, found guilty of high treason, and sentenced to 15 years. Freed in an amnesty in 1963, he died in Bucharest three years later.

[43]General Nicolae Marinescu's actual title in the Sănătescu cabinet was Minister of Labor, Health, and Social Services.

[44]General Ion Boiteanu's actual title was Minister of National Culture and Religion.

The Minister of Justice is Pătrăşcanu, head of the Communist Party[48]

It is presently a provisional government as the name itself implies. Its scope is simply that of taking care of the situation now existing in time of emergency.

A mission was sent to Moscow some day ago to sign the Armistice and it is reported that the actual signing was yesterday. (Not signed yet according to latest dope early 1 Sept. W.R.)[49] This was the same mission that had been in Cairo but upon demand they had to move to Moscow to talk business. The mission was made up of Prince Ştirbey,[50] who had been Prime Minister and Mr. Vişoianu,[51] the late minister to the Hague and also to Warsaw.[52]

---

[45]General Aurel Aldea (1887-1949), an artillery officer, had retired in 1940. Closely associated with military planning for the coup of August 1944, he served as Minister of the Interior in the first Sănătescu cabinet. In 1945 he began to participate in anticommunist resistance, eventually forming the central command of the National Movement of Resistance. In 1946 he was arrested on charges of "plotting to destroy the unity of the Romanian state," found guilty, and sentenced to hard labor for life. He died in Aiud Prison in 1949.

[46]General Constantin Eftimiu died in Aiud Prison in 1950.

[47]Dimitrie D. Negel (1890-?), an apolitical lawyer and businessman. May 1941, Subsecretary of State in Ministry of National Economy and Supply under Marshal Antonescu; 1942 Administrator of the Royal Estates. Minister of Agriculture in first Sănătescu cabinet. In November 1944 became Marshal of the Royal Court.

[48]See endnote 37 above.

[49]This parenthesis is handwritten and initialed by Ross at the top of the page with a line indicating where to insert it. In actual fact the armistice was not signed in Moscow until September 12th, some three weeks after the coup. This foot-dragging allowed the Soviet army to occupy Romania, while technically a state of war still existed between the two countries.

[50]Prince Barbu Ştirbey (1873-1946), descendent of Romanian nobility, close confidant of royal house and Queen Marie, Liberal politician briefly Prime Minister in 1928. Marginalized by Carol II and Marshal Antonescu, Ştirbey made unsuccessful attempt to negotiate an armistice for Romania with the Anglo-American allies in Cairo in June 1944. King Michael's efforts to appoint Ştirbey again Prime Minister in March 1945 foundered because of Soviet opposition. Active in 1945 organizing resistance to the communist authorities, he died the following year.

[51]Constantin Vişoianu (1897-1994), career diplomat, minister to the Netherlands and Poland in the 1930s. Followed Prince Ştirbey to Cairo to meet with Anglo-American representatives. Foreign Minister in Sănătescu's second cabinet and the Rădescu cabinet. At Maniu's urging, he fled Romania in 1945, settling initially in Switzerland and then the United States where he became active in refugee affairs, leading the Romanian National Council after the death of General Rădescu. Died in the United States.

Another mission was later dispatched to negotiate the terms of the armistice. This was headed by Pătrăşcanu, already mentioned and the logical choice.

Today I saw Georgescu again and he had just returned from Constanţa where he met some Russky's and tried to do something with them about the rate of exchange on the lei and the ruble. He was very unhappy over the outcome and told me he thought they were tough as pig iron.

As would be expected the Russians are not liked and the new crowd had high hopes of being able to negotiate with the Americans and the British rather than the Russians. They are afraid of what Russia will lay down for them, naturally.[53]

Enough for now. Will try to pass along more dope as I get it.

s/ Walter M. Ross
Walter M. Ross, Major AGD

On September 1st, Ross appears to have written only a brief note to Green:

1 Sept 1944

Ed,

This morning a Dutch Admiral checked in with a Dutch Lt. and they want a ride to Italy so that they can get back to England.[54] They are:

L.A.C.M. Doorman, Royal Netherlands Navy
D.W. Baron van Lynden, Lieutenant R.N.N.

The Admiral was taken from Holland in 1942 to Stanislawow in Poland, which is a prison camp. He escaped from there in Jan 44 with the Lieutenant and walked thru the Rumanian frontier. They were later picked up by the Roumanian police and placed in a prisoner of war camp at Timişul de Jos. They were liberated when the government changed.

There will be a lot of French turn up in all probability and others of the above type from time to time. So, I think you had better get with the Fifteenth or BAF and decide upon a policy as to other nationalities and let us know what the procedure is to be.

If you can get a signal to us thru Cairo let us know on this as soon as possible.

---

[52]There is a vertical pencil line in the left margin of this and the following paragraph.

[53]There is a vertical pencil line in the left margin of this paragraph.

/s/W.M.R.

W.M.R.[55]

Ross's fourth and final communication with Green concerning the situation in Romania is the longest in the series:

2 Sept 1944
(Secret)
Lt. Cdr. Edward Green
Hq Co B 2677th Regt OSS
APO 534, % PM NY

Dear Ed:

I hardly know what to start on, there is so much to write about from over here.

But, of course, the most important thing is the evacuation. After I wrote to you yesterday, we got off sixteen planes with an average of twenty-five per plane or about 380 more boys. This total added to the approximate 741 the other day makes a total of something like 1125 people. Pretty good and pretty fast but a very satisfying performance. Tomorrow we have

---

[54]The odyssey of Admiral Doorman and Lieutenant van Lyndon is one of the fascinating adventures of World War II. Prisoners of war after the 1940 German occupation of the Netherlands, the two Dutch sailors were shunted around prisoner of war camps in the Third Reich, finally arriving at a camp (probably Stalag 371) in Stanislau (Stanislawow in Polish), Galicia, General government (occupied Poland). The town, which is Irano-Frankivs'k in the present day Ukraine, is situated some 80 miles north of the Romanian frontier across the Carpathian mountains. In January 1944 the Dutch prisoners of war were placed in cattle cars prepared for a move probably into the heart of the Reich to escape the advancing Soviet army. In the confusion of that move a number of the Dutch escaped, including in all likelihood Admiral Doorman and Lieutenant van Lynden. The two made their way into Romania, a considerable accomplishment for a sixty-five year old moving by foot in January over the Carpathians, but it was doubtless facilitated by the admiral's putative knowledge of five languages.

Their apprehension in Romania presented the authorities with an interesting problem in international law. The Germans, of course, wanted their erstwhile prisoners returned. The Romanians, then allies of the Germans, might have been expected to comply with this demand were it not for the fact that the Netherlands and Romania had never declared war on each other and, thus being at peace, had no right to detain the other's subjects as prisoners of war. The compromise that finally evolved was to intern the two officers for the duration of the war with the American POWs at Timişul de Jos. (Caradja, *op. cit.*, p. 135; Britt, *op. cit.*, pp. 155-157; Dugan and Stewart, *op. cit.*, pp. 236, 255). Information concerning Stalag 371 comes from a secret report 4 January 1945 from "Saint Bari" to "Saint & DH/125 Washington," sourced to a Dutch officer who escaped from the camp in the January 1944 move and made his way to Hungary and then Italy. (NARA, RG-226, E-154, B-27)

[55]Beneath the initials and to the left is handwritten: "Above answered JSD."

three more planes to come which will take out from 30 to 50 depending upon how many show up between now and the time the planes show. There will also be a C-47 with a wing panel for the B-17 which blew upon landing the other day.

Everything went smoothly and it was a great show. The Fortress which blew a tire the other day was repaired and could take off with the others in place of the one which blew a wing yesterday. Col. Kraigher is also leaving tomorrow and I will stay on to finish up the job. There is plenty to do altho the total will be small. Just today we ran on to one boy in a small town hospital who is in such bad shape that we signalled for a doctor to come in tomorrow.[56] Three others were located by Kraigher, Rodrigo, and myself this afternoon at Ploieşti in a hospital and we haven't even been able to see them yet. So, there will be many like that and some of them are in bad shape, I am afraid.

Lt. Forbes the Field Photo guy is coming in tomorrow to get some of his film in the works but he is leaving Paris here. There is plenty of story yet, so it is well worth his while to stay. I[57] am going to send Sgt. Horvath back also. I really don't need him now, but I will keep Dubes and Stavanjos for a while, one to do radio and the other to help round up the fliers.

Rodrigo and his crew got in yesterday on the B-17's which carried the men out. As I understand it, they are only here for a week so to do the Ploieşti thing and have no other job. Wisner arrived at Popeşti on a plane which hedge hopped from Istanbul and which arrived while we were at the field waiting for our planes to show. After Rodrigo leaves the show for OSS will settle down to the SI crowd with Wisner at the top and it will consist of Wisner, the four which came with me (Vǎllimǎrescu, Hagigogu, Bookbinder, and Fehrenback), plus three others which Wisner has waiting in Cairo to go when

[56]This is most likely a reference to T/S Peter Tierney. A memorandum by Lieutenant R.H. Dorr, USNR on September 2, 1944, reports locating Tierney "in a small rural hospital south of Ploieşti about 7 or 8 miles." Severely wounded on August 10th by anti-aircraft fire which necessitated multiple operations, Tierney was suffering from phlebitis and septicemia with uncertain prospects for survival by the time Dorr found him. The memorandum requests urgently that an American doctor with penicillin and sulfa drugs be sent out immediately. (NARA, RG-226, E-190, B-118)

[57]This sentence through "don't need him now, but" in the following sentence is crossed out in the Ross manuscript version, and in the retyped version the text reads: ...worth his while to stay. I will keep Dubes..." The implications of this deletion are unclear, perhaps a bureaucratic desire not to appear to be overmanned.

another plane can get out. Wisner seems to be just what I have heard of him, a very good gent.[58]

This place is wild with information and Wisner is in his glory. We have a beautiful entree to the government and plan to use it fast while it is available and hot stuff. This morning we went at eight fifteen to see Georgescu and the lesser lights, we meaning Kraigher Rodrigo, Wisner, and myself. Kraigher and I have already seen everyone in the new set up so it was not a new deal for us. After Georgescu, it was the Foreign Minister, Buzeşti, then it was the President, Maniu and finally the Prime Minister, Sănătescu. The visits were mostly for the purpose of identifying the Rodrigo and Wisner units as compared to the evacuation deal and to pave the way for going to Ploieşti with the whole crowd. Rodrigo arranged for a lot of stuff to be picked up in Bucharest to complete his deal on Ploieşti. For your information, in case it wasn't passed on to you, he is on a MAAF[59] deal and not OSS.

---

[58]Frank Gardiner Wisner (1910-1965), unlike Ross, made a career as an American intelligence officer, rising to high rank in the Operations Division of the Central Intelligence Agency. He became a legend in his own time for his work in covert operations during the Cold War, and he figures prominently in all histories of the CIA in the years before his retirement in 1963. The stresses and depressions associated with this work most likely account for his tragic death at his own hands. He is buried in Arlington Cemetery.

The Wisner whom Ross first met in September 1944 was very much a star in ascendancy, fresh from a successful tour in Istanbul repairing the damage to a station thoroughly penetrated by German intelligence and hand picked by General Donovan for the Bucharest assignment. See Burton Hersh's *The Old Boys: the American Elite and the Origins of the CIA* (New York et al.: Charles Scribner's Sons, 1992). See chapter 12, "The Redeemer from the West," pp. 189-210 for a description of Wisner's early life through his assignment to Bucharest.

Probably the most complete account of Wisner's career was written by Evan Thomas in *The Very Best Men: Four Who Dared: The Early Years of the CIA* (New York et al.: Simon & Schuster, 1995). Wisner's time in Bucharest is covered in pp. 19-23. Thomas, however, falls into the frequent error of attributing the success of the evacuation to Wisner: "His first assignment was to organize the return of 1800 American fliers shot down over the Ploieşti oil fields (a success: Wisner commandeered every bus in the city)..." (Ibid., p. 20).

As this paper has made clear Major Ross is entitled to this praise not Commander Wisner, who had nothing to do with the planning or execution of the evacuation and arrived in Romania only on September 1st in time to observe the last day of the operation. Such misplaced praise is perhaps understandable in earlier accounts not written with benefit of the declassified OSS records (eg. Ernest Volkmann, *Warriors of the Night: Spies, Soldiers, and American Intelligence,* New York: William Morrow and Company, Inc., 1985, p. 37) but less understandable ten years later.

Here is a matter on Wisner which should be given serious consideration and straightened out at once, I think. He is somewhat inclined, and I don't blame him in view of the situation, to regard the Cairo team as step children.

He has a WT operator coming from Istanbul and even before that he has his own signal plan with Istanbul which he has given to Capt. Rinker of Rodrigo's team and he is going to send his stuff straight thru to Istanbul. It is good and hot so Istanbul is going to get all the credit unless something is done about it. Wisner is already in to the provisional government boys, is smart and is plenty senior to any other SI man here. You will recall and so will Joyce, that last Sunday in talking with the General he verbally agreed that Roumanian stuff should be centered in Bari, because of lift, etc. I think Wisner is a fine selection, from all I know of him, to head the SI deal but something should be done to coordinate the Cairo and Istanbul teams. I am going to see him tomorrow and try to get him to take the Cairo crowd over and at least give them all he gets for signal to both spots but since he is in the gravy and has the skids greased for him presently, he may prefer to cut the Cairo crowd out. I don't mean that he would be malicious, but it would be an easy thing to do. While I am trying to get them to work together and exchange information and assignments, why don't you get busy and see if you can't get Gen. Donovan to place all Roumanian stuff in Bari and order Wisner to report accordingly.[60]

Things here are as tense as the devil. Last night the Russky's placed a curfew at nine whereas the city before had been on eleven and it doesn't suit the Roumanians at all. There are plenty of tales, of loot, rape, theft, etc, most of them untrue or exaggerated to beat the devil. We have a lot of people come to us who are American citizens and have stayed here thru the war, or who were helpful to the American fliers and now want our help in keeping their property from the Russians. It is of course out of the question for us to do anything about it even

---

[59]Mediterranean Allied Air Force, apparently Rodrigo's cover as an OSS officer. This entire sentence is crossed out in the Ross manuscript version and does not appear in the retyped version, probably reflecting a concern about compromising Rodrigo's cover story.

[60]This entire paragraph is crossed out. There are brackets in both margins with "OMIT" written in the left margin of the Ross manuscript version. This paragraph does not appear in the retyped version, possibly because it reveals too much of OSS's internal procedures and rivalries.

if the stories they tell are true. We know seizing of cars and trucks is going on in a rather rough shod and indiscriminate manner for we had a truck which was given to us and it was out with a Roumanian driver this afternoon and was taken by the Russkys. Also, tonite, we came back after dusk from Ploieşti and were stopped on two occasions by Russians who quite obviously had ideas of seizing the car but did not do so when we identified ourselves. One time we even had to produce our American AGO cards. The man who owns the house we live in, a Mr. Bragadiru, owns a brewery and had three trucks picked up today. It is going on plenty and there isn't anything anyone can do about it.[61]

This morning we also went to see the Chief of Staff of the Roumanian army and some of his staff. The C. of S. is a George Mihail[62] and his S-2 is a Col. Runceanu and the S-3 person is a Col. Leonidas. They really gave us everything and Wisner being SI[63] fell heir — giving such things as the Russian communique of last night announcing the curfew, turning in of arms, radios, etc. Also they are preparing for him an overlay on the order of battle on the Hungarian border which is fine stuff for anyone to have right now. I[64] don't like to see it go to Istanbul but Wisner is sure to send it there unless I can get Rodrigo to convince him it should go to Caserta as I know Bari would die a trying between Istanbul and Caserta. In any event, we are getting it but I would like to see it all centered in Bari. I think Wisner might even like for me to stay on to help him because I have already made the connections and a Major looks like he might be more valuable than all the second Lts. around. Most

---

[61] In the left margin of this paragraph is written "Control," which is underlined. Underneath this is written "curfew," "Anti-Russian rumors" and an illegible line, possibly "Req of cars," meaning "requisitioning of cars."

[62] General Gheorghe Mihail (1887-1982), infantry officer, 1937-1939 Chief of the Royal Military Household, 1939 Subsecretary of State in the Ministry of National Defence in the cabinets of Armand Călinescu and Constantin Argetoianu, Vice President of the Council of Ministers under Ion Gigurtu, Chief of the General Staff for 2 weeks in August-September 1940 and again in August-October 1944. Arrested at his home in Sinaia in 1948 and accused of having "a hostile, anti-Soviet, and anti-democratic attitude," he remained imprisoned on various charges until 1957. He died in Bucharest.

[63] Secret Intelligence.

[64] From this point in the Ross manuscript version to the end of the paragraph, the text has been crossed out and written in the left margin is "OMIT." These lines do not appear in the retyped version, probably for the reasons already noted in endnote 56 above.

of the boys here in the government speak either English or French so the language situation isn't difficult at all.

At noon we went to a luncheon given by a person who is acknowledged by the ones who know to be the leader of the underground movement in Roumania. He is a very powerful person financially and politically. If certain plans the crowd has in mind should work out, he might conceivably run the government some day, either from behind the scenes or in the open. His name is Nicky Caranfil.[65] He was Minister of Air under Carol but was thrown out by Antonescu. He is a sort of a utilities tycoon, has been in the telephone company, the water company and the light company and is still in one or more. He is sharp as the devil, very intelligent and a very high grade, cultured person. He is the one who knows a lot about the Hungarian underground (they undoubtedly have their connections), and I am meeting him Monday afternoon at his home for lunch to see what he has to offer. If[66] in the meanwhile Chapin or one of his crowd shows up, I can take him along.

This underground thing is very important in the whole set up right at present.[67] To illustrate — at this luncheon given by Caranfil was on my left Baron Stircea, who is Marshal of the Palace and about as close to the King as anyone can be. Along with him, across the table, was the Foreign minister Niculescu-Buzeşti, whom I have previously mentioned. So, there you have the link, Stircea, who is the King's confidant and right hand guy, Buzeşti, the Foreign minister and aligned with them is Georgescu, all previously mentioned. They all check into Caranfil, who is the money, power, suaveness, etc. And also, Caranfil is tough. Joe Morton is going to see the King tomorrow and it is wholly thru Caranfil. Caranfil asked Stircea to

---

[65]Nicolae G. Caranfil, engineer, was appointed Subsecretary of Aviation in the Ministry of National Defense in April 1935 and Minister of Air and Naval Forces in November 1936 by Prime Minister Gheorghe Tătărescu. The latter portfolio Tătărescu assigned to Radu Irimescu in January 1937. Contrary to the information that Ross reports, Caranfil's departure does not appear to have been the results of Ion Antonescu's efforts.

A pencilled question mark and a red vertical line appear in the left margin of this paragraph where Caranfil is first mentioned.

[66]This sentence is crossed out on the Ross manuscript and does not appear in the retyped version possibly because of the implied identification of Chapin as an OSS officer.

[67]In the left margin of this sentence is a question mark with a vertical line, and below is written and then crossed out "patron of Caranfil."

arrange it. The King left Bucharest a couple of hours before the bombing started on the morning of the 24th by the Germans.[68] He is out in the country some 100 miles and I am informed Joe will go by plane with Stircea to see him. He will be the first of the writers to see the King and there are half a dozen others sitting around the Ambassador Hotel tonite who would give their eye teeth for the same deal. And without asking for bouquets, it hasn't hurt Joe any to be out here at the house with us in getting his deal set up. He might have gotten in anyway but we have had a chap very close to us who did a lot of the liaison, if I am not mistaken.

In connection with the King, I understand the Russian General who is in charge of the Russkys in Bucharest refuses to see anyone less than the King. Buzești, the foreign minister has called on him but the Russky refused to see him and asked for the King.[69] What the King thinks about that or will do remains to be seen. This is pretty straight dope for, after all, I had lunch with Buzești and Stircea today.[70]

The Baron Stircea is a nice looking, highly cultured, smart chap who is young (not over 37 or 38) and eager to go places. Buzești is also young (close to forty) and Caranfil is not over 42 or so.[71] It is a pretty powerful combination in connection with the King and certain headliners in the provisional government such as Georgescu.[72]

---

[68] King Michael, who was himself driving the second of four cars in the convoy, left the royal palace in Bucharest shortly after 3:00 a.m. August 24th. Moving swiftly but circuitously southwest, the convoy passed through Alexandria, Roșiorii de Verde and about 10:00 a.m. that morning paused to refuel in Craiova. Proceeding on through Tîrgu-Jiu, they reached the village of Bumbești-Jiu at about 4:00 p.m. and there in the Carpathian foot-hills prepared to await events. The party was joined that evening shortly before 10:00 p.m. by the Queen Mother, Helen, who had been in Sinaia and came in a separate convoy. Thus the interview with Joe Morton likely took place in Bumbești-Jiu as the royal family did not depart the village until the evening of September 9th and arrived in Bucharest by train the following day. (Arthur Giould Lee, *Crown Against Sickle: The Story of King Michael of Rumania*, London et al.: Hutchinson & Co. Ltd., no date (ca. 1949), pp. 82-89.)

[69] This presumably on the example and orders of General Vladislav Petrovici Vinogradov, Chief of the Soviet Mission and Chairman of the Allied Control Commission for Romania.

[70] In the left margin of this paragraph is a vertical line and the word "Control."

[71] In actual fact Baron Mocsonyi-Styrcea, born in 1909, was 35 or 36 at the time Ross wrote this; Niculescu-Buzești, born in 1908, was 36 or 37.

[72] In the left margin of this paragraph is a red vertical line and "Person" has been written.

My informant and I know he is close because he was also at lunch is one I.G. Mathiescu. He is a brother in law to the person mentioned above who is the A-2 for the Roumanian army. He also has a brother in the Foreign office in London, although I don't know if that means anything.[73]

My honest opinion is that this is pretty straight stuff and no one will get it out any sooner than this reaches you. Morton will have a story on the same plane but it will be censored some before it reaches print.

Enough of that, here is what the Roumanians want bombed:

in order of importance:

1. Marshaling yards of Tg. Mureş (Two German divisions are reported on the way of being concentrated there.)

2. Reghin, railway junction and roads concentration of German troops.

3. Oradea and Dej. Marshaling yards and roads German troops reported to be there with a view to concentration in the Cluj-Huedin zone.[74]

Col. Kraigher may get in with these same targets as soon as you get this letter but in any event they are the very latest today and I suggest you get the information to the Fifteenth as quickly as possible. I will also put them on the air, but this may reach you first.

The Ploieşti thing is almost a story in itself but Bowie is getting it along with the host of boys from Caserta, also Johnson. We were in place today and the damage is terrific, you simply can't visualize it, yet surprisingly enough, they keep up a certain amount of production. It is a wrecked area though, if there is one in the world today.

One refinery, the Creditul Minier, has been out of production completely since the raid of 1 Aug 1943. Up to that date the output was about 140 wagons (tons) per day for crude and 50 wagons of gasoline per day was produced by the cracking plant. This plant normally employs five hundred men and the raid was on a Sunday when there was a small shift and those on duty for the most part got to shelters so that only four casualties (dead) resulted. Crude oil for this plant came from Moreni.[75]

---

[73]There is a vertical line in the left margin of this paragraph.

[74]There is a red vertical line in the left margin of this paragraph.

The largest refinery in the group of six was the Astra-Română (Anglo-Roumanian), which got most of its crude from Tinta. This plant reputedly produced some five hundred wagons per day but was cut down to about 100. It employed 3000 people. It was also first bombed on 1 August 1943 and supposedly suffered about thirty bombings all together. It was bombed by the Russians as well as the Americans. Only about 35 people were killed at this plant.[76]

Some more dope from the General Staff Meeting which I failed to mention earlier —

The Roumanians captured some 50000 prisoners according to their claims and this had previously been reported to us by the Red Cross so it may be pretty close to right.[77] In the bag were 9 German generals.[78] In Roumania the GS claims all territory was cleared by Roumanian troops except a couple of small places near Ploieşti. The report that the Russians liberated or conquered Bucharest is resented like the devil here.[79]

The Russians in this area are now identified as the Sixth Armored Army and are in Bucharest proper and vicinity.[80] Most of the equipment they have is American except the tanks and they seem for the most part to be English. It looks like a non-descript outfit and it is hard to picture them as winning a battle against anyone. Without exception though, they look rugged as hell and they maintain good order and discipline.[81]

---

[75]"Econ" has been written with a vertical pencil line in the left margin of this and the following paragraph.

[76]Ross is correct on the Creditul Minier damage. The refinery went from a monthly fuel production of 35,000 metric tons in July 1943 to zero and so remained through August 1944. He is less well informed concerning Astra Română where production went from 155,000 metric tons in July 1943 to 65,000 in August 1943 as a result of Operation Tidal Wave. By November of that year, however, production had risen to 205,000 tons and only declined significantly again in April 1944 when bombing was resumed and production ceased altogether. (Leroy W. Newby, *Target Ploieşti: View from a Bombsight*, Novato, California: Presidio, 1983, pp. 238, 244.)

[77]"Mil" is written in the left margin of this paragraph.

[78]Axworthy (*op. cit.*, pp. 187, 191) indicates in the week before the Soviets arrived in Bucharest, the Romanian army captured and disarmed 70,832 Germans within Romania and an unknown number who were in the rear areas of Army Group South. Of these some 7000 were captured in the vicinity of Bucharest, including 7 generals.

[79]This is a near universal complaint in Romanian and Anglo-American memoirs of the period. Ivor Porter, for example, recalls that "...repeated BBC announcements that the Red Army had 'liberated' yet another Transylvanian town eventually began to get on our nerves." (Porter, *op. cit.*, p. 221.) See also endnote 30 above.

We saw them today between here and Ploieşti by the bushelful. Many, many of them were in horse drawn peasant wagons and on horseback.[82]

The Roumanians claim that the Russians are actually hindering their own efforts by hindering rail and truck transportation.[83]

Six or seven correspondents came in on the plane from Istanbul yesterday with Wisner. They all tried to broadcast tonite over the Roumanian radio for pick up by BBC or AP. I read the broadcast of Sam Brewer AP and Chicago Tribune and it represented the tone of the lot. The main theme is (1) the Russians seem to take all the credit for "liberating" Bucharest and in turn the Rumanians claim their own armies did it and all the Russians had to do was march in. There is a great deal to be said for the Roumanians on this point.[84] (2) The apprehension felt by the average Roumanian regarding the treatment he may get from the Russians. (3) The evacuation. No names are mentioned altho there was a reference to the evacuation mission being the only Americans left in town.

This is a scrambled letter but it represents the general conditions here tonight. The situation is tense and there is no doubt about it but will probably simmer down and no trouble will result. I don't know when, now, I may be able to get another long report out to you but will do so at the first opportunity. In the meantime, I will keep you posted by radio as it is finally working, thank heavens.

I neglected to mention to you that Killinger, the German Gestapo chief who was caught here when the government

---

[80]On August 23rd the Soviet Sixth Armored Army was operating within the Soviet 2nd Ukrainian Front in the salient just north of Bârlad. In the following days it penetrated the Axis lines as the Romanian 4th Armored Corps fell back to Bucharest from positions north of Adjud in Sectorul 209. The Soviet Sixth Armored Army passed north of the fortified line of Focşani-Nămoloasa-Brăila and advanced in a southwesterly direction to Bucharest. (Constantin Popa, *Armata Română în Războiul Antihitlerist*, Bucureşti: Editura militară, 1980, pp. 58-61.)

[81]Ross shows here apparent ambiguity, in one sentence calling the Sixth Armored Army "a non-descript outfit" difficult to imagine "winning a battle against anyone" and in the next sentence describing them as "without exception... rugged as hell" and maintaining "good order and discipline."

[82]"Control?" with a vertical pencil line appears in the left margin of this paragraph, probably reflecting concern at the less than favorable description of the Soviet allies.

[83]There is a vertical pencil line in the left margin of this paragraph.

[84]See endnotes 30 and 79 above.

changed, committed suicide today and so did his secretary.[85] That is official.[86]

Got your signal late tonight about returning some radio equipment but I may not be able to do it tomorrow. We are starting at six in the morning and it is now nearly three a.m. I will be able to get it out in two or three days on the repaired B-17, if not tomorrow.

Best Wishes,
s Walter
Walter M. Ross

I had a later talk with Wisner this morning and believe he is okay so far as Bari is concerned. Says he regards Istanbul as dead anyway and he prefers to funnel stuff thru Bari for speed and attention. So I suggest you try to make it official on this basis and continue the Cairo and Istanbul teams.

Wisner is sending a long hot memo to Joyce today and there is no need for me to report too much of the same thing.

W.M.R.

Looks now like the radio stuff will get here to go with the C-47 whenever it goes.[87]

With Wisner now in command in Bucharest, the Ross-Green correspondence ceases. Major Ross stayed on for several days to oversee the stragglers and stretcher cases still being evacuated. As implied in the letter of September 2nd, Ross may also have been hoping that Wisner would ask for him to be permanently assigned to OSS's Bucharest team, now code-named the "Hammerhead Mission."

On September 11th and 12th Ross and a doctor drove into Bulgaria to ascertain the situation with respect to American POWs being held there. They found three wounded POWs in the hospital at Rus,

---

[85]Manfred von Killinger (1886-1944) was the German minister in Bucharest, not a Gestapo chief. A torpedo boat commander in World War I, he joined the Nazi party in 1928 and rose rapidly through the ranks in the SA. He entered the German Foreign Office as a professional Nazi diplomat and was the minister to Slovakia in December 1940 when he was appointed to Bucharest. After the August 1944 coup, von Killinger and his secretary, Hella Peterson, committed suicide in the legation on September 2nd rather than become Soviet prisoners.

[86]A vertical line appears in the left margin of this paragraph and an illegible note, possibly "oa."

[87]In the Ross manuscript version this entire *post scriptum* is crossed out and is bracketed in the left margin with the word "OMIT." It does not appear in the re-typed version, probably for the reasons noted in endnote 60 above.

but the prison camp at Schumen, where most of the prisoners were believed to have been kept, was empty when the Americans arrived, all the POWs having already left by train for Istanbul. With no work to be done in Bulgaria, they returned to Bucharest on September 12th. Two days later with no further excuse for delay and apparently no move by Wisner to integrate Ross in the Hammerhead Mission, he returned to Italy where, on September 16th, he filed his final reports on the Romanian and Bulgarian missions.[88]

By any standards the Bucharest mission was a success for which Ross deserves much of the credit. Not only did he, in a very short time, get an intelligence operation up and running successfully, despite serious initial difficulties and his priority assignment, the evacuation of nearly 1200 former POWs. This accomplishment was recognized almost immediately, for on September 4th General Hap Arnold radioed to the various units involved: "worthy of the highest commendation is the efficient and rapid manner with which the actual return of our interned airmen in Romania was effected. All personnel connected with this operation are to be informed of the appreciation of the AAF in the recovery of these airmen."[89]

Ross's personal efforts had clearly earned him the respect of the OSS, for when LCDR Green, the commanding officer of Company B, was transferred on October 18, 1944, Major Ross was appointed commanding officer in his place.[90] When Frank Wisner was transferred from Bucharest at the end of January, 1945, Ross finally got the posting at which he had broadly hinted six months before and became commanding officer of the Hammerhead Mission. By that spring he had been promoted to lieutenant colonel and had added the OSS commendation award to his bronze star.

Ross left the Army of the United States in 1946 to resume his business career, first as vice-president of the First National Bank in Louisville. In 1950 he moved to the Chemical Bank in Manhattan. By the time he retired in 1968 he was the executive vice-president. In that year he moved from Greenwich, Connecticut, to Palm Springs, Califor-

---

[88]Two reports (subject: "Evacuation of Air Crew Men from Rumania" and "Evacuation of American Fliers from Bulgaria") by Major Ross to Commanding Officer Co. B, 2677th Regt. OSS (Prov), both dated September 16, 1944. (NARA RG-226 E-190 B-118)

[89]See endnote 1 above.

[90]Memorandum "To the Staff of OSS — Bari" from LCDR Edward J. Green, 18 October 1944. (NARA RG-226 E-190 B-118)

nia, where he was associated with the ISI Corporation. At the age of 86, he died of cancer on November 10, 1990.[91]

Ross's letters from Bucharest are an important documentary source for one of the most interesting and successful American operations in the Second World War, the evacuation of over 1200 military personnel hundreds of miles behind enemy lines. As commanding officer of the OSS unit which carried out the task of assembling and transporting these men, Major Ross provides a generally accurate eye-witness account of the overall operation.

The letters also provide descriptions and evaluations of some of the key personalities of the Sănătescu government in its first week in power. There is nothing startling or unexpected here; they are the initial, hurried observations of a skillful intelligence officer trying to sort out the power structure of a new government.

Likewise the initial contact with the Russians is not surprising or unusual. The Red Army would soon be famous throughout central Europe for its ruthless requisitioning and for the difficulty its officers frequently had in maintaining discipline when the army was in contact with civilians. The loss of the American truck with a Romanian driver the afternoon of September 2nd perhaps may be blamed on the confusions and exigencies of a war zone. Nevertheless the two attempts the same evening to requisition Ross's automobile with American uniformed personnel were extreme even by Red Army standards.

In a sense, however, the letters are more than the sum of their parts, for one can see fleetingly on their pages the long foreshadows of the coming Cold War. There was, of course, the massive use of American airpower which would be again demonstrated four years later in the Berlin Air Lift.

The rough shod behavior of the Red Army operating outside the Soviet Union in contact with the civilians of central Europe has already been noted. To American eyes it would become all of a piece with the conduct of the Soviet army in Poland, Hungary, Berlin, or Vienna and a host of other situations in the antechamber of the Cold War. The ruthless disregard of individual, human rights in American eyes paralleled Soviet behavior throughout the Cold War.

More intriguing than these obvious parallels, however, were the events the forenoon of August 29th when Cantacuzino returned to Romania from Bari. He had been instructed to have assembled and readied at the airport that afternoon some 20 ex-POWs to fly out on

---

[91] See endnote 15 above.

the two B-17s that would land with Ross and his team. Disregarding his instructions, Catacuzino immediately upon landing instead drove into Bucharest to consult with the Romanian authorities. One senses in the letter of August 30th Ross's disappointment when he is greeted not by the expected POWs but by a delegation of ingratiating Romanian officials. One cannot help suspecting that Cantacuzino was encouraged or even ordered by these same charming, obliging Romanian officials to ignore the American instructions. One notes also that Ross had been ordered to establish his headquarters at the airfield in Popeşti, orders he ignored in favor of a villa in downtown Bucharest "for many reasons," which he declined to elaborate. Similar pursuits of different agendas, working to cross purposes while giving mixed signals would all too frequently bedevil the American-Romanian relationship in the next few years with tragic results.

One does not want to press on this point too hard. Ross was a bright and talented intelligence office, not a prophet. Nevertheless, if current scholarship by such historians as Elizabeth Hazard[92] and Eduard Mark[93] is borne out and Romania is to be seen as the cradle of the Cold War because it was here the Anglo-Americans and the Soviets first met in an essentially post-war relationship, then the Ross letters do provide an uncanny preview of some of the major themes in the East-West conflict to come.

---

[92]Hazard, *op. cit.*, pp. 240-241.

[93]Eduard Mark, "The OSS in Romania, 1944-45: An Intelligence Operation of the Early Cold War," Intelligence and National Security, Vol. 9 (April 1994), No. 2, pp. 321-344, see especially pp. 321 and 333-334.

American-Romanian Relations
1953-1998

Joseph Harrington
Framingham State College

During the 45 years of Radu Florescu's tenure at Boston College, Romanian-American relations made great progress, a progress that moved from no diplomatic relations to an official White House invitation by President William Clinton to President Emil Constantinescu in the summer of 1997. No one could be more pleased by this progress than Radu, who has labored throughout his life to bring Bucharest and Washington closer together.

Ever since the Allies decided at the Teheran Conference in 1943 that Romania would come under the Soviet sphere of influence, Romanian relations had gradually deteriorated with her Western neighbors, including the United States. As the Cold War evolved, Washington treated Romania as she did Moscow, and all the Soviet satellites, as part of a monolithic "bloc", which was a threat to the "free world." The United States decided to use all power at hand, especially her economic and technological prowess, to weaken this Soviet Bloc.[1] In 1949, the United States Congress passed the Export Control Act, designed to prohibit the export of any materials viewed as contributing to the economic or military potential of the Communist world. The prohibiting mechanism was a license. Any company that wanted to export goods to the Soviet Bloc had to apply to the Commerce Department for a license to do so.[2] Throughout the 1950s and early 1960s, the Commerce Department invariably refused such license requests.

However, export controls could only be effective if Western Europe supported America's position. Washington used Marshall Plan funds as leverage to force her Western allies to adopt similar, although not identical, export controls. Washington was aware that these actions were in violation of her pledge to the United Nations that she would promote free trade and submit copies of all trade agreements to the international body.[3] Consequently, the United States coerced her allies into "voluntarily" supporting the trade prohibitions, and institutionalized this voluntarism through a Coordinating Committee or COCOM, which met secretly, kept no minutes, and established lists of commodities prohibited for export to the Communist world.[4] In 1951, in the midst of the Korean War, the United States Congress passed the Mutual Defense Assistance Act. Commonly called the Battle Act, after its sponsor Laurie Battle, this legislation gave the President the right to punish Western allied countries if they exported materials to Communist countries.[5] While all of this legislation would directly impact American-Romanian trade, none did as much damage to Bucharest as

---

[1]For a summary of the period 1940-1990, see Joseph F. Harrington and Bruce Courtney, *Tweaking the Nose of the Russians: Fifty Years of American-Romanian Relations, 1940-1990* (Boulder, Colorado: East European Monographs, published by Columbia University Press, 1991). For a summary in Romanian see 1993 monthly issues of *Magazin Istoric*. For the period 1989-1994, see Joseph F. Harrington, Edward Kams, and Scott Kams, "Romanian Human Rights and American MFN, 1989-1994," *South East European Monitor*, II, No. 4, 1995; and by the same authors, "American-Romanian Relations, 1989-1994," *East European Quarterly*, Vol. XXIX, No. 2, pp. 207-235.

[2]See U.S. Congress, House, Hearings before the Committee on Banking and Currency, Export Control Act of 1949, H.R. 1661, 81st Congress., 1st Session., 1949; U.S. Congress, Senate, Hearing before the Subcommittee of the Committee on Banking and Currency, Extension of Export Controls, S. 548, 81st Congress., 1st Session., 1949.

[3]Report "Status of Controls over Exports to the Soviet Union and its Satellites, April 17, 1950," p. 4, Box 19, Record Group 469, Special Representative, Paris, Trade and Finance Division Subsection Files, 1949-1951, Trade E, National Archives.

[4]Report, "Understandings on Export Control in East-West Trade," p. 4, NSC, No. 46, May 3, 1949, Folder 206, President's Secretary Files, Harry S. Truman Presidential Library.

[5]For a discussion about this see Gunnar Adler-Karlsson, *Western Economic Warfare, 1947-1967: A Case Study in Foreign Economic Policy* (Stockholm: Almquist and Wiksell, 1968). America's export controls applied not only to the Communist world, but to the free world as well. Some critics questioned whether the real motive of America's export controls was to cripple Russia, or to insure that America maintained her preponderant economic position which in 1950 accounted for 52% of the world's gross national product.

Congress's decision on August 31, 1951, to suspend Romania's Most-Favored-Nation (MFN) product treatment on imports to the United States.[6]

These congressional actions ignored the traditional "bread-basket-workshop" relationship that existed between East and West Europe. The East produced food, and the West manufactured products. This exchanges had kept Europe economically vibrant for centuries. Further, America's export controls were at odds with Washington's stated goals of facilitating Western Europe's economic recovery. This recovery was impossible without East-West trade, and consequently America's allies complained bitterly about export controls and Washington's threatened sanctions.

In the early 1950s, the Soviets exploded their first hydrogen bomb, which served as vivid proof that the export controls were not working. Further in 1953, hostilities in Korea ended and the Soviets introduced a "New Course," designed to create a new image following Stalin's death. These developments, coupled with Europe's successful efforts to establish intra-European unions, encouraged the Western powers to pressure the United States to relax its export controls.

President Eisenhower finally agreed, principally because he did not want to support any program that did not work, and the controls were not working effectively. Western businessmen, including some Americans, had found ways to circumvent the licensing mechanism through transshipments. Further, Eisenhower was committed to a balanced budget, and increased trade was a major means to achieve this goal. This commitment produced the "New Look" which included possible trade with the Soviet Bloc, especially of surplus American agricultural products.

Meanwhile, postwar developments in Romania had produced a Socialist Republic in Bucharest, which by 1952, was led by Gheorghe Gheorghiu-Dej, a Stalinist by personality, but a Romanian nationalist by conviction. Gheorghiu-Dej wanted Romania to pursue her own national path to Communism, not a path dictated by Moscow.[7] As Gheorghiu-Dej simply stated, he was tired of Romania sending corn to Poland, so that Poland could raise pigs to trade to the West for manu-

---

[6]Telegram, Termination of US-Rumanian Commercial Agreement of August 20, 1930, 3 pp., September 19, 1951, File 411.6631/9-1951, Box 1854, Record Group 59, NND862903, National Archives.

[7]Report of the Delegation of the Rumanian Workers' Party to the 22nd Congress of the CPSU delivered by Gheorghe Gheorghiu-Dej at the Plenary Meeting of the C.C. of the R.W.P. held over November 30-December 5, 1961, December 10, 1961.

factures and technology. He wanted Romania to trade directly with the West, independent of Moscow and CMEA directives.[8]

As a result of the "New Course," "New Look," and developments in Romania, an environment existed which enabled Bucharest to notify Washington that Romania would like to establish normal relations with the United States.[9] Negotiations developed slowly since the United States refused to talk about trade until Romania agreed to compensate American citizen and corporate claims concerning lost ownership of properties following Bucharest's nationalization policies adopted in 1948. In 1956, the White House established a Foreign Claims Commission that began work on Romanian claims.[10]

In 1960, the United States and Romania signed a claims settlement agreement that gave each of the claimants about $1,000 or approximately 38% of their entitlement. Shortly thereafter, Bucharest pressed Washington for a trade agreement. President Kennedy supported expanded East-West trade. However, his efforts to secure appropriate legislation failed. The combined effects of the Bay of Pigs, the Khrushchev-Kennedy Vienna talks, and the Cuban Missile Crisis prompted Congress to pass legislation that severely curbed East-West trade.

The Nuclear Test Ban Treaty in 1963 eased Congress's Cold War mentality and permitted Kennedy to again press for greater East-West trade. He appointed William Crawford as America's Minister to Bucharest and Crawford was more committed to improving Romanian-American relations than any of his predecessors. Crawford's work, aided by his close relationship with Averell Harriman, a personal friend of the President, made American-Romanian trade possible. Crawford used his influence directly on the White House, bypassing the normal State Department channels. He believed that the Department was

---

[8]Statement according to William Crawford, America's Minister and later Ambassador to Romania. William A. Crawford recorded interview by William A. Moss, March 12, 1971, John F. Kennedy Presidential Library, Oral History Program, p. 14. CMEA, the Council for Mutual Economic Assistance, was the Soviet counterpart to the Marshall Plan. CMEA insured that Moscow controlled the economies of member satellites.

[9]Telegram, London to Secretary of State, December 15, 1954, File 411.6631.12-1554, Box 1854, Record Group 59, NND862903, National Archives; *New York Times*, October 12, 1955, p. 2; Transcript of News Conference, Silviu Brucan, April 30, 1956, p. 1, File 215 Rumanian Government, Box 886, Office Files, White House Central Files, Dwight D. Eisenhower Presidential Library.

[10]Report, Patterns of Rumanian Claims Settlements with Western Countries, October 30, 1959, pp. 1-4, Bureau of Intelligence and Research, Report 8143, Box 1787, OSS R&A Reports, National Archives.

made up of people who still thought in Cold War terms and who were unable to realize that significant changes were occurring in Romania.[11] Gheorghiu-Dej desperately sought economic independence from Moscow, and Crawford wanted the United States to reward his efforts. The Minister saw trade as a means to affect change in Romania; trade was for political purposes, not for any considerable economic gain. To Gheorghiu-Dej, trade was important for a variety of reasons. An agreement with Washington would first give greater legitimacy to his government; second, enable Bucharest to secure Western technology; and third, provide Romania with the means to pursue her own national goals.[12]

Crawford's efforts brought results. Just prior to his assassination, President Kennedy authorized the Administration to move forward on expanding East-West trade, particularly with Romania. Lyndon B. Johnson accepted the Kennedy proposal, and in April, 1964, the White House formally notified Bucharest that the United States was willing to begin trade talks.[13]

This announcement came at the same time that the Romanian Communist Party Congress passed a decree generally viewed as Romania's Declaration of Independence from Moscow. Taking a number of Moscow statements out of context, Gheorghiu-Dej proclaimed, as had the Kremlin, that each socialist country was free to pursue its own road to Communism. The Party decree certainly reinforced Washington's decision to trade with Bucharest, and bilateral talks began in May and continued throughout the month.

On June 1, the two countries issued a joint communique that indicated that they would try to increase trade, and raise the level of their respective diplomatic missions from Legations to Embassies. The White House agreed to press Congress to pass legislation granting Romanian products MFN treatment, and to authorize the Ex-Im Bank to extend financial credits to Romania. Finally, Washington agreed to establish a general export licensing procedure which would permit

[11]Crawford, Oral Interview, March 12, 1971, p. 20; Crawford interview with author, Metropolitan Club, Washington, D.C., April 18, 1979.

[12]Orville Freeman Papers (former Secretary of Agriculture), Notes 5, Box 8, Trip to Communist Countries, pp. 77-79; Report at Eforie dated August 4, 1963, pp. 1-3, John F. Kennedy Presidential Library.

[13]Agerpress, April 26, 1964, Supplement, 4 pp. Moscow's statements were not directed at Romania, but rather at trying to emphasize Communist unity in an effort to downplay the developing Sino-Soviet rift. However, Gheorghiu-Dej chose to take the letter rather than the spirit of the announcements and apply them to Romania.

American companies to export most items to Romania without having to apply for individual licenses.[14] This 1964 agreement laid the groundwork for MFN. However, neither side could envision that Romania would have to wait eleven years before her products received MFN treatment.

President Johnson wanted to "build bridges" to Eastern Europe — bridges that would bring democracy and Western values to the satellite states, bridges that would undermine Communism and decouple these states from Moscow.[15] However, Johnson's pursuit of the Vietnam War, totally derailed his "building bridges" program. Congress would never consider increasing trade with Communist Romania. What would prevent Bucharest from transshipping American technology to North Vietnam, a fraternal communist country, which could be used to kill American G.I.s? There were no supporters on Capitol Hill for granting Romania MFN as long as there was a war in Vietnam.

As a matter of fact, Romania did transship equipment to its socialist brother in North Vietnam, but, at the same time, Bucharest offered its services to mediate an end to the bloody conflict. Romania's Ambassador to the United States, Corneliu Bogdan, agreed to carry messages via Bucharest to Hanoi. The White House agreed and initiated a plan called the "Packers", named after the successful football team, the Green Bay Packers. Bogdan continued to mediate until the Tet offensive in early 1968, which put an abrupt end to all negotiations. Unfortunately for Romania, "Packers" was a covert operation, and Congress was unaware of its existence, thus preventing Capitol Hill from rewarding Bucharest for its assistance.[16]

In 1969, Richard Nixon took office as President of the United States with a clear mandate to end the Vietnam War. One of his first appointments was Henry Kissinger as National Security Council Advi-

[14]See, U.S. Congress, House, Hearings before the Subcommittee on Trade of the Committee on Ways and Means, United States-Romanian Trade Agreement, 94th Congress, 1st Session, 1975.

[15]Public Papers of the Presidents of the United States, Lyndon B. Johnson, 1963-1964 (Washington, D.C.: U.S. government Printing Office, 1965), I, 709. Zbigniew Brzezinski was the author of the "building bridges" idea (J.F. Brown, Eastern Europe and Communist Rule (Durham, N.C.: Duke University Press, 1981, p. 108).

[16]Richard Allen (ed.), Yearbook on International Communist Affairs, 1968 — (Stanford, CA: Hoover Institution Press, 1969), p. 516; The Secret Diplomacy of the Vietnam War: The Negotiating Volumes of the Pentagon Papers, ed. George C. Herring (Austin: University of Texas Press, 1989), pp. 522-523; Lyndon B. Johnson, The Vantage Point: Perspectives of the Presidency, 1963-1969 (New York: Holt, Reinhart and Winston, 1971), p. 268; Author interview with Cornelieu Bogdan, March 19, 1987.

sor. Both men shared a common view, that American foreign policy had to change from a bipolar view to a multi-polar view. Beijing, Tokyo, and the Common Market were all viable players on the geopolitical scene; the world was more than Soviet-American relations. Further, Nixon did not see the Communist world as a monolithic "bloc." To the contrary, he supported a policy of differentiation. While this was not totally new, since America has differentiated in favor of Yugoslavia nearly twenty years earlier, the Nixon Administration would be the first to adopt differentiation as a policy.

An opportunity to explore this new policy appeared in the summer of 1969. Kennedy's promise to send a man to the moon within the decade came to fruition. Nixon decided to meet the Apollo moon mission members in the Pacific, and to return home via Bucharest, to visit a country which had treated him most cordially in 1967, when he was not in political office. He also wanted to irritate Moscow.[17] While he had a soft spot for Romania, his main goal in foreign policy was linkage. Nixon and Kissinger wanted to capitalize on the Sino-Soviet split. The President wanted to link Soviet-American progress in one area, with Soviet-American relations in another. Quite specifically, Nixon wanted Soviet support to end the Vietnam War, and in return, he was willing to talk about strategic arms limitations. But one was a Quid pro quo for the other. A visit to Bucharest, the Soviet Union's maverick satellite, might put the Kremlin on notice, that there was a new regime in the White House.

Nixon was the first American president to visit Romania in the near 100 year history of American-Romanian relations. He received a hero's welcome in Bucharest; people lined the streets, and Nixon followed a time honored campaign practice jumping out of his car, kissing babies and shaking hands with the crowd, forcing Romanian President Nicolae Ceaușescu to do similarly, for the first time in his life. In his talks with Ceaușescu, Nixon did not promise the Romanian leader MFN, but he did promise to improve relations between the two countries.[18] Within weeks of his return, Nixon did increase Romania's credit line with the Ex-Im Bank and supported Romania's application for membership in the International Monetary Fund and the World Bank.

[17] Author interview with Corneliu Bogdan, March 19, 1987.

[18] While there was some discussion at the time as to whether Nixon had promised Ceaușescu MFN, the author interviewed Robert Haldeman, John Erhlichman, and Brent Scowcroft at the Nixon Presidential Conference sponsored by Hofstra University, November 19-21, 1987, and all agreed that no such promise was made.

Nixon's Romanian visit caught the attention of a number of liberal Congressmen who interpreted the action as a sign that the time was right to introduce East-West legislation. Within a couple of days of Nixon's visit, Senator Walter Mondale of Minnesota proposed that Washington accord Romania MFN product treatment. Similar legislation appeared in the House. However, the House effort needed the support of Wilbur Mills, the Chairman of the House Ways and Means Committee. Ambassador Bogdan talked with Mills and was convinced that the Congressman had no knowledge of where Romania was, and was not terribly informed as to the nature of MFN. However, Mills made his price quite clear: if Nixon called and requested him to move Romanian MFN legislation, he would insure that the bill would leave his committee and be approved by the House. All Mills required was a personal call from the President.[19]

However, there would be no call. The Soviets refused to play at linkage and the Kremlin would not intercede in the Vietnam peace process. Nixon was angry with the Communists and his feelings broadened to include all Communist countries, including Romania. By 1971, Bogdan saw the handwriting on the wall and knew that no call would be made. Romania simply was not important enough to establish an IOU with the powerful Chairman of the House Ways and Means Committee; there were much more important issues that might require Mills' support.[20]

Meanwhile, the Vietnam peace negotiations had progressed and as they did so, Nixon's anger towards Moscow abated. The successful SALT talks led to a Soviet-American Trade Agreement in October 1972. The accord, if approved by Congress, provided MFN treatment for Soviet products in return for Moscow repaying her lend-lease debts incurred during World War II.[21] This agreement angered conservative legislators in both houses of Congress. Since the Trade Agreement was signed at the close of the 92nd session of Congress, opposition legislators had time before the opening of the 93rd Congress to prepare their attack, and they did so under the leadership of Senator Henry "Scoop" Jackson of Washington and Representative Charles Vanik from Ohio.

[19] Author interview with Corneliu Bogdan, March 19, 1987

[20] Ibid.

[21] This agreement ended any thoughts of Romanian MFN. Nixon could not reward Romania for her maverick position toward Moscow and, at the same time, develop cordial relations with the Soviets. Memorandum, Larry Brady to Bob McDermott, July 10, 1972, Folder ExCo 125, Romania 1/1/71, Box 63, Co Subject Files, White House Central Files, Nixon Presidential Materials Project.

While there was some discussion at the time as to whether Nixon had promised Ceauşescu MFN, the author interviewed Robert Haldeman, John Erhlichman, and Brent Scowcroft at the Nixon Presidential Conference sponsored by Hofstra University, November 19-21, 1987, and all agreed that no such promise was made.

Jackson and Vanik received substantial support from numerous American groups opposed to dealing with the Soviets, including the Jewish lobby, which urged restraint on Soviet-American relations until the Kremlin permitted free emigration of Jews from the Soviet Union. Both men were attracted to this issue because it would prick the Communist countries in a vulnerable area. Moscow and the East European countries opposed emigration because they saw it in terms of lost assets and a brain drain. Their governments had paid for the education of those who wanted to leave, and, generally speaking, those applying were people who were better educated or more highly skilled.

Jackson and Vanik had to wait for appropriate legislation to which they could attach their amendment. They did not want to limit their language solely to the Soviet Trade Agreement. In 1973, Nixon urged Congress to pass a Trade Reform Bill that would give greater authority to the president to reduce tariffs and increase America's export markets. 1971 was the first year that America had a trade deficit, and Nixon wanted power to reduce the imbalance. Jackson and Vanik quickly went to work. Their efforts became known as Section 402 of the Trade Bill of 1974. This section stipulated that America could not grant MFN product treatment to any non-market economy that did not permit free emigration. The amendment language did not require a country to pass legislation stipulating free emigration. Rather, the mechanics simply required the President of the United States to tell Congress that he had received assurances that a particular country would improve its emigration practices and this improvement would lead to the objectives of Section 402. This assurance would then enable Congress to grant and/or extend MFN. The extension would be annual and could be terminated if either house passed a resolution disapproving a further extension. Liberals joined conservatives in both houses in support of the amendment and in December Congress passed the Trade Reform Act of 1974 with its Jackson-Vanik amendment. In January 1975, President Gerald Ford signed the legislation into law. The importance of the amendment was not in Jewish emigration, but in the power that it gave Congress to veto foreign policy. The White House could no longer accord MFN treatment to a Communist country without the approval of both houses of the legislature. Watergate and the

Vietnam War had shifted power from one end of Pennsylvania Avenue to the other.

While the Soviets saw the Jackson-Vanik amendment as a tool to interfere in the domestic policies of a country, Bucharest saw it as a formula to achieve MFN. Two weeks after Moscow notified Washington that it was no longer interested in the 1972 Trade Agreement, Bucharest informed Harry Barnes, the United States Ambassador to Romania, that she was ready to comply with the terms of Section 402. If MFN required Jewish emigration, Ceauşescu could let more Jews emigrate. Negotiations between the two countries began quickly and on August 2, 1975, Ford and Ceauşescu signed the Romanian-American Trade Agreement that gave Romanian products MFN treatment in the United States.[22]

American-Romanian relations from 1976 through 1988, when Romania lost MFN, are easily divided by the Carter and Reagan Administrations. Throughout both periods, there was a rhythm to the relations, a rhythm produced by the mechanics involved in the Jackson-Vanik language. Simply put, the President would annually ask Congress by June 3 to extend Romanian MFN for another year. Each house had until September 3 to pass a resolution of disapproval to deny the request. If neither house took any action, MFN was automatically renewed. Therefore, every year between March and August, Romania would increase emigration, especially Jews, and wine and dine congressional and business delegations in Bucharest. After September 3, Romanian-American relations would go on the back burner until the following Spring.

During the Carter years, academicians such as Radu Florescu, then President of the Society for Romanian Studies,[23] and representatives from corporate America supported Romanian MFN at the various congressional hearings. By 1980, the trade agreement had resulted in over a billion dollar two-way trade, with the United States enjoying a $400 million trade surplus. The Commerce and State Departments also supported MFN renewal. The former, because it was good for business, the latter, because it gave Washington leverage to affect political change in Bucharest, especially in the area of emigration.

[22]Author interview with Harry Barnes, July 19, 1987; Harry G. Barnes, Jr., "Impression of Romania," *The United States and Romania*, ed. Paul D. Quinlan (Woodland Hills, CA: American-Romanian Academy of Arts and Sciences, 1988), p. 126.

[23]U.S. Senate, Committee on Finance, Subcommittee on International Trade, Continuing Most-Favored-Nation Tariff Treatment of Imports from Romania, 1977. Hearing, 95th Congress., 1st Session., June 27, 1977, p. 134.

While Romanian MFN survived all of the hearings, every summer produced a discussion about Jewish emigration. Finally, in an effort to put an end to this issue, representatives from B'nai B'rith and the Presidents of the Major American Jewish Associations went to Bucharest in June, 1979. They met with government leaders and, with the help of former Romanian Ambassador Bogdan, worked out a formula for Jewish emigration. The formula, according to Bogdan, stipulated that almost any Jewish person who wanted to leave Romania could do so. The only restrictions concerned those with state secrets or those who could be a threat to Romania's national security.[24]

With the Jewish issue resolved, there appeared to be no further impediments to the annual renewal of Romanian MFN. However 1980 was not 1974. In 1974, the Jackson-Vanik amendment meant Jewish emigration; in 1980, it began to mean human rights. In the wake of Watergate and Vietnam, Jimmy Carter had campaigned and won on a banner of moral consciousness and human rights. Soon committees appeared in Congress that aimed to monitor human rights activities in foreign countries, especially those receiving aid from the United States.

At the outset, Romania was not a target of these committees. Human rights were essentially confined to gross violators, mainly governments that tortured and executed its citizens. President Carter had an interesting view of human rights. He disapproved of them in rightist regimes, but tolerated them under Communist governments because he believed that Communism intrinsically denied people human rights. Consequently, he refused to expand the definition of the Jackson-Vanik amendment to include human rights; instead, he preferred to use MFN renewal as a means to improve Romanian human rights.[25]

The 1980 presidential election focused on the Islamic Revolution in Iran, the seemingly never-ending hostage crisis, and the Soviet invasion of Afghanistan and brought Ronald Reagan to the White House with the support of a "moral majority." Reagan rhetoric announced a new day: the Soviet Union was an "evil empire" and he did not want to deal with satans in Moscow. Unlike Carter, human rights violations in geostrategically friendly rightist regimes would be tolerated, but they would not be tolerated in Communist countries. Congress saw

[24]Author interview with Corneliu Bogdan, January 11, 1989.
[25]Jimmy Carter, Keeping Faith: Memoirs of a President (New York: Bantam Books, 1982), p. 143.

the Reagan landslide and knew that human rights was the new currency for dealing with the Soviet Union and its satellites.

Beginning in 1981, Congress changed the rules. Romania had
signed the Helsinki Accords, and that meant that she was committed to
human rights. Congress redefined the Jackson-Vanik amendment to
mean not only emigration, but also a broad spectrum of human rights.
Ceauşescu's cult of personality, which permitted no dissidence, would
not do well within this framework. To make matters worse, Romania
had incurred a massive foreign debt. Ceauşescu's decision to import
Western technology in the 1970s with the hope of making Romania a
major industrial country backfired. Although Romania had her own
oil, her industrialization demanded more energy than she could produce. Consequently, she made arrangements to purchase oil from Iran.
This worked well until the Shah fell, and with that the price of oil sky-
rocketed and continued to do so with the ensuing Irani-Iraqi war.
Romania had to import oil from the Soviet Union, making her dependent on Moscow, the one development Ceauşescu had vigorously tried
to prevent.[26]

Further, without oil exports to provide her with Western currency,
Romania had to borrow to pay for her technological imports. By
1981, she owed the West 11 billion dollars. Ceauşescu decided to pay
off the debt as quickly as possible. He would make Romania self-suffi-
cient. Bucharest would slash imports and increase exports, especially in
foodstuffs. This decision, of course, lost Romania the support of the
American business community, and when annual MFN hearings
occurred in the early 1980s, the bulk of the testimony came from those
who opposed extending MFN. They argued that Romania was ineligi-
ble for MFN on the basis of her maltreatment of her national and religious minorities, especially Hungarians and neo-protestants. By 1983,
there was sufficient support in the House to pass a resolution disapproving the President's recommendation to renew MFN. However, out
of nowhere, Romania received a reprieve.

In June 1983, the United States Supreme Court made a decision
in the Chadha vs. the Immigration and Naturalization Service that stipulated that the vote of one house of the legislature could not override a

---

[26]Richard F. Staar (ed.), *Yearbook on International Communist Affairs, 1982* (Stanford, CA: Hoover Institution Press, 1982), p. 461; U.S. Congress, *Joint Economic Committee, Selected Papers, East European Economies: Slow Growth in the 1980s.* Vol. 11: Foreign
Trade and International Finance, 99th Congress., 2nd Session., 1986, p. 33; and Vol. III:
Country Studies on Eastern Europe and Yugoslavia, 99th Congress., 2nd Session., 1986,
pp. 492ff.

presidential recommendation. An override could only be achieved if both houses passed a resolution and presented the resolution for the President's approval or veto. If vetoed, both houses would have to override the veto in the same manner as they would with any veto. Since the Senate was far less eager than the House to terminate Romanian MFN, no negative actions developed in either house for the next three years.[27]

However, congressional hearings did continue in Washington, and those that testified began to tell stories of arbitrary arrest, the denial of basic rights, and massive food and energy shortages. The American Ambassador to Romania, David Funderburk, appointed in 1981, resigned in protest in 1985. He believed that the American State Department was in league with the Romanian Communists to thwart the human rights concerns of the United States. At the hearings, Funderburk testified that the conditions in Romania were as inhuman as the witnesses suggested.[28]

Further, the continued growth of Ceauşescu's cult of personality, which seemed to be aimed at establishing a family dynasty in Romania, incurred the wrath of thousands of people who fled to Austria and neighboring Hungary with stories of torture and starvation. Ceauşescu incurred the wrath of even the indifferent when he destroyed architectural treasures in order to build his palace, a building measuring nearly three football fields in length, one field wide, and 13 stories high. The structure was filled with marble and crystal, an opulence few felt that Romania could afford since most of its inhabitants lived with a single 40 watt light bulb per house, with the only meat available in the form of animal heads, and temperature controlled at 50 degrees during the winter. The only salvation was the "second economy," or black market, for those who could participate, and the currency there was Kent cigarettes.

By 1986, with the erosion of business support and the growing concern with human rights, congressmen in both houses set about finding legislation to which they would attach a resolution suspending Romanian MFN. The bill chosen was the Omnibus Trade Bill, which would take three years to pass. However, Congress knew it had the

---

[27]For details about the Chadha case, see Barbara Hinkson Craig, *Chadha: The Story of an Epic Constitutional Struggle* (New York: Oxford University Press, 1988); and her work, *The Legislative Veto: Congressional Control of Legislation* (Boulder, CO: Westview Press, 1983), pp. 139ff.

[28]See David Funderburk, *Pinstripes and Reds* (Washington, D.C.: Selous Foundation Press, 1987).

votes to override any presidential veto. Consequently, supporters in both the Senate and the House attached amendments to the bill that called for suspending Romanian MFN.[29]

As the enormous bill wandered through Congress in 1987, human rights advocates focused their attention on the bill's passage and ironically ignored the President's continued recommendation to renew Romanian MFN, which was extended through July 1988. However, Ceauşescu knew that the end was near and rather than have the United States take away MFN, he decided to "cut his losses" and abrogate the agreement himself.[30] In February 1988, Ceauşescu informed Washington that Romania was no longer interested in retaining American MFN product treatment. On July 3, MFN ended.

Although Ceauşescu would pay off all of his country's foreign debt by April 1989, he did so on the backs of the Romanian people. His economic austerity programs coupled with his willingness to violate everyone's human rights to eliminate criticism produced a climate of hatred and fear; a situation which could only be changed by the death of the President. Events that began in Timişoara on December 16, 1989, quickly escalated and ended with the death of Nicolae and Elena Ceauşescu which was announced on Christmas Day.

A new government quickly formed, and in many ways it was old wine in new bottles. The National Salvation Front (NSF) was led by Ion Iliescu, a former Communist who had fallen out of favor with Ceauşescu. On January 9, 1990, the NSF notified Washington that it would like to begin negotiations to restore MFN. Iliescu noted that his principal foreign policy goal was to join the European house; but the road to Brussels led through Washington. As Romanian Ambassador Mircea Geoană noted "the MFN debate was essential to put Romania back on the American Congressional agenda, a position lost in 1988."[31] Little did anyone realize that it would take Romania nearly 4 years to regain MFN, and nearly 6 years to have it permanently restored.

Relations between the new Romanian government and Washington resembled a roller-coaster between January 1990 and the summer

[29]U.S. Congress, House Committee on Foreign Affairs, Hearing before the Subcommittee on Human Rights and International Organizations, Human Rights in Romania and Its Implications for U.S. Policy and Most Favored Nation Status, 100th Congress., 2nd Session., 1987, pp. 18ff. See also U.S. Congressional Record, 100th Congress., 1st Session., CXXIII, S8788-8789, S9963.

[30]Author interview with Corneliu Bogdan, January 11, 1989.

[31]Author interview with Mircea Geoană, November 22, 1996.

of 1992. In March 1990, hundreds of Romanians attacked Hungarians in the Transylvanian city of Târgu Mureş producing criticism from Washington.[32] Two months later, Bucharest won plaudits for its freely run May elections the first in over forty years. However, a month later, the newly elected government, still under Iliescu, called in miners from the Jiu Valley to remove student demonstrators from Bucharest protesting the recent elections. The miners clad in overalls, wearing their hard hats and lamps, and wielding clubs, iron bars and coal picks made great story lines for Western media. On June 14, President Bush denounced Bucharest's actions as "government inspired vigilante violence," and he suspended all non-humanitarian aid to Romania.[33]

While Romania would win Western approval for her support of the United Nations actions during the Iraqi-Kuwaiti War, the image would be compromised by the growing number of stories about black-marketeering of Romanian babies, AIDS children, and anti-semitism.[34] In 1992, relations revolved around local and national elections. When Romania supported United Nations' sanctions against Yugoslavia, she did so aware that it would cost her substantially in lost trade.[35] The White House appreciated the move and Bush urged Congress to grant Romania MFN product treatment.[36] However, such approval would be contingent on the degree of freedom exhibited in the forthcoming national elections.

As the September 27 election day approached, supporters of Romanian MFN tried to unlink the results of the election with the legislation and pressed for an early vote on MFN. House Ways and Means

---

[32]*Manchester Guardian Weekly*, April 1, 1990, pp. 7, 13; Foreign Broadcast Information Service, Daily Report, East Europe, March 16, 1990, p. 53. Hereafter cited as FBIS, EEU.

[33]Weekly Compilation of Presidential Documents (Washington, D.C.: U.S. Government Printing Office), June 18, 1990, p. 949; FBIS, EEU, August 2, 1990, pp. 35. 37 U.S. Congress, House Committee of the Judiciary, Hearing before the Subcommittee on International Law, Immigration and Refugees, Romanian Adoptions, 102nd Congress., 1st Session., June 5, 1991.

[34]Editors' note: Please consult author for documentation.

[35]The Romanian Foreign Ministry anticipated that Romania would lose at least $550 million in trade through the sanctions. And this figure was especially significant since Romania's industrial production had already dropped almost 18% in the first five months of 1992 compared to the preceding year (*Wall Street Journal*, June 26, 1992, B6:3).

[36]U.S. Congress, House Document 102341, 102nd Congress, 2nd Session, Extension of Waiver Authority, Message from the President of the United States (Washington, D.C.: U.S. Government Printing Office, 1992), p. iii.

Chairman Dan Rostenkowski called for a decision on September 22. Tom Lantos, a frequent naysayer concerning Romania, challenged the Chairman and won Congressional support to postpone any decision on MFN until after the election.[37] On September 30, in spite of well-run elections, Congress chose not to consider Romanian MFN in 1992.

Why did Congress say no? Many blamed Lantos, the Hungarian born California Congressman. However, in an interview with the American Ambassador to Romania, John Davis, the reason Congress refused to consider the resolution had little to do with Lantos, and much to do with the perception that the Romanian government was not legitimate; the revolution of 1989 had only eliminated Ceauşescu, not the Communists. Further, Romania's press image in the West did little to attract support: miner violence, blackmarketeering of babies, and AIDS children. These were sufficient reasons not to support MFN.[38]

1993 saw Bucharest still willing to be the principal Balkan enforcer of United Nations sanctions against the former Yugoslavia. Iliescu, who won the 1992 presidential elections, wanted to capitalize on the West's appreciation of Romania's contribution. However, he knew that Romania needed a new image and Bucharest began a full fledged public relations campaign including inserts in weekly news magazines in America, such as *Newsweek*, which featured a 16 page insert on "Romania: Rebuilding the Nation."[39] In March, Iliescu accepted an invitation to attend the opening of the Holocaust Museum in Washington, in the process deliberately underscoring the fact that anti-Semitism was not an issue in Romania. In addition, the visit enabled Iliescu to spend a few minutes with President Clinton and with other ranking government and congressional members to lobby for MFN.

Iliescu's efforts met with success. On July 2, 1993, Clinton asked Congress to grant Romania MFN, with a request for fast-track approval. Representative Richard Gephardt of Missouri introduced Joint Resolution 228, and the House Ways and Means Committee asked for written comments. Reminiscent of the 1970s, 60 firms sent letters supporting Romanian MFN. In reviewing all of the correspondence received, over 90% supported the immediate restoration of MFN.[40] On September 28, the Council of Europe approved Romania's request for membership, and while this meant little to most people in

---

[37]U.S. Congressional Record, 102nd Congress, 2nd Session, pp. H8850ff.

[38]Author interview with John Davis, March 25, 1994.

[39]*Newsweek*, April 12, 1993.

the United States, government officials knew that this meant that the Romanian government had agreed to adopt Western human rights standards.[41]

On October 12, Rostenkowski brought MFN to a vote. This time Lantos supported the measure "in view of Romania's improved human rights record." The House approved the resolution by voice vote and action in the Senate was equally quick. On November 2, President Clinton signed the bill as Public Law 102-133 giving Romania MFN product treatment effective November 8, 1993.

In analyzing the difference between the votes of 1992 and 1993, several issues become clear. According to Ambassador Davis, supporters of the 1992 legislation misplayed their hand. They assumed it was a "sure thing" and ignored the fact that they were pressing for approval in the midst of Romania's elections and also ignored the fact that Chinese MFN was on the floor at the same time; Congressmen could approve one and disapprove the other thereby accommodating all of their constituents. In 1993, Romania's image had significantly improved. If people wanted bloodshed and inhuman rights, they only had to look to Bosnia. Romania had also resolved the blackmarketeering of babies and reduced the incidence of AIDS.[42] Aurel Munteanu, the former Romanian Ambassador to the United States, told me that there may have been another reason. He believed that the failure in 1992 was designed to send a message to the Chinese that once MFN was lost, it was difficult to have it restored. So China ought to improve its human rights record.[43] In 1993, Washington decided to support the Iliescu regime to thwart conservative forces in Romania who wanted a return to the past, and closer links to Moscow. Finally, if Ceaușescu's Romania had MFN and Iliescu's did not, what did this say about the Iliescu government?

Romanian-American relations progressed normally during the next couple of years. Bucharest pressed to have Washington grant Romania permanent MFN, rather than the annual renewal. In 1995, when President Clinton recommended yet another annual renewal, the Romanian government began to aggressively lobby Congress. Mihai

---

[40]U.S. House of Representatives, Subcommittee on Trade of the Committee on Ways and Means, Written Comments on a Trade Agreement Between the United States and Romania, September 20, 1993.

[41]Author interview with Cristian Popișteanu, November 9, 1993. Popișteanu is the editor of the Romanian publication *Magazin Istoric*.

[42]Author interview with John Davis, March 25, 1994.

[43]Author interview with Aurel Munteanu, January 28, 1994.

Botez, the Romanian Ambassador, made his presence known on Capitol Hill. In September, President Iliescu visited the White House and although it was not an official state visit, it did give him the opportunity to raise the issue of permanent MFN with Clinton. This time, Clinton indicated that he had already begun to address that issue. A month later, Iliescu again visited the United States, this time for the opening of the United Nations session in New York. While in America, he visited businessmen in Houston and, due to the efforts of Radu Florescu, he met with academics and corporate leaders at the Kennedy School at Harvard.[44]

Clinton's promise materialized in March 1996, when several Congressmen, led by Representatives Phil Crane of Illinois, Sam Gibbons of Florida and Barbara Kennelly of Connecticut, introduced legislation granting Romanian products permanent MFN treatment.[45] The new Romanian Ambassador Mircea Geoană lobbied Congress while Bucharest wined and dined American businessmen and government officials, including the mercurial Lantos who finally announced his support for permanent MFN in April.

The Romanian efforts succeeded. The House agreed in July to consider the legislation and after some debate,[46] the House approved the bill 334 to 86. Two days later, on July 19, the Senate did likewise and on August 3 President Clinton signed the legislation into law. This opened the door not only for MFN, but also for extended credit lines from the Ex-Im Bank, the International Monetary Fund and the World Bank.

Why did Romania succeed in 1996? The United States decided to support Iliescu, in part, because the devil you know is better than the devil you do not. Washington also thought they were supporting Iliescu's reelection bid, but Romanians had a far different perception as evidenced by Emil Constantinescu's victory in the Fall 1996 elections. However, independent of Iliescu, Washington also wanted to reward Romania for its steps toward democracy and a free market economy, and to support a stable country in an unstable area of the world.

---

[44]FBIS, EEU, September 27, 1995, p. 64; Open Media Research Institute Digest (OMRI) *Daily Digest II*, No. 187, September 26, 1995. OMRI reached via internet "OMRIL@UBVM.cc.buffalo.edu."

[45]U.S. Congress, 104th Congress, 2nd Session, House of Representatives, Report 104-269, Most-Favored-Nation Treatment for Romania.

[46]U.S. Congress, Congressional Record, 104th Congress, 2nd Session, July 16, 1996, pp. H75897597.

Further, what was to be gained by denying Bucharest MFN? The carrot and stick policy pursued for decades had produced little and had not brought down Ceauşescu. Moreover, by 1996 the Clinton Administration had already divorced human rights from trade in its dealings with China, so why should there be linkage with Romania? Finally, there was the business lobby, who found it quite difficult dealing with Romania when annual renewal was dependent on Congressional whim. In September 1994, America was Romania's number one investor. In 1995, she was number eight. So the award of permanent MFN was designed to encourage Romania's progress toward a free market economy, one in which the United States could gain a larger share. While the MFN award did not help Iliescu's political career, it did assist all of America's other goals. And from the Romanian side, permanent MFN set the stage for Bucharest's bid to join NATO. As Ambassador Geoană said in November, 1996, "American MFN was the compulsory prerequisite for NATO membership; if Romania is not trustworthy enough to receive MFN status, how could Romania be trusted as a military ally?"[47]

In November 1996, the Romanians elected Emil Constantinescu their new president. He certainly was new wine in new bottles. His principal goal was to bring Romania into NATO and later the European Union. He initiated a major lobbying campaign in all 16 NATO nations' capitals to secure an invitation to join at the July 8, 1997 NATO meeting in Madrid, Spain. A significant voice in this campaign was Radu Florescu, recently appointed Honorary Consul of Romania in Boston. He, along with Stephen Fischer-Galaţi, Armand Scala, leading academicians including Paul Quinlan, Robert Weiner, and Ernest Latham, along with organizations such as the Society for Romanian Studies, American-Romanian Academy, Congress of Romanian-Americans, American-Romanian Chamber of Commerce and the East European Research Center urged congressmen and businessmen to support Romania's bid to join NATO. Kurt Treptow's *Romanian Civilization*, a publication of the Center for Romanian Studies, dedicated its Spring-Summer issue to NATO.[48] Florescu frequently visited Washington to lobby Senators Kennedy and Kerry and spoke to NATO officials in Brussels concerning Romania's value in the Euro-Atlantic alliance.

[47]Author interview with Mircea Geoană, November 22, 1996.

[48]*Romanian Civilization: A Journal of Romanian and East Central European Studies*, Vol. VI, No. 1, Spring-Summer, 1997, Special NATO Issue.

In Bucharest, Constantinescu sent his principal cabinet members to visit their counterparts in all of the NATO countries. Further, he worked furiously to eliminate problem areas by signing treaties with Hungary, the Ukraine, and Moldova. In April, Constantinescu announced that Romania, Moldova, and the Ukraine would establish two "Euro-Regions" to increase economic and cultural contacts.[49] By early Spring 1997, Romania had a champion. France led nine countries in support of Romania's inclusion in NATO. While this action was probably in part due to France's efforts to balance NATO between Washington and Paris, Bucharest was delighted by the support.[50] However, there were still two holdouts, Germany and the United States. In part, due to the efforts of Ambassador Geoană, Senator Alfonse D'Amato, Chairman of the Commission on Security and Cooperation in Europe announced his support of Romania's inclusion in the first tier of NATO enlargement. The New York Senator wanted to reward the government of Constantinescu for its rapid progress toward democracy, military security and a free market economy.[51]

However, the White House was not ready to support Romania. At a preliminary meeting of NATO foreign ministers in Sintra, Portugal, on May 29, Madeline Albright, the American Secretary of State, noted that "NATO's enlargement was not a scholarship program" and she would only support the candidacy of Poland, the Czech Republic, and Hungary.[52] The handwriting was on the wall and on June 12 President Clinton supported Albright's announcement.[53] The reasons America would not support Romania's candidacy, according to Radu Florescu, were that the new government has only been in place a short time, the economy is still poor, and some political dissidents who fled Ceaușescu and came to America are still not permitted back into Romania. Florescu believes that there are still too many pro-Ceaușescu Securitate members in the middle echelons of government that prevent the return of anti-Ceaușescu forces.[54]

---

[49]Radio Free Europe/Radio Liberty Newsline, Vol. 1, No. 21, Part 11, April 29, 1997. Hereafter cited as RFE/RL. On Internet "Rferl-Lậlistserv.acsu. buffalo.edu"

[50]The Economist, July 5, 1997, pp. 18-19.

[51]Romanian Press Review, 2.27, Week of May 26, 1997. On Internet "romprâhat-cyon.com"

[52]RFE/RL, Vol. 1, No. 42, Part II, May 30, 1997.

[53]RFE/RL, Vol. 1, No. 52, Part II, June 13, 1997.

[54]Author interview with Radu Florescu, August 8, 1997.

The same day, Bucharest received another setback. On June 11, Romanian Prime Minister Victor Ciorbea announced that the German Chancellor, Helmut Kohl, had given his support to Romania's inclusion in the first round of enlargement.[55] On June 12, Kohl denied that he had made any such endorsement, noting that his message was meant to convey Germany's "sympathy" for Romania's case, not literal support.[56]

While Bucharest would continue its lobbying efforts, Constantinescu began to accept the reality that Romania would not be invited to join NATO in the initial enlargement. On June 18, Victor Ciorbea met with American Vice President, Al Gore, and they agreed to set up a "special strategic partnership" between Washington and Bucharest.[57] Further, Clinton invited Constantinescu to an official visit to the White House at a date to be determined. The result of these exchanges was that Constantinescu learned that Washington would probably support Romania's inclusion in NATO at a later date.

On July 8, representatives from 44 nations met in Madrid, Spain, 16 NATO countries and 28 partner countries representing lands from Central Europe to Central Asia. Following the invitation to Poland, the Czech Republic, and Hungary, Clinton announced that he would visit Bucharest. The United States wanted to help Romania join NATO "if they can stay on the path of democracy and freedom."[58] Romania did get a sort of "pat on the back" for her efforts to qualify and suggestions were made that she, along with Slovenia and Austria, might be invited for the second round of invitations in 1999.[59] On July 9, Constantinescu announced at the first meeting of NATO's newest organization, the Euro-Atlantic Partnership Council (EAPC),[60] Romania's "irrevocable desire" to join NATO as soon as possible.[61]

Romania's initial reaction to the NATO rejection was mixed. While some immediately blamed Bill Clinton, far more believed that the real culprit was the preceding governments of Iliescu. They had

---

[55]*RFE/RL*, Vol. 1, No. 51, Part II, June 12, 1997.

[56]*Romanian Press Review*, 2.30, Week of June 16, 1997.

[57]*RFE/RL*, Vol. 1, No. 56, Part II, June 19, 1997.

[58]*RFE/RL*, Special Reports: The Madrid Summit.

[59]*The Economist*, July 12, 1997, pp. 19-20.

[60]NATO established the EPAC at the May meeting in Sintra, Portugal. The EPAC includes the members of NATO and the 27 members of the Partnership for Peace program.

[61]*RFE/RL*, Special Reports: The Madrid Summit: Rom.

failed to implement the needed reforms necessary for Romania to participate in NATO. This view proved the more compelling following President Clinton's visit to Bucharest on July 11. As the first American President to visit Romania in 20 years, Clinton received an overwhelming ovation by the more than 50,000 Romanians who gathered in University Square.[62] Clinton told his audience that "I have come to Romania for everything you have already done, I have come for everything you can do, I have come for everything we shall do together to fulfill your dream and to secure you a place in the family of free states."[63] The President concluded that "NATO promises to reexamine the candidates in 1999 — and Romania is one of the most serious candidates."[64]

Without question, Clinton's visit reassured the Constantinescu government that American-Romanian relations were on solid ground. As for the future, the Romanian Foreign Minister, Adrian Severin, announced that Bucharest would maintain its present policies and establish closer relations with NATO and neighboring countries. To facilitate this process, Severin set up a NATO Information Office in Bucharest to keep abreast of current developments in Brussels.

As for the future, Romania must continue to implement democratic and free market reforms. Looking at the progress Bucharest has made since the arrival of the Constantinescu regime, Romania was unfortunate to have the NATO enlargement meeting so soon. Had the Madrid enlargement process taken place in January 1998, without question Romania would have been invited. So for Bucharest, the goal is to be prepared for the next invitation in 1999. As for the Honorary Romanian Consul, Radu Florescu will have a full time job working with Bucharest and the Romanian Embassy in Washington to bring his native country into the Euro-Atlantic community of NATO.

---

[62]Florescu believed the number was closer to 100,000 and the ovation Clinton received was similar to that received by President Nixon in his 1969 visit to Bucharest, an event Radu also attended. Author interview, Radu Florescu, August 8, 1997.

[63]*Romanian Press Review*, 3.04, Week of July 14, 1997; see also *Washington Post*, July 12, 1997: "AO 1."

[64]Ibid.

The Impact of Gorbachev's "New Thinking" on Eastern Europe

Anthony R. DeLuca
Emerson College

Gorbachev's "New Thinking,"[1] his frequent travels abroad and his "new style" of public diplomacy generated such an overwhelmingly enthusiastic reception, that his reputation as an agent of change quickly spread throughout Europe and gave birth to the political phenomenon of "Gorbymania."[2] After decades of fear and skepticism, it suddenly seemed that Europe was experiencing "a sea change," that presaged an end to the Cold War and a resolution of the "nuclear nightmare." Moreover, the signs of political change and the prospects for arms control also suggested a new beginning in Europe and the creation of a new climate of opinion where people believed that "hopes and possibilities" could be turned "into facts and certainties."[3]

There was also widespread "speculation that Gorbachev's flexibility as a member of the new generation of Soviet leaders might challenge the conventional wisdom concerning Soviet domination in Eastern Europe."[4]

---

[1]Walter Laqueur, *The Long Road to Freedom* (hereafter cited as Laqueur, *The Long Road to Freedom*), New York: Macmillan, 1989, p. 221.

[2]Stephen White, *Gorbachev and After*, Cambridge: Cambridge University Press, 1991, pp. 210-211.

[3]Laqueur, *The Long Road to Freedom*, pp. 232-234.

But in what may have been the ultimate irony, Gorbachev's reformist inclinations were driven not by geopolitical considerations of Realpolitik or the Stalinist-Brezhnevite legacy of Soviet hegemony in Eastern Europe, but by crowds of East Europeans who greeted him enthusiastically with "shouts... posters, signs, and banners," welcoming him as a natural ally[5] and hailing him as "Mikhail the Liberator."[6]

Gorbachev, of course, was shrewd enough to capitalize on this infectious wave of "Gorby fever" and transcend the "endemic" popular distrust of the Soviet Union.[7] Among members of the "Shestidesiat-niki," the Soviet generation of the Sixties who supported reform, the Czechoslovak invasion of 1968 had remained the primary symbol for the nightmare of Soviet repression and a rallying point for political dissidence.[8] During his visit to Prague in April, 1987, Gorbachev managed to transform the resentment of the 1968 invasion into "grudging admiration" and "genuine public affection for (the) new Soviet leader."[9] The Czechs, who were excited about perestroika and glasnost were also enthusiastic about Gorbachev's new style of leadership, which reflected elements of "the model adumbrated by Dubcek... in 1968."[10] And. as Gorbachev made his way through the crowds "jubi-

---

[4]Condoleeza Rice, "The Soviet Alliance System," in Alexander Dallin and Condoleeza Rice, eds., *The Gorbachev Era*, Stanford: Stanford Alumni Association, 1986, p. 162.

[5]Eduard Shevardnadze, *The Future Belongs to Freedom*, translated by Catherine A. Fitzpatrick (hereafter cited as Shevardnadze, *The Future Belongs to Freedom*), London: Sinclair-Stevenson Limited, 1991, pp. 116-117.

[6]Doder and Branson, *Gorbachev: Heretic in the Kremlin*, p. 377. Gorbachev realized that his popularity in Eastern Europe might create political problems, as he glibly quipped in reference to Zdenek Mlynar's favorable portrayal of Gorbachev, that "A Prague Spring intellectual issuing a very positive verdict on me could cause some tongues to wag." Gorbachev and Mlynar had become friends while they were students at Moscow State University during the 1950s. Seweryn Bialer, *The Soviet Paradox: External Expansion, Internal Decline* (hereafter cited as Bialer, *The Soviet Paradox*), New York: Alfred A. Knopf, 1986, p. 113.

[7]As an agent of reform Gorbachev was, in effect, able to dispense with Brezhnev's fear that the Czech spring and Dubcek reforms might spread throughout Eastern Europe and eventually into the Soviet Union. Jerry Hough, *Russia and the West: Gorbachev and the Politics of Reform*, New York: Simon & Schuster, 1990, p. 139.

[8]Giulietto Chiesa, *Cronaca del Golpe Rosso*, Milano: Baldini & Castoldi, 1991, p. 47. In his *Memoirs*, Gorbachev would eventually admit that "We felt viscerally deep down, that (the invasion) was indignantly rejected by the people." Mikhail Gorbachev, *Memoirs* (hereafter cited as Gorbachev, *Memoirs*), New York: Doubleday, 1995, p. 100.

[9]Donald Morrison, et al., ed., *Gorbachev: An Intimate Biography* (hereafter cited as Morrison, et al., ed., *Gorbachev: An Intimate Biography*), New York: Time, 1988, p. 144.

lantly pressing the flesh" he was greeted with "shouts of 'Druzhba! Druzhba!,' the Russian word for friendship, from the normally Russophobic residents of Prague."[11] Gorbachev's reception did, however, prompt one of his own supporters to observe tartly: "Isn't it a shame that Gorbachev is understood better abroad than at home."[12]

Nonetheless, given the strained and sometimes hostile relations between the two states in the past, the new, relaxed political atmosphere, generated by Gorbachev's visit, made it clear that the "public relations" campaign he had set in motion was beginning to produce tangible results.[13] When Gorbachev's spokesman, Gennady Gerasimov, was asked during a press conference to comment on "the difference between the ousted reformer Dubcek and Gorbachev's New Thinking," he glibly responded: "Nineteen years."[14] In keeping with the Dubcek theme, Alexander Yakovlev, one of Gorbachev's closest advisers, stressed the need for the Soviet Union's new foreign policy to incorporate a "moral and humanitarian" system of values and avert a repetition of "the tragedy of August 1968."[15] The fact that the Soviets eventually issued "a nicely timed retrospective condemnation of the 1968 Warsaw Pact invasion" also served as heady encouragement for the Prague reformers.[16]

But what most appealed to Gorbachev's Czechoslovak audience was the emphasis he placed on consultation and an approach favoring "the velvet glove rather than... the iron fist."[17] This did not mean, however, that he was ready in 1987 to loosen the Soviet grip in Eastern Europe and sacrifice the Soviet Union's most vital security zone in the

---

[10]Hannes Adomeit, "Gorbachev and German Unification, Revision of Thinking, Realignment of Power," in Dallin and Lapidus, eds. *The Soviet System: From Crisis to Collapse* (hereafter cited as Dallin and Lapidus, eds. *The Soviet System*), Boulder: Westview Press, 1995, p. 468.

[11]Morrison, et al., ed., *Gorbachev: An Intimate Biography*, p. 183.

[12]Doder and Branson, *Gorbachev: Heretic in the Kremlin*, pp. 232-233.

[13]Morrison, et al., ed., *Gorbachev: An Intimate Biography*, p. 183.

[14]Doder and Branson, *Gorbachev: Heretic in the Kremlin*, p. 229.

[15]Alexander Yakovlev, *The Fate of Marxism in Russia*, translated by Catherine A. Fitzpatrick, Binghamton: Bail-Vallou Press, 1993, p. 226.

[16]Timothy Garton Ash, *The Magic Lantern: The Revolution of '89 Witnessed in Warsaw, Budapest, Berlin, and Prague* (hereafter cited as Ash, *The Magic Lantern*), New York: Random House, 1993, p. 141.

[17]Dev Murarka, *Gorbachov: The Limits of Power*, London: Hutchinson, 1988, pp. 396-398.

west.[18] He did choose, however, in his April speech to the people of Prague to appeal directly to his vision of a "common European home," and he chided critics who labeled his European idea a "pipe-dream" for failing to realize that it was "a serious analysis of the situation on the continent."[19] To reinforce his message he invoked the image of mountain climbers, knitted together by one rope who were dependent upon one another for their safe arrival at "the summit or crash(ing) down into the abyss together."[20] But when it came to the realities of European integration, he acknowledged the complexities facing countries divided by different social systems and membership in opposing military and political blocs. Though lacking in specifics, he nonetheless reiterated his call for "an accord on medium-range missiles," for reductions in conventional forces and armaments that were a menace to European security,[21] and for the creation of non-nuclear and chemical free zones in Europe.[22] He also spoke of expanding cooperation in scientific and technological progress as part of his "all-European" vision and of the need to deal with environmental pollution as "an all-European problem,"[23] — and a particularly acute one within Czechoslovakia, given the country's notoriously high pollution levels. He even quoted Lenin on the need "to polish (or) re-do many things in our system" in order to stimulate greater popular initiative and innovation.[24] In *Perestroika: New Thinking for Our Country and the World*, which appeared in the summer of 1987 following his visit to Prague, Gorbachev reasserted the principle of "absolute independence" among socialist states and the need to respect the "traditions (and) political institutions" of each nation.[25] As a good European, he also emphasized

---

[18]"The military value" of "Soviet force" stationed in Eastern Europe gave the Soviets a "first line of military strength against the West and... serve(d) as a constant reminder of Soviet power to recalcitrant populations or governments." Rice, "The Soviet Alliance System," in Dallin and Rice, eds., *The Gorbachev Era*, p. 157.

[19]In his speech Gorbachev appropriated de Gaulle's image of a Europe stretching "from the Atlantic to the Urals" to strengthen his argument. Mikhail S. Gorbachev, "Speech at Rally in Prague to mark Czechoslovak-Soviet Friendship," (10 April 1987) in Robert Maxwell, ed. *M.S. Gorbachov: Speeches and Writings,* Vol. 2, Oxford: Pergammon Press, 1997, p. 200.

[20]*Ibid.*, p. 196.

[21] *Ibid.*, p. 197.

[22]*Ibid.*, p. 198.

[23] *Ibid.*, p. 200.

[24]*Ibid.*, p. 192.

participation in "non-socialist" associations and "above all... the EEC."[26]

Given its political and strategic importance, Poland stood at the crossroads of Soviet influence in Eastern Europe. Control over the new post-World War II Polish corridor had enabled the Soviets to seal off "the historic route of invasion from the West" and create a buffer zone against an attack by NATO and/or a renascent Germany.[27] When faced in 1981 with worker unrest in the Polish trade union movement Solidarity under the leadership of Lech Walesa, the Soviets decided against a bloody crackdown in favor of restoring order from above in the person of General Wojciech Jaruzelski, a "stern military figure"[28] who promoted his ability to spare Poland the more painful consequences of direct Soviet military intervention. But when a Canadian representative of "Polish extraction" asked Gorbachev during his visit to Canada in 1983 why the Soviet Union was not doing more to help the Poles, Gorbachev "bristled" and testily reminded his audience that the "economic blockade of Poland" originated in the west and that the Soviets were doing everything possible to help their "Polish friends."[29]

The topic of Poland resurfaced in the spring of 1988, when Gorbachev agreed to meet with representatives of the American press in advance of the Moscow summit. The interview was conducted by a team of editors and reporters from *The Washington Post* and *Newsweek* magazine. The fact that the interview was published in the May 23, 1988, issue of *Pravda* was a tribute to glasnost and Gorbachev's view of the summits as a stabilizing influence in the "peaceful competition" between the two countries.[30] In his remarks Gorbachev insisted that a peaceful future needed to be structured not only upon "nuclear deter-

---

[25]Mikhail Gorbachev, *Perestroika: New Thinking for Our Country and the World* (hereafter cited as Gorbachev, *Perestroika*), New York: Harper & Row, 1987, pp. 165-166. See also Doder and Branson, *Gorbachev: Heretic in the Kremlin*, p. 231.

[26]Gorbachev, *Perestroika*, p. 167.

[27]Condoleeza Rice, "The Development of Soviet Military Power," in Alexander Dallin and Condoleeza Rice, eds., *The Gorbachev Era*, Stanford: Stanford Alumni Association, 1986, p. 131.

[28]Thomas G. Butson, *Gorbachev: A Biography* (hereafter cited as Butson, *Gorbachev: A Biography*), New York: Stein and Day, 1986, p. 55.

[29]Ibid., p. 11 and pp. 84-85.

[30]Mikhail Gorbachev, "Replies to Questions from the Washington Post and Newsweek, Pravda, May 23, 1988," in Mikhail Gorbachev, *At the Summit*, New York: Richard Steirman & Black, p. 201.

rence" but also upon conventional force reductions and "reciprocity."[31] When asked if he would tolerate the creation of "a pluralistic system" that denied the Polish Communist Party its "leading role" in government, he replied as a true reconstructed liberal that it would be best to "put that question to the Polish leadership," since the Soviets "recognize the right of each people... to choose its own way of developing its society."[32] While his response raised the possibility of a green light for further political reforms in Poland, it also spoke volumes about his attempts to distance the Soviet Union from its image as the oppressor in Eastern Europe. When Poland again emerged as "the main engine of change" in Eastern Europe in the spring of 1989, all the deft management both from within and without could not prevent the outcome of free and open elections that were "a triumphant result for Solidarity and a disaster for Jaruzelski's Communists." Only a few days later and as a harbinger of things to come, Gorbachev "replied enigmatically" to a question concerning the Berlin Wall during a West German press conference that "Nothing is eternal in this world," adding that the wall was built under certain conditions, "which would not last forever."[33]

As for Poland's future, many believed that the political presence of Pope John Paul II would serve as a beacon for Polish nationalism and protection against Soviet repression. In his ministerial role as the spiritual voice of Catholics in Poland, his visits to his native land generated a thunderous response. His stature within the international community also suggested that the road to Polish independence had suddenly been altered and that it would now have to pass through Rome, as long as he remained Pope.[34] But Gorbachev was not about to make a pilgrimage to seek the Pope's forgiveness in 1989. Rome was not Canossa.[35] Moreover, the mood of the Italian people was euphoric as the citizens of Rome greeted Gorbachev with an enthusiastic "welcome worthy of a Russian czar" and staged "a street spectacle," unlike anything "this indifferent city" had seen since John F. Kennedy's visit in the sixties.[36] But while the official version of the historic meeting stressed reconcilia-

---

[31]Ibid., pp. 204-205.

[32] *Ibid.*, p. 219.

[33]Robert Kaiser, *Why Gorbachev Happened: His Triumphs and His Failures* (hereafter cited as Kaiser, *Why Gorbachev Happened*), New York: Simon & Schuster, 1991, pp. 297-298.

[34]For a discussion of how Gorbachev and the Pope combined to influence the popular ferment in Poland see Ash, *The Magic Lantern*, pp. 133-134.

tion with the Polish Pope,[37] diplomats, reporters, and everyday citizens were struck by the symbolic significance of the conservative head of the Catholic Church receiving "the apostle of communism,"[38] who headed a state — once synonymous with "atheistic communism."[39] One can only imagine how Stalin, who purportedly asked "How many divisions does the Pope have?" might have reacted to the sight of the Soviet head of state conferring with the Polish Pope, who served as beacon of national independence in Eastern Europe and whose divisions were not military, but spiritual and political.

Still, despite the initial euphoria, perestroika also produced discord within the East European leadership.[40] The pro-reform camp, made up of Poland and Hungary greeted "the reforms... with official applause,"[41] while other East European regimes found the implications of "cultural freedom," "glasnost and democratization" most unsettling.[42] Nor had Gorbachev fully considered the demoralizing impact his "gamble on liberalization" would have on the communist parties of Eastern Europe, which were being asked to forfeit their "monolithic character"[43] and compromise their power. The split also produced a dramatic example of role reversal, since Moscow suddenly found itself in the unusual position of spearheading "the liberalization

[35]Sheehy paints a picture reminiscent of the Holy Roman Emperor Henry IV's appealing to Pope Gregory VII for reinstatement at Canossa in 1076. But Gorbachev's admission that "we no longer think that we are always right" and his decision to discard "State atheism and totalitarianism and pledge(d) his country to the principle of freedom of choice" hardly suggested the submission of secular authority to ecclesiastical authority. Gail Sheehy, *The Man Who Changed the World: The Lives of Mikhail S. Gorbachev.* (hereafter cited as Sheehy, *Gorbachev: The Man Who Changed the World*), New York: Harper Collins, 1990, p. 220.

[36]*Ibid.*, p. 219.

[37]Kaiser, *Why Gorbachev Happened*, pp. 306-307.

[38]Sheehy, *Gorbachev: The Man Who Changed the World*, p. 220.

[39]These remarks clearly sent a message that the world and East European politics had changed dramatically. Sheehy described the event as Gorbachev's public "confession on international television of the Soviet Union's "mistake in treating religion superficially." Ibid., pp. 34-35.

[40]Laqueur, *The Long Road to Freedom*, p. 247.

[41]Doder and Branson, *Gorbachev: Heretic in the Kremlin*, p. 230.

[42]A perfect example of this obdurate attitude was the official dismissal of Abuladze's film, *Repentance*, as "'historically incorrect,' 'nihilistic,' (and) 'inhumane,'" and for providing aid and comfort to the anti-communist enemy. Laqueur, *The Long Road to Freedom*, pp. 246-247.

[43]Henry Kissinger, *Diplomacy*, New York: Simon & Schuster, 1994, p. 794.

drive, while the East Europeans were dragging their feet."[44] Czechoslovak hardliner and party leader Gustav Husak "was conspicuously cool"[45] to liberalization, as was East Germany's Erich Honecker, who cracked down on political dissidents.[46] None of this localized opposition deterred Gorbachev from pursuing his reformist course. For example, in a 1987 speech delivered in Bucharest, he did not hide "his distaste for Ceauşescu's megalomaniac style and his corrupt leadership."[47] It is important to note that Gorbachev's relationship with Ceauşescu was different from that of any of the other East European leaders. Gorbachev found Ceauşescu to be an arrogant, vain, overconfident man — an autocrat who ruled through terror. One bizarre incident occurred in Hungary, when Gorbachev claims Ceauşescu faked a fall so that he could be seen "chatting" with Gorbachev before television cameras suddenly and magically appeared on the scene. Gorbachev referred to Ceauşescu's project to build the Bucharest-Danube Canal as part of a grandiose scheme to turn Bucharest into a major seaport. He also criticized Ceauşescu's forced resettlement of the Hungarian minority population; his poorly conceived investment policy; his gross mismanagement of Romania's foreign debt; and the shortages of food, electricity, industrial products, and consumer goods as examples of Ceauşescu's failed leadership and bankrupt policies. Moreover, Ceauşescu's personality and his imperious manner served as an apt example for Gorbachev of the "degradation" of an "authoritarian-bureaucratic system" built upon "monopoly, tyranny, (and) stagnation"[48] — the same system he had challenged within the Soviet Union, when he condemned the privileges and self-serving attitude of the apparatchiks.

Given the Soviet Union's military leverage within the Warsaw Pact and its role as the primary benefactor in the region, Gorbachev was not overly concerned about alienating the leaders of the more autocratic regimes in Eastern Europe. And despite their best efforts to stem the reformist tide, the East European conservatives quickly began to lose control over the political situation[49] and the wave of popular enthusiasm that ultimately swept them away. It was, however, left to

---

[44]Doder and Branson, *Gorbachev: Heretic in the Kremlin*, p. 232.

[45]*Ibid.*, p. 229.

[46]Laqueur, *The Long Road to Freedom*, p. 246.

[47]Doder and Branson, *Gorbachev: Heretic in the Kremlin*, p. 230.

[48] Gorbachev, *Memoirs*, pp. 473-478.

one of Gorbachev's advisers, the polyphonic Gennady Gerasimov, to record the significance of the moment in the summer of 1989, when he glibly referred to "My Way" as "Moscow's new Sinatra doctrine" to signal that "all satellite countries would be allowed to go their own way." The mischievous reference to Sinatra, which was obviously designed to demonstrate how in tune the new Soviet leadership was with cosmopolitan popular culture, played like music upon Western ears. But the tone was by no means frivolous, since it marked "the death knell to Brezhnev's concept of limited sovereignty" which had been invoked to legitimize the invasion of Czechoslovakia and protect the common interests of the socialist commonwealth.[50] By the fall of 1989, the pace of change had simply overwhelmed the entire Empire, as Solidarity triumphed in Poland. In Hungary church bells tolled, as citizens "peacefully overthrew" the government and shouted "Russians go home!" and "Gorby! Gorby!" In November, the Berlin wall fell, Bulgaria's hard-line regime "collapsed,"[51] and Czechoslovakia's "velvet revolution" led to the formation of a new democratic government led by Vaclav Havel,[52] who proved that, unlike the failed revolutions of 1848, it was possible for "a poet in politics" to emerge as the leader of his country. In Romania, however, a totally different form of poetic justice led to the summary execution of Ceauşescu and his wife Elena on Christmas day.

But the full impact of Gorbachev's imprint on the affairs of Eastern Europe was most significant during the debate over Germany's future and the status of Berlin. In *Perestroika* Gorbachev had concentrated upon the political aspects of "two German states with different social and political systems" and with each possessing "values of its own." He also postulated that it might take "a hundred years... for history to decide" the outcome and warned against engaging "in incendiary speculations."[53] To say the least, his timetable was off the mark and his own public declarations elevated "the public consciousness" of the German people and prompted them to move more quickly and in a

[49]Shevardnadze, *The Future Belongs to Freedom*, p. 116. The situation prompted Henry Kissinger to remark that "it quickly became obvious that the Communist Party — even where it still controlled the media — was not designed for democratic contests." Kissinger, *Diplomacy*, p. 793.

[50]Doder and Branson, *Gorbachev: Heretic in the Kremlin*, p. 387.

[51]Kaiser, *Why Gorbachev Happened*, p. 306.

[52]Sheehy, *Gorbachev: The Man Who Changed the World*, p. 218.

[53]Gorbachev, *Perestroika*, p. 200.

way that no one could have imagined. His involvement had helped transform what had been "a question for the distant future" into one of immediate significance.[54] Ironically, at the outset Honecker and other members of the DDR's leadership "seemed to be genuinely annoyed by events in Moscow" and confident that "Gorbachev would not last long."[55] However, when Gorbachev visited Berlin in October 1989 to celebrate the fortieth anniversary of the founding of the DDR, the mood "was tense," as his arrival had raised expectations and fanned the flames of public discontent. The shouting by members in the crowd of "Freedom! Freedom!," while others chanted "Gorby! Gorby! Help Us!," fed the speculation about a possible split between the two parties. For his part, Gorbachev tried to stay apart from the fray, although his cryptic remark in public that "Life itself punishes those who delay..." was widely taken as a warning to Honecker.[56] The fact that Gorbachev also let it be known to the East German leadership that "Soviet troops were not available for purposes of domestic repression" obviously sent a clear political signal and a chill up and down the old guard's spine.[57]

Marshall Goldman believes that Gorbachev actually nudged Honecker to "liberalize some of (his) hardline positions in order to ward off an explosive reaction and violence."[58] Gorbachev's efforts to avoid "inflammatory statements"[59] and underscore "his hands-off policy" were designed to make it clear that matters related to the DDR were "not decided in Moscow, but in Berlin." How ironic that nearly thirty years after Jack Kennedy had visited Berlin and proclaimed for all the world to see and hear: "Ich bin ein Berliner!" Gorbachev, with the same city serving as a backdrop, seemed to have reversed Kennedy's dictum and matter-of-factly declared: "Ich bin kein Berliner!" The effect, however, was in a way the same, since Gorbachev's remarks sug-

---

[54]Bialer, *The Soviet Paradox*, p. 341.

[55]Walter Laqueur, *The Dream that Failed: Reflections on the Soviet Union*, Oxford: Oxford University Press, 1994, p. 169.

[56]See Kaiser, *Why Gorbachev Happened*, p. 302. See also Adomeit, "Gorbachev and German Unification: Revision of Thinking, Realignment of Power," in Dallin and Lapidus, eds., *The Soviet System*, pp. 471-472.

[57]Ash, *The Magic Lantern*, p. 141.

[58]Marshall Goldman, *What Went Wrong with Perestroika* (hereafter cited as Goldman, *What Went Wrong with Perestroika*), New York: W. W. Norton & Company, 1991, p. 198.

[59]Kaiser, *Why Gorbachev Happened*, p. 302.

gested he was giving the green light to democratic forces in Germany and leaving Honecker with "the kiss of the Godfather... Eleven days later Honecker was gone."[60] The euphoric, exuberant, and ritualistic celebration of tearing down the Berlin wall on November 9, 1989 was a pivotal symbolic event. And the subsequent sale of parts of the wall as "solid mementos of a (modern day) miracle" resembled to some degree the ritualistic sale of "holy relics of other eras."[61] But the collapse of the wall did not solve the larger German problem, which continued to boil "uncomfortably on a diplomatic backburner." Given the "high price" the Soviets had paid to defeat Hitler and the fear of a reunified Germany's participation in NATO, the Soviets understandably sought substantive concessions in return for ceding their dominant strategic position in Central and Eastern Europe.[62] In a matter of a few months, even weeks, the issue of German unification became an elaborate diplomatic dance, in which a "plethora of proposals" revealed Moscow's indecision on how best to adjust to the new German reality.[63]

As part of his effort to seize what remained of a diplomatic initiative in the summer of 1990, Gorbachev invited German Chancellor, Helmut Kohl, to join him in the Soviet south, where they would be able to engage in some old-fashioned horsetrading. For Gorbachev, the decision to return to his native Stavropol and seize "his electric moment" was extremely important.[64] Here at the foot of the majestic Caucasus range and in the shadow of his early successes, he hoped to obtain German financial and technical aid in return for German unification and membership in NATO. Kohl eagerly accepted Gorbachev's terms and "in a single stroke and for a relatively small sum (of) 21 billion deutsche marks, Gorbachev relinquished Josef Stalin's World War II conquest."[65] The transaction also lent new meaning to Thatcher's early dictum about Gorbachev: "We can do business together."[66] While

---

[60] Sheehy, *Gorbachev: The Man Who Changed the World*, p. 217.

[61] Goldman, *What Went Wrong with Perestroika*, p. 17.

[62] Kaiser, *Why Gorbachev Happened*, p. 356.

[63] Adomeit, "Gorbachev and German Unification: Revision of Thinking, Realignment of Power," in Dallin and Lapidus, eds. *The Soviet System*, p. 477.

[64] Sheehy, *Gorbachev: The Man Who Changed the World*, pp. 227-229.

[65] For Dusko Doder and Louise Branson's discussion of the Kohl-Gorbachev meeting see Doder and Branson, *Gorbachev: Heretic in the Kremlin*, pp. 434-435.

[66] Morrison et al., ed., *Gorbachev: An Intimate Biography*, p. 129.

it is true that Gorbachev was not in an ideal situation to leverage his position with Kohl, the haste with which he concluded the agreement suggested that his own short-term political survival was more important than larger geopolitical concerns. Later, in a "Dear Friends" letter addressed to the German people and published in *Stern* magazine, he managed to add insult to injury by asking for meat, vegetables, and noodles to help cope with shortages for the 1990-91 winter. Many of the brave and proud Soviet citizens, who recalled the heroic siege of Leningrad in the face of Nazi encirclement during World War II, were disgusted at the thought of having to turn to "Russia's former arch enemy" for food and assistance and angry with Gorbachev for having almost single-handedly reversed the verdict of the War.[67]

Upon his return to Moscow following the August coup, a weary Gorbachev took time to reflect upon recent events and defend his record against those who criticized him for handing over the gains of the Great Patriotic War. He reminded them that before perestroika the Soviet Union was "a super-power with an inefficient economy" and that his foreign policy initiatives were necessary to end the confrontation with the West and preserve the Soviet Union's status as great power.[68] He also sought to assert pride of authorship for the changes in Eastern Europe and portray them as a desirable outcome of perestroika and glasnost. While most observers agreed that Gorbachev did not engineer the collapse of Communist governments in Eastern Europe, there is little doubt that Gorbachev, as the Prime Mover who "set the whole process in motion," had inspired East European reformers and allowed "the revolution in Eastern Europe"[69] to run its course. But it is also clear that he "miscalculated" the desire among the peoples of Eastern Europe to seize the opportunity and "break with the communist system completely." (And the same could be said of the Soviet Union.)[70] When the old regimes began to crumble, Gorbachev could do little more, short of direct military intervention, than give his all-important permission to let the changes in Eastern Europe proceed.

Others, however, were not as magnanimous, since they did not share Gorbachev's noble intentions concerning popular sovereignty and

---

[67] Kaiser, *Why Gorbachev Happened*, p. 378.

[68] Mikhail Gorbachev, "Appendix C," in Mikhail Gorbachev, *The August Coup: The Truth and the Lessons*, New York: Harper Collins, 1991, pp. 117-119.

[69] Sheehy, *Gorbachev: The Man Who Changed the World*, p. 218.

[70] Goldman, *What Went Wrong with Perestroika*, p. 198.

national self-determination. They rued Gorbachev's having let slip the East European jewel from the crown of the Soviet Empire. The decision obviously cost Gorbachev politically, as conservatives derisively referred to him and his Foreign Minister, Eduard Shevardnadze, as the "Knights of Malta" who ceded the Soviet Union's foreign policy interests to the West.[71] Moreover, not everyone greeted with the same philosophical detachment and optimism as Gorbachev the sight of East Europeans dancing in the streets, celebrating the overthrow of the communist political establishment from Warsaw to Sofia. It also became painfully obvious that there had been little, if any, conceptual assessment of the impact the reforms might have on the Soviet Union's security. Particularly hard hit were members of the military, who felt "unappreciated" and humiliated, and who were reluctant to wear "their military uniforms in public for fear of being insulted."[72] But while critics continued to blame Gorbachev for the "collapse of the socialist system" and the needless sacrifice of the strategic "buffer zone" in Eastern Europe, figures such as Georgi Arbatov attributed these recidivist attitudes to the unresolved legacy of Soviet "imperial thinking."[73]

Others such as Shevardnadze defiantly dismissed the charges of having "demolished the political structure in Europe" and for having facilitated the unification of Germany.[74] He maintained that a military intervention comparable to the ones in which Soviet tanks had "brought order to Hungary" in 1956 and "crushed the Prague spring" in 1968[75] would have led to a bloody encounter and perhaps put "the entire world... at risk."[76] He was, however, willing to admit that the "collapse of socialism in Eastern Europe" had a traumatic impact on the Soviet people and undermined their belief in the Soviet Union's standing as a world power.[77] But he compared the popular mood to "a kangaroo court," that wanted to try "perestroika" as "the root and cause of all evil and misfortune."[78] Timothy Garton Ash, however, dis-

---

[71] Shevardnadze, *The Future Belongs to Freedom*, p. 217.

[72] Goldman, *What Went Wrong with Perestroika*, p.199.

[73] Georgi Arbatov, *An Insider's Life in Soviet Politics: The System*, New York: Times Books, 1992, pp. 58-59. For further discussion of the loss of "the gains" during World War II see also Goldman, *What Went Wrong with Perestroika*, p. 199.

[74] Shevardnadze, *The Future Belongs to Freedom*, p. 119.

[75] *Ibid.*, p. 125.

[76] *Ibid.*, p. 118.

[77] *Ibid.*, p. 124.

putes Shevardnadze's claim that perestroika was not responsible for the changes in Eastern Europe, since had it not been for Gorbachev's policies, the events of 1989 and 1991 would not have occurred.[79] Nor can one avoid the conclusion that Gorbachev's charismatic personality and energetic appeal for reform and renewal aroused a new wave of hope and popular enthusiasm that contributed to the breakup of the Soviet Empire in Eastern Europe.

[78]*Ibid.*, pp. 119-120.

[79]Ash, *The Magic Lantern*, pp. 160-161. See also Kaiser for a discussion of how Gorbachev cause(d) the revolution in Eastern Europe. Kaiser, *Why Gorbachev Happened*, p. 299.

Postcommunist Romanian Foreign Policy at the U.N.

Robert Weiner
University of Massachusetts at Boston

Introduction

Postcommunist Romanian foreign policy at the United Nations is characterized by both elements of continuity[1] and discontinuity. For example, Romania has continued on as a member of the Group of 77, which consists mostly of Third World countries. But a significant discontinuity emerges because Romania no longer votes as frequently with the Third World as it did during the Ceauşescu era. However, Romania has continued its identification with Latin America,[2] maintaining its membership in the Latin American subgroup of the Group of 77.

Although the Revolution of 1989 resulted in a realignment of its foreign policy, some of the principal elements of Romanian foreign policy

---

[1]For a discussion of communist foreign policy at the United Nations, see Robert Weiner, *Romanian Foreign Policy and the United Nations* (New York: Praeger, 1984).

[2]For example, at the 50th session of the General Assembly of the U.N., Romania was a co-sponsor of a draft Resolution that granted observer status to the Central American Integration System in the General Assembly. For the Romanian statement of support for Central American efforts at regional integration which Bucharest linked to its own efforts at the promotion of regional integration in Eastern Europe, see U.N. Document, A/50/PV.30 (12 October, 1995), p. 16.

141

still consisted of traditional factors rooted in the interwar model of foreign policy established by the brilliant Romanian diplomat Nicolae Titulescu. Some of these elements encompass such factors as support for the principles of collective security, the resolution of conflicts through peaceful means, support for the basic principles of international law and organization, the pursuit of friendly relations with one's neighbors, and the importance of geopolitics. Romania's geostrategic position has assumed greater significance with the emergence of new postcommunist states in a region marked by conflict and characterized by the potential for future conflict. For example, as Foreign Minister Meleşcanu pointed out in 1993, "Romania finds itself in a geopolitical zone where things are in movement."[3]

Other traditional elements of Romanian foreign policy consist of support for regional and subregional organizations,[4] and most important of all, the primacy of national interest. But it is also important to point out that the United Nations did not rank very high[5] as one of the most important priorities in the strategy of Romanian foreign policy after the Revolution. A more important foreign policy goal consists of integration in the Euro-Atlantic institutional structure of postcommunist Europe. Special emphasis has been placed on trying to resolve Romania's security dilemma by obtaining full membership in NATO and the European Union (in 1997 Romania was informed that it would be considered for admission to NATO in the second wave of expansion of members and it was not invited to become a full member of the European Union, but continued on as an associate member), the normalization of relations with the United States, the establishment and consolidation of friendly relations with neighboring states,[6] the ending of Romania's isolation from the international community, and securing economic aid from such international financial institutions as the International Monetary Fund (IMF) and the World Bank. However, it is also necessary to point out that postcommunist Romanian

[3]*Libertatea*, 29/30 June 1993, p. 1.

[4]Ibid.

[5]But postcommunist Romania has also been very supportive of the United Nations and has contributed to the United Nations Development Program, UNICEF, the U.N. Fund for Population Activities, the U.N. Habitat, the U.N. Fund for Industrial Development, the U.N. Drug Control Program, the U.N. Fund for Science and Technology for Development, and the United Nations Environmental Program.

[6]Romania signed basic treaties of friendship and cooperation in 1997 with Hungary and Ukraine.

participation in the United Nations was designed to serve the function of helping Romania to achieve some of its primary foreign policy goals such as integration in the Euro-Atlantic security architecture.

Postcommunist Romanian foreign policy at the U.N. was also supposed to be based upon more openness toward the world,[7] as opposed to the closed foreign policy of the Ceaușescu era. Furthermore, postcommunist Romanian foreign policy was supposed to be de-ideologized. It was hoped that Bucharest's new foreign policy would not represent the interests of any particular group, but rather would be based on a national consensus that was focused on the pursuit of the national interest of the country.

Regionalism

Another major element of postcommunist Romanian foreign policy is recognition of the need for cooperation between the United Nations and such regional organizations as NATO,[8] the OAS[9] (the Organization of American States), the OSCE (the Organization for Security and Cooperation in Europe), and the European Union. Romania viewed such cooperation as "beneficial to the system of collective security based on the U.N. Charter."[10] However, Romania also expressed its dissatisfaction with the inability of European regional organizations such as the OSCE to successfully resolve conflicts in Moldova, Chechnya, and Nagorno-Karabakh.[11]

Moreover, since 1993, Romania has cooperated closely with the EU at the U.N., as an associate member of the organization. Therefore it is to be expected that Romania would identify with some of the elements of the common foreign policy of the EU, since the representatives of the EU at the U.N. speak on behalf of Romania and other associated states. For example, at the 51st session of the General Assembly in 1996, Romania voted for an EU supported Resolution that called for the end of the US economic embargo against Cuba.[12] At the

---

[7]*Libertatea*, 29/30 January, 1993, p. 1.

[8]See U.N. Document, A/C.1/47/PV.10 (4 November, 1992), p. 42. Romania participated in NATO peacekeeping operations in Bosnia.

[9]For example, Romania supported the efforts of the OAS to work with the U.N. Security Council to restore democracy in Haiti. See U.N. Document, S/PV.3011 (3 October, 1991), p. 43.

[10]U.N. Document, A/50/PV.94 (18 December, 1995), p. 16.

[11]Ibid.

previous session of the General Assembly, Romania had abstained on the vote that took place on a somewhat similar Resolution. On the other hand, at the 10th Emergency Special Session of the U.N. in July 1997, Romania abstained while all of the members of the European Union voted for a Resolution that condemned Israel for building new settlements in Jerusalem.[13] So it is fair to conclude that Romania does not always follow the EU's common foreign policy at the U.N., but rather follows its own national interest. Maintaining good relations with Israel took precedence over EU common foreign policy.

Romania has also expressed its concern at the U.N. about allowing regional organizations like the CIS (the Commonwealth of Independent States) to be used by Russia to maintain its hegemonic position in the former Soviet Union.[14] Romania was not enthusiastic about U.N. recognition of the CIS as a "regional arrangement" falling under the scope of Article 52 of the Charter, which allows regional organizations to engage in peacekeeping as long as such activities conform to the basic principles of the U.N. Charter. Bucharest would prefer that Russia follow the guidelines that are set forth in Chapter VIII of the U.N. Charter which deal with "Regional Arrangements." From the perspective of peace and security, this is an important issue, because as the U.N. discovered that it had overextended itself in taking on too many peacekeeping and peace enforcement operations in the post-Cold War period, it found it more expedient to regionalize peacekeeping by entering into arrangements with organizations like the CIS. Romania has adopted the position that a regional organization should only take enforcement action according to the terms of Article 53 (1) of the Charter, which stressed the need to secure the approval of the Security Council for such activities. The Romanians have also argued that Russian peacekeeping activities should be supervised by the Security Council according to the terms of Article 54 of the U.N. Charter.[15] Of particular concern to Romania in connection with this is the situation in Transdniester in Moldova. Transdniester had been occupied by the Russian 14th Army, an action that could be interpreted as an example of

---

[12] See U.N. *Press Release, GA/9164* (12 November, 1996).

[13] http://www.un.org/.

[14] See U.N. Document, A/C.4/49/SR.25 (5 February, 1994), p. 8.

[15] Article 54 reads: "The Security Council shall at all times be kept fully informed of activities undertaken or in contemplation under regional arrangements or by regional agencies for the maintenance of international peace and security."

Russian "peacekeeping." Consequently, Romania has consistently called for the withdrawal of Russian troops from Transdniester.[16]

Peacekeeping

Postcommunist Romania has been rather supportive of U.N. peacekeeping and peace enforcement activities and has also complied with U.N. sanctions against Iraq and the former Yugoslavia, at a substantial cost to its own economy. As far as peace enforcement is concerned, Romania faced its first real test when the U.N. Security Council had to deal with the Iraqi invasion of Kuwait in August of 1990. Romania supported the actions taken by the Security Council against Iraq because it believed that peaceful means should be used to settle disputes between nations.[17] Romania also supported efforts on the part of the Security Council to create a system of controls that would prevent Iraq from developing a nuclear weapons capability and Bucharest urged Iraq to comply with the provisions of the relevant Security Council Resolutions.[18] Romania also criticized Iraq's harsh treatment of foreign nationals, as well as foreign diplomats.[19] It was just accidental that Romania was presiding over the Security Council. Romania was elected to serve a two-year term on the Security Council beginning October 18, 1989[20] when it considered the conflict in the Persian Gulf. But skillful Romanian diplomacy at the time provided it with an opportunity to enhance its international reputation.

Romania was also a member of the Security Council when it considered the conflict in Yugoslavia. Romania consistently urged that peaceful means[21] be used to settle the conflict. Moreover, after the conclusion of the Dayton Peace Accords, Romania supported the return of

---

[16]U.N. Document, A/50/PV.9 (27 September, 1995), p. 39. Russia had agreed in 1994 to withdraw its troops from the Transdniester.

[17]U.N. Document, S/PV.2932 (2 August, 1990), pp. 24-25. Romania stated that the "occupation of Kuwait by Iraq has no legal validity." See U.N. Document, S/PV.2934 (9 August, 1990), p. 3.

[18]U.N. Document, S/PV.2995 (26 June, 1991), pp. 19-20.

[19]U.N. Document, S/PV.2940 (16 September, 1990), p. 21.

[20]Romania was elected to serve a two-year term on the Security Council beginning October 18, 1989.

[21]Romania had also expressed its willingness to participate in OSCE peace missions dispatched to the former Yugoslavia, and even offered to lead such a mission. See U.N. Document, A/PV.94 (18 December, 1995), p. 17.

Federal Yugoslavia (Serbia and Montenegro) to the U.N., as well as its reintegration into European regional and subregional organizations.[22] The Romanians consistently took the position that the Yugoslavians themselves had to resolve the conflict rather than being forced to reach an agreement by external actors.[23] On the other hand, Romania also expressed its support in the Security Council for the Vance-Owen peace plan, which, if implemented, would have divided Bosnia-Herzegovina into a number of ethnically based cantons.[24]

Romania has also participated in a number of U.N. peacekeeping operations, most recently in Albania in 1997. Romania took part in U.N. peace-enforcement and peacekeeping operations in Iraq and Kuwait, Somalia, Rwanda, and Angola.[25] By 1997, Romania had become the 12th largest[26] contributor to U.N. peacekeeping operations. As a significant troop contributing country, Romania has called for more negotiations between the Security Council and the countries which contribute troops to U.N. operations, in order to keep them informed of decisions taken by the Security Council which deal with the peacekeeping mission concerned.[27]

Moreover, since its troops have also suffered casualties in such places as Angola, Romania has supported U.N. efforts to create an international legal framework that will help to ensure the safety of the "blue helmets." For example, in September 1995, Romania signed an International Convention on the Safety of U.N. and Associated Personnel.[28] Romania has also developed programs that are designed to train its military and police to respond quickly to requests from the United Nations for peacekeepers. Romania also supports the idea that the United Nations should have a rapid deployment capability in order to prevent reliance on the *ad hoc* types of peacekeeping operations which have not succeeded in the post-Cold War international system. Therefore, in connection with this, Romania also stressed that the U.N. should further develop its preventive diplomacy and preventive

---

[22]Ibid.

[23]U.N. Document, S/PV.3009 (25 September, 1991), p. 42.

[24]U.N. Document, S/PV.3201 (19 April, 1993), p. 63.

[25]As of March 1997, there were 792 Romanian troops participating in the U.N. peacekeeping operations in Angola, which is known as the United Nations Angola Verification Mission III.

[26]http://www.un.org/.

[27]U.N. Document, A/C.4/50/SR.20 (8 January, 1996), p. 8.

[28]Ibid.

deployment capabilities. Romania has also expressed its concern about the growing complexity of U.N. peacekeeping operations that have stemmed from the U.N.'s increasing involvement in civil conflicts.[29] Therefore, Romania urged that more attention should be given to the decisions that are made by the U.N. to set up new peacekeeping operations in the first place or to renew the mandates of those that are already operating.[30]

The Security Council

Most students of international relations agree that the reputation of a nation is an important characteristic of the foreign policy behavior of a country. Postcommunist Romania earned the reputation at the U.N. of being a good international citizen. For example, an analysis of Romania's voting behavior in the Security Council over a two-year period (1990-91) indicates that it was quite supportive of efforts by the U.N. to maintain international peace and security. Romania voted for every single Security Council Resolution (Resolutions 647-725) which was adopted by that body (admittedly, this took place during a period of rather extraordinary consensus in the Security Council). This provided Romania with a good opportunity to further establish its reputation as a responsible diplomatic actor.[31]

As a member of the Security Council, Romania had to deal with such serious threats to the maintenance of international peace and security as the situation between Iraq and Kuwait and of course, the situation in the former Yugoslavia. But Romania also had to cope with such important peace and security issues as the situation in the Middle East, the situation in Afghanistan, the situation in Cyprus, and efforts at peace-making in Central America. Furthermore, while serving on the Security Council, Romania had the opportunity to vote for the election of Boutros Boutros Ghali as Secretary-General of the United Nations.[32] Romania was also represented in the Security Council at a critical period in the history of the U.N., a period which was marked by an

---

[29] U.N. Document, A/50/PV.9 (27 September, 1995), p. 40.

[30] Ibid.

[31] For a breakdown of the votes, see *Index to the Proceedings of the Security Council, Forty-Fifth Year–1990* (New York: U.N., 1991); *Index to the Proceedings of the Security Council, Forty-Sixth Year–1991* (New York: U.N., 1992); *Resolutions and Decisions of the Security Council. Official Records: Forty-Fifth Year* (New York: U.N., 1991).

[32] See Security Council Resolution 720 (1991).

expansion of membership. Consequently, Romania had the chance to vote for the admission to the U.N. of such states as Namibia,[33] Liechtenstein,[34] the Democratic People's Republic of Korea and the Republic of Korea, the Federated States of Micronesia, the Marshall Islands, Estonia, Latvia, and Lithuania.

But Romania's tenure on the Security Council was not without some pressure to deal with other controversial issues. For instance, in connection with some issues dealing with Palestine, Romania voted in favor while the United States voted against allowing the representatives of Palestine to participate in the debates of the Security Council.[35] Romania had to maintain a fine balance between its friendship for the United States and Israel, and its support for the Palestinians. For example, in May of 1990, Romania voted in the affirmative while the U.S. vetoed a draft Resolution that called for the U.N. to provide more protection for the Palestinians living in the Occupied Territories.[36]

As mentioned earlier, Romania had to use all of its diplomatic skill to deal with the delicate issue of the conflicts in the former Yugoslavia. Thus, in 1991, Romania supported the decision of the Security Council to impose an arms embargo against all of the parties to the conflict in the former Yugoslavia, although Romania also stressed that as a neighbor of Yugoslavia, the solution to the conflict had to be reached internally by the parties themselves.[37] But Romania recognized that all states had to comply with the embargo according to the terms of Article 25 of the U.N. Charter.[38]

Democratization

Participation in the U.N. has also provided Romania with the opportunity to deal with its "image problems" and to persuade the world community that the postcommunist transition was progressing

---

[33]For Romanian comments emphasizing its past support for the Namibian struggle for independence, see U.N. Document, S/PV.2918 (17 April, 1990), p. 37.

[34]Romania supported the admission of Liechtenstein because it contributed to the universality of the world organization. See U.N. Document, S/PV.2936 (14 August, 1990), p. 11.

[35]U.N. Document, S/PV.2910 (15 March, 1990), p. 7.

[36]U.N. Document, S/PV.2926 (31 May, 1990), p. 36.

[37]U.N. Document, S/PV.3009 (25 September, 1991), p. 42.

[38]Article 25 stipulates that all of the members of the U.N. must carry out the decisions of the Security Council.

along the path toward democracy. Postcommunist Romania sought to use the U.N. as a forum to legitimize its standing in the world community as an emerging democracy.[39] For example, in 1997, Bucharest hosted the U.N. sponsored Third International Conference of the New or Restored Democracies on Democracy and Development, from June 2-4. The conference was designed not only to discuss the different experiences which countries were undergoing in the consolidation of democracy, but also to analyze the regional and subregional characteristics of democracy in the Balkans.[40] It is clear that regardless of the internal problems that Romania was experiencing in consolidating democracy[41] at the time, it at least supported efforts at the U.N. to create a framework for the globalization of democracy. For example, Romania endorsed the efforts of the U.N. Security Council to restore democracy in Haiti.[42] In 1991, Romania also supported a western version of a Resolution rather than a rival Resolution advocated by Third World governments, to provide electoral assistance for nations making the democratic transition. The Third World viewed such electoral assistance as an infringement on the national sovereignty of the members of the U.N.[43]

Romanian delegates to the U.N. observed that Romania had established a rule of law state[44] based on respect for human rights and free and fair elections.

At the U.N., Romania also advocated the liberalization of trade so that it could have more access to markets and expressed the desire for more technical assistance from the U.N., especially to help it cope with the losses that it had suffered in complying with the application of U.N. sanctions.[45] Furthermore, Romania also focused on the need for its transitional economy to be integrated into the world economy.[46]

---

[39]For more discussion of the problems which Romania faces in consolidating democracy, see Robert Weiner, "Democratization in Romania," in *Romania in Transition*, ed. Lavinia Stan (Aldershot: Dartmouth Publishing Company, 1997), pp. 3-23.

[40]See U.N. Document, A/50/PV.55 (10 November, 1995), p. 2.

[41]See Robert Weiner, *Change in Eastern Europe* (Westport: Praeger, 1994), pp. 119-131.

[42]U.N. Document, S/PV.3011 (3 October, 1991), p. 43.

[43]For example, at the 50th session of the U.N., the General Assembly adopted the Third World Resolution by a vote of 91-57-21. The western version, Resolution 50/185, was adopted by a vote of 156-0-15.

[44]U.N. Document, A/50/PV.9 (27 September, 1995), p. 37.

[45]U.N. Document, A/C.2/46/SR.6 (14 October, 1991), p. 4.

The Romanians hoped that this would allow them to improve the flow of their exports and also generate increased foreign investment. Romania especially stressed the need for its integration into the European Union.[47]

Arms Control and Disarmament

Postcommunist Romania also supported efforts at the U.N. to strengthen post-Cold War Arms Control and Disarmament measures. For instance, Romania backed the indefinite extension of the Non-Proliferation Treaty that was designed to prevent the spread of nuclear weapons. Bucharest endorsed the idea that non-nuclear weapon states could be protected by the negative and positive security assurances given by all five nuclear weapon states in the form of a Security Council Resolution. The relevant Security Council Resolution increased the number of permanent members of the Security Council providing security assurances[48] from three to five. Romania believed that such assurances were particularly important given the emergence of a power vacuum in Eastern Europe.[49] Romania also suggested that the safeguards system of the International Atomic Energy Agency should be strengthened by improving its international inspection machinery.[50]

Romania is also a member of the Zangger Committee, an informal group that is committed to preventing the export of products which can be used to produce nuclear weapons by countries which are not parties to the Non-Proliferation Treaty and which also have not placed themselves under the International Atomic Energy Agency (IAEA) safeguards system.[51] Romania is also following the norms established by the Missile Technology Control Regime[52] which are designated to regulate the export of missiles. Romania emphasized that it was necessary for the world community to move in the direction of the complete elimination of all nuclear weapons as well as to complete the negotiations for a Comprehensive Test Ban Treaty (CTB), which

---

[46]U.N. Document, A/C.2/47/SR.32 (18 November, 1992), p. 5.

[47]U.N. Document, A/C.2/46/SR.39 (29 November, 1991), p. 13.

[48]U.N. Document, S/PV.3514 (11 April, 1995), p. 8.

[49]Ibid.

[50]U.N. Document, A/50/PV.47 (1 November, 1995), p. 6.

[51]U.N. Document, NPT/CONF.1995/21 (20 April, 1995) in http://www.un.org/.

[52]U.N. Document, A/C.1/46/PV.8 (22 October, 1991), p. 64.

would eliminate underground testing.[53] However, it should be pointed out that Romania did not vote for a U.N. Resolution accepting an Advisory Opinion of the International Court of Justice that states should immediately fulfill their obligations to pursue good faith negotiations on nuclear disarmament. But Romania was in good company, because it abstained in the vote along with about 19 other countries, including the United States and the United Kingdom.[54]

Generally, though, Romania has also supported U.N. efforts to control and eliminate other weapons of mass destruction, such as chemical, biological, and bacteriological weapons. Romania signed a major chemical weapons control convention in 1993 and is also working with the Australia Group, which is designed to control the use of chemical and biological weapons. Romania also called for the strengthening[55] of the verification regime that dealt with the Convention on Bacteriological and Biological Weapons.

Bucharest also supported efforts on the part of the United Nations to control and regulate trade in conventional weapons. Romania backed the idea of transparency or openness in the arms trade and furnished information to the United Nations Register on Conventional Arms.[56] Romania associated itself with the position of the European Union on this issue.[57]

Sanctions

Most important of all, postcommunist Romania has supported the application of U.N. sanctions according to the conditions set forth in Chapter VII of the U.N. Charter. However, Bucharest found that support for the enforcement of U.N. sanctions against Iraq, the former Yugoslavia, and Libya has been very costly in economic terms. The U.N. Charter did not adequately envisage the adverse effects which participating in economic sanctions would have upon the economy of a state like Romania. The relevant article in the U.N. Charter in this case

---

[53]U.N. Document, NPT/CONF.1995/SR.5 (26 April, 1995) in http://www.un.org/.

[54]*UN Press Release, GA 9196* (10 December, 1996) in http://www.un.org/.

[55]U.N. Document, A/C.1/46/PV.8 (22 October, 1991), p. 67.

[56]This revealed that Romania had supplied Moldova with some armored cars in 1995. See http://www.un.org/.

[57]http://www.un.org/.

is Article 50. As the Romanians pointed out, there were no provisions in Article 50 to provide "automatic assistance"[58] to states that needed it. The Romanians estimated that they had lost billions of dollars by participating in the sanctions regimes, without receiving adequate financial compensation from the international community. In the case of sanctions enforcement against the former Yugoslavia, since Romania was a Danubian riparian state that bordered on Serbia, it could be viewed as a "frontline" state[59] and therefore should be entitled to special compensation. Romania had disrupted its trading relations with Serbia, a country with which it had traditionally maintained friendly and neighborly relations. Moreover, before U.N. economic sanctions against the former Yugoslavia were partially lifted, Romania had had to cope with a great deal of pressure from the United Nations[60] to enforce Security Council Resolutions prohibiting the transshipment of products on Yugoslavian barges. Some friction ensued when some Romanian barges were seized on the Danube by Yugoslavians. The Security Council clearly condemned the seizure of the Romanian barges.[61]

The Security Council did allow some exceptions to the sanctions regime regarding the former Yugoslavia, which were requested by Romania. For example, the U.N. sanctions committee dealing with Serbia allowed repair work to take place on the locks of the Iron Gates system, fuel to be shipped to the former Yugoslavia in order to allow icebreakers to operate along the Danube, and electric energy to be shipped across Serbia to Albania. The Romanians also requested that exceptions to the sanctions regime imposed against Serbia be granted to allow for the shipment of humanitarian aid. However, in the case of the former Yugoslavia, Romania believed that the requests for exceptions to the sanctions were not always handled in a transparent and expeditious manner by the sanctions committee, which had been established under Security Council Resolution 724. In 1993, Romania

---

[58]U.N. Document, A/C.6/49/SR.11 (13 October, 1994), p. 2.

[59]A Romanian governmental task force was set up to oversee the implementation of the embargo. See U.N. Document, S/25228 (3 February, 1993), p. 2.

[60]See U.N. Document, S/25227 (3 February, 1993), p. 1. For a Romanian explanation of its efforts along with Bulgaria to enforce U.N. sanctions against vessels which were traversing the Danube, whereby Romania "appealed for an increased international presence for sanctions monitoring... see Ibid. Also see Security Council Resolution 992 (1995), which requested the Government of Romania to deny passage through the locks of the Iron Gates system to any vessel which was suspected of breaking the U.N. sanctions.

[61]See RFE/RL Research Institute (1 March, 1993), p. 3.

sought and received international assistance to enforce the sanctions against the former Yugoslavia along the Danube, in the form of a sanctions assistance mission drawn from the Western European Union and the Conference on Security and Cooperation for Europe.

But Romania and a number of other states[62] called for the creation of a Compensation or Trust Fund which would be paid to those third states whose economies had suffered because they participated in the application of the sanctions.[63] Romania stressed that such a fund would make it more possible for it to support Security Council efforts to deal with conflicts.[64] Romania enjoyed some success in persuading the U.N. to adopt a Resolution calling for the establishment of such a fund. The envisaged Compensation or Trust Fund could be drawn from a percentage of the dues which were assessed from each country by the United Nations, as well as voluntary contributions from international financial institutions outside the United States, member states, Non-Governmental Organizations, and even individuals.[65] Laying the framework for the creation of such a Compensation Fund, Romania co-sponsored a Resolution that pointed out that Article 49 of the U.N. Charter called upon U.N. members to provide mutual assistance to countries which were implementing Security Council decisions.[66] Romania also argued that before the Security Council decided to apply sanctions against a state, the effects of such sanctions on other states should first be discussed, or at least Security Council discussions vis-à-vis the application of sanctions should be held in a more transparent fashion. Critics of the Romanian position[67] argued, however, that there might not be enough time to engage in a detailed discussion as to how the implementation of sanctions would affect states like Romania. Nonetheless, Romania managed to engage in the skillful diplomatic balancing act of complying with its obligations under the Charter of

---

[62]For example, see the letter to the Secretary-General of the U.N., sent by Romania, Bulgaria, Greece, the Republic of Moldova, and Ukraine. U.N. Document, A/50/189,S/1995/412 (24 May, 1995).

[63]See the statement by the Romanian Foreign Minister, U.N. Document, A/47/PV.9 (2 October, 1992), p.118.

[64]U.N. Document, A/C.1/47/PV.10 (4 November, 1992), p.48.

[65]See the *Report of the Special Committee on the Charter of the United Nations and on the Strengthening of the Role of the Organization* (New York: United Nations, 1994), p. 13.

[66]Ibid., p. 11.

[67]U.N. Document, A/50/361 (22 August, 1995), p. 4.

the U.N. while simultaneously maintaining good relations with all of the states of the former Yugoslavia. Following the conclusion of the Dayton Peace Accords in 1995, Romania advocated the admission of Federal Yugoslavia (Serbia and Montenegro) to the U.N., as well as its return to regional and subregional organizations in Europe.[68] The Secretary-General of the U.N. had also reported[69] on the problem of how sanctions affected non-target states and had also recommended the establishment of a Compensation or Trust Fund.

One can conclude that Romania has been somewhat effective in bringing this issue before the United Nations, even if it has not benefited to the extent that it had hoped to. Over the past several years, the U.N. General Assembly has adopted Resolutions calling on the international community to deal with the negative economic effects of sanctions on "third countries" like Romania. For example, U.N. Resolution 48/210 called upon the Secretary-General to devise mechanisms that would allow international organizations and countries to help states such as Romania.[70] U.N. Resolution 50/58E (1995) focused on the effects which sanctions were having on the established transportation and communications patterns of the Danubian riparian states in the region.

By the 51st session of the General Assembly of the U.N., which took place in 1996, the Secretary-General of the U.N. reported on the actions which had been taken by states and international organizations to alleviate the adverse economic consequences of participating in the U.N. embargoes. Several governments and international agencies, such as the European Bank for Reconstruction and Development, the European Union, the U.N., and Russia as well, described the financial and technical assistance which they had provided to Romania to cope with the effects of the sanctions. But Romania was particularly interested in receiving more economic aid from the international community to help deal with the damage that had been done to its economy and its balance of payments.[71] International financial institutions such as the IMF and the World Bank provided loans for Romania, mostly in the context of helping it with the transition to a market economy, rather than pro-

---

[68]U.N. Document, A/PV.94 (18 December, 1995), p. 7.

[69]U.N. Document, A/50/361 (22 August, 1995), p. 4.

[70]See the *Report of the Special Committee on the Charter of the United Nations and on the Strengthening of the Role of the Organization* (New York: United Nations, 1994).

[71]U.N. Document, A/50/189,S/1995/412 (24 May, 1995), p. 2.

viding any special relief for the losses suffered from the sanctions. For example, I have not been able to discover any evidence that the IMF provided Romania with any aid from its Compensation and Contingency Facilities Funds.

After the lifting of U.N. sanctions against the former Yugoslavia in 1995, Romania co-sponsored a draft Resolution to help the affected states participate in the postwar reconstruction of Bosnia. The Romanians believed that "Geographical proximity and economic complementarity recommend Romania as a valid partner in the process of economic reconstruction in the area of Southeast Europe."[72]

Charter Reform

Finally, another consistent element of postcommunist Romanian foreign policy at the U.N. has been support for Charter Reform. Since the old bipolar[73] international system had been replaced by a multipolar one, Romania suggested that the structure of the United Nations should also be adapted to reflect the changed conditions of the new post-Cold War international system. There was a great deal of interest in revamping the structure of the U.N. at its 50th anniversary session in 1995, especially in view of the post-Cold War wave of global democratization. One target of reform focused on the enlargement of the size of the Security Council. Of particular concern was the distribution of permanent seats on the Security Council. Permanent seats on the Security Council had been allocated in 1945 to just five countries – the US, Russia, France, China, and the United Kingdom. A permanent seat on the Security Council also carried with it special privileges and rights, such as the use of the veto. Postcommunist Romania supported the enlargement of the Security Council so as to reflect the overall increase that had taken place in the membership of the U.N. since its foundation in 1945. Romania believed that enlargement of the Security Council would endow it with a more representative nature.[74] Consequently, Romania supported the addition of Germany and Japan as permanent members of the Security Council.[75] Bucharest also sup-

---

[72]U.N. Document, A/PV.94 (18 December, 1995), p. 17.

[73]Romania stressed that "released from the fetters of bipolarity and of the Cold War, the international system has regained its natural freedom of movement." See U.N. Document, A/50/PV.37 (23 October, 1995), p. 12.

[74]U.N. Document, A/C.6/49/SR.11 (13 October, 1994), p. 12.

ported a moderate increase in the overall size of the Security Council[76] from 15 to about 25. This would mean increasing the number of non-permanent seats that were allocated to various regions of the world, with particular emphasis on the Third World. Romania stressed that developing countries should by no means find themselves marginalized as a result of reform.[77] Romania, not surprisingly, also advocated an additional nonpermanent seat on the Security Council for the East European region, thus increasing its representation from one to two non-permanent members. But Romania also suggested that consideration should be given to the extent to which a state has contributed to international peace and security before it is added to the Security Council.[78]

In connection with the reform of the U.N. Charter, Romania also advocated the deletion of those clauses in Articles 53, 77, and 107 of the Charter, which referred to "enemy states." These clauses were objectionable, among other reasons, because they provided a legal basis for members of the U.N. to take action against "enemy states." For example, Article 53[79] allowed regional agencies to take enforcement action against "enemy states". Article 77 referred to the U.N. Trust Territories that had been detached from "enemy states." Article 107 legitimized the right of states to take action against states that had been designated as "enemy states." One could therefore understand why Romania and other "enemy states" such as Germany and Japan would advocate the deletion of the objectionable clauses. Consequently, the General Assembly of the United Nations adopted a Resolution at its 50th session which called for the amendment of the U.N. Charter to delete the "enemy states" clauses, according to the procedure described in Article 108.[80] The sections in the Charter referring to "enemy states" were seen as "anachronistic" by Romania because they also contradicted those articles of the U.N. Charter which emphasized that dis-

---

[75] Ibid.

[76] See U.N. *Press Release, GA/7147* (30 October, 1996) in http://www.un.org/.

[77] U.N. Document, A/C.6/49/SR.11 (13 October, 1994), p. 12.

[78] See U.N. *Press Release, GA/9147* (30 October, 1996) in http://www.un.org/.

[79] Article 53, Section 2 of the Charter referred to enemy states as "any state which during the Second World War has been an enemy of any signatory of the present Charter."

[80] Article 108 stipulates that the Charter can be amended by a 2/3 vote of the members of the General Assembly, which must include the permanent members of the Security Council.

putes between nations should be solved by peaceful means rather than through force.[81]

Conclusion

In conclusion, postcommunist Romanian foreign policy at the U.N. has been based on some traditional elements, the most important of which is national interest. The Romanians have also tried to enhance the authority of the U.N. in the post-Cold War world by supporting and participating in its peacekeeping activities, and even participating in U.N. sanctions regimes at great cost to itself. Romania has also supported U.N. efforts at Arms Control and Disarmament. Postcommunist Romania's foreign policy priorities have focused on resolving its security dilemma through integration into the Euro-Atlantic institutions. Participation in the U.N. has helped it to try and achieve these objectives as Romania has proceeded along the painful road toward democratization and a market economy. Finally, Romania has continued to support Charter reform, in an effort to transform the U.N. into a more democratic and representative organization in a multipolar, post-Cold War world.

---

[81]In connection with this, Romania referred to Article 1, paragraph 1, and Article 2, paragraphs 3 and 4 of the U.N. Charter. See U.N. Document, A/C.6/49/SR.11 (13 October, 1994), p. 13.

Ecumenism, Religious Freedom, and the National Church: Controversy in Romania

Earl A. Pope
Lafayette College

The religious situation in Romania defies any brief or simple analysis. In the 1980's the religious communities, both the registered and the unregistered, found themselves in the midst of a complex and volatile world. Increased breathing space was a profound concern of the churches, but the communist state showed no signs that it would begin to respect its citizens' civil and religious rights. All the religious communities, including the Romanian Orthodox Church, were carefully monitored by the Securitate which perceived them as potentially destabilizing forces for the socialist society. They had remained the only social structures which had not been fully integrated into the Romanian political system because of their basic ideological incompatibility. The extent to which some of the religious leaders collaborated with the communist state as well as the role which some of the international ecumenical agencies played, however, remains a very sensitive issue.[1]

Until December 1989 Romania was under the control of a ruthless communist dictator in charge of a large, well-armed security force with an

---

[1]Stephen Brown, "Konrad Raiser Defends WCC's Cold War Record," *Ecumenical News International*, No. 23 (November 26, 1997), pp. 6-7.

extensive informant system which penetrated every part of the society, an abysmal human rights record, an economic crisis of catastrophic proportions, and a reign of terror in which human beings were the last priority in a nightmare world.[2] Laszlo Tokes, a 36-year-old minister of the Reformed Church in Timişoara and a rare outspoken critic of the Ceauşescu tyranny, became the catalyst for the Romanian revolution.

The revolution brought about important changes within the Romanian society at large and for the religious communities in particular. Two of the most significant decisions made by the National Salvation Front, which initially served as the provisional government, were to relegalize the Greek Catholic Church, popularly known as the Uniates, which had been suppressed by the communist state and now found itself involved in a struggle to regain approximately 2,000 churches, and to maintain the legal status of the other fourteen religious communities which had been recognized under the Ceauşescu regime and to permit them to have an amazing amount of freedom. For the first time in more than forty years it was now possible for the churches to govern themselves, to set their own agendas, to revise their structures, and to live out their own lives and articulate their own missions in the fullest way. They were totally unprepared for the unparalleled opportunities which had now arisen for their ministries and for their service, although they had helped to pave the revolution's way by keeping alive the spirit of democracy and a belief in the innate dignity of every human being.[3] Unfortunately, more than eight years after the upheaval of December 1989, the ecumenical situation in Romania leaves much to be desired; new religious legislation has not been finalized and there are even mounting fears that there could be restrictions on religious freedom in the new era.

After the revolution there was a tremendous feeling of euphoria, particularly among some of the minority churches. All the religious communities took steps to use this new freedom effectively in the light of their particular perspectives. There have been extensive restoration and building programs, new confessional schools and theological institutes with a large number of candidates for the priesthood, many new church periodicals and publications, opportunities on radio and televi-

---

[2]Earl A. Pope, "Review of The Silent Escape: Three Thousand Days in Communist Prisons" by Lena Constante to be published by *Canadian-American Slavic Studies*, 1998.

[3]Laszlo Tokes, "The Possible Role of Romania's Churches in the Social Upheaval of the Country," *Occasional Papers on Religion in Eastern Europe*, ed. Paul Mojzes, X (October, 1990), p. 30.

sion, and openings for ministries in all the state institutions. To be sure, there was more than a little discomfort among the minority churches because the Romanian Orthodox Church was rapidly beginning to fill all the openings. Religious believers who had been severely persecuted suddenly found themselves free to practice their faith openly without fear of reprisal. The state continued to provide subsidies for the salaries of pastors and administrators of the traditional churches, but these were not considered adequate given the serious economic problems. Some of the churches refused to receive such state subsidies because of their views of the separation of church and state.

The evangelical churches (Adventists, Baptists, Brethren, and Pentecostalists) were enthusiastic about the new freedom which they were experiencing for the first time in their history, whereas the traditional or Reformation Protestant churches were more restrained in their enthusiasm because of the slow pace at which their property was being restored. Some of the religious associations, given their historical experience with only provisional approval, initially used this new freedom in a very cautious way, waiting for the moment when they would have full constitutional recognition. The formerly illegal groups such as the Lord's Army, the Nazarenes, the Reformed Adventists, and Jehovah's Witnesses were recognized as religious associations, but to this day there is still serious concern because the full significance of their "recognition" has not been fully clarified. Historically, religious associations have not had the same constitutional rights as approved religious communities and have been far more vulnerable to decisions made by local officials. The four evangelical bodies were regarded as religious associations before the emergence of the communist regime and their rights were severely restricted in the inter-war period. There is no question but that there still needs to be a dialogue between them and the Romanian Orthodox Church which they perceive as their oppressor in the past.

Following the revolution approximately seventy religious associations were approved by the Ministry of Cults (now referred to officially as the State Secretariat for Cults or Religious Affairs — SSRA). At the present time there are approximately 400 registered associations with reports that many more are functioning openly throughout the country. These groups are also developing an ecumenism of their own which has yet to be adequately studied and have become a very sensitive issue, particularly for the Romanian Orthodox Church which views them as intruders in their world. Most of the registered religious associations have relationships with the fifteen approved religious communities, now including the Uniates, and presumably enjoy the freedom which these groups provide. The unaffiliated religious associations have been anxiously awaiting the approval of new religious legislation so that they may request full religious status.

The contemporary religious situation in Romania continues to be very complex. New forms of ecumenical ventures have emerged, and one of the major priorities has been new religious legislation to replace the 1948 Law of Cults imposed by the communist state. The Hungarian Protestant churches (Lutheran, Reformed, and Unitarian) joined in a rare coalition with the Latin Rite Catholic Church in Transylvania immediately after the revolution and adopted a document which called for a free church in a free society. This involved not only the removal of the 1948 Law of Cults but also the restitution of their archives, libraries, confessional schools, and social institutions; freedom to train their pastors and publish their literature; access to the mass media; and religious education in the public schools.[4]

The Protestant churches (with the exception of the Unitarians) together with the German Lutheran Church have formed an Ecumenical Association with the Romanian Orthodox Church under the guidance of the World Council of Churches and the Conference of European Churches to assess their needs and conduct their missions more effectively among the Romanian people. This association is to some extent a reflection of the interconfessional theological meetings permitted by the communist regime and has the same membership but a much larger agenda. The platform of this association initially had three objectives: (1) helping inter-church dialogue on matters of common concern; (2) providing an ecumenical instrument through which the members could make a public statement; and (3) discussing priorities for ecumenical cooperation and witness. The representatives of these churches recognized the critical importance of developing trust and confidence within the country so that "freedom and democracy" could be fully achieved through "non-violent and reconciliatory means." They also stated as priorities: (1) the development of "national-ethnic reconciliation" whereby the churches would have a special responsibility for providing models for a "multi-racial, multicultural society;" (2) issues related to new religious legislation; (3) religious education in the public schools; (4) the reevangelization of the Romanian people; and (5) a joint ecumenical witness involving ecolog-

---

[4]Letter to Gheorghe Vlăduțescu from representatives of the Roman Catholic, Evangelical Lutheran, Reformed, and Unitarian Churches, October 30, 1990.

ical concerns, and the transformation of life for the most underprivileged within the society.[5]

In February 1991, AIDROM (Ajutor Interbisericesc Departamentul România), a social agency organized by these same churches and coordinated by the Committee on Interchurch Aid and Refugee World Service (CICARWS) of the WCC began its operations to achieve the objectives on its agenda. In November, 1993, this body was officially registered as the Ecumenical Association of Christian Churches in Romania.[6] Its program has been only partially successful for several reasons: trust still has not been achieved, national ethnic reconciliation still has a difficult road to travel, the churches at times have become contentious rather than positive models for their society, and the reevangelization of the Romanian people was a much greater challenge than originally anticipated and the modest efforts in this area have become divisive and are marred by charges of proselytism further poisoning the ecumenical climate. The evangelicals have had second thoughts regarding the significance of mass evangelism which has been offensive to the Orthodox, and now they, too, have raised serious questions regarding its effectiveness. Most of the so-called converts disappeared after the flamboyant evangelists went home, but it is possible that some of those who attended the meetings are developing a renewal movement in their own churches.[7]

The priorities set forth for AIDROM represented a long-term program which would require close cooperation among the churches and the continued leadership of their sponsoring ecumenical bodies to help the leaders of the Romanian churches to fully trust and work with one another. Tensions among the founding churches have emerged, but the ecumenical bodies apparently have been too involved in other international crises to give the serious attention which is imperative for the ecumenical dilemma in Romania. Then, too, these agencies have internal problems of their own and are preparing for an universal

[5]"Romanian Churches Meet to Set Ecumenical Priorities," *Lutheran World Information*, XXVI (July 12, 1990), 16; Robert C. Lodwick, "Romanian Trip Report and Romanian Roundtable Meeting," June 18-25, 1990; "National Ecumenical Platform Set Up in Romania," *Keston News Service*, No. 356 (August 9, 1990), p. 11; "Romania: Eastern Orthodox, Lutherans, Reformed Plan Cooperation," *Ecumenical Press Service*, November 4, 1990.

[6]AIDROM, *Statute of the Ecumenical Association of Churches in Romania* (Bucharest, Romania: AIDROM, 1993), 8 pp.

[7]Josef Tson, "Towards Reformation in Romania," *East-West Church and Ministry Report*, I (Spring, 1993), p. 1.

Christian council which would include the major families of churches — Catholic, Orthodox, Protestant, and Evangelical Pentecostal — to discuss issues which divide them and to develop a common confession of faith.[8] This could have an important impact on the Romanian religious situation.

Unquestionably, the work of AIDROM, in spite of its highly qualified staff and the programs it has developed in a wide range of areas, has been seriously hampered by the tensions which have surfaced among the churches. It should be noted that most of the churches are individually beginning to develop extensive social programs to address the appalling needs of the marginalized within Romanian society, such as the orphans, the street children, the homeless, the disabled, and the elderly. Increasing attention is also being given to the specific needs of the Roma minority which have been too long ignored but are now on the AIDROM agenda.[9]

There has been a measure of cooperation in the area of religious education in the state schools, but this has not been an unqualified ecumenical success. Courses in "moral-religious education" were introduced into the state schools as a result of a joint decision by the Minister of Science and Education and the SSRA. All of the theological schools have been invited to train teachers to fill the tremendous number of positions available. It is readily obvious, however, that there needs to be more careful attention as to what is meant by "moral-religious education" and how it can be taught by the representatives of the various religious bodies in what the "joint decision" called an "irenic spirit."[10]

At the present time each of the various religious communities has the opportunity to appoint teachers to present the essentials of its own tradition if there are ten or more of its own faith registered in a course. The minority faiths have complained that when their views have been discussed they have not been adequately presented by some of the teachers who identify with the majority faith. There is no common core course in which the history and faith of each of the religious com-

---

[8]"WARC Official Welcomes Proposal to Discuss Church Divisions," *ENI* Bulletin, XIII (July 9, 1996), p. 5.

[9]N. Barney Pityana, "The Plight of the Roma," *One World*, November, 1991, pp. 14-15.

[10]Gheorghe Ştefan and Gheorghe Vlăduţescu, "The Introduction of Moral-Religious Education in Public Schools," *Romanian Orthodox Church News*, XX (September-December 1990), pp. 27-28; "The Revival of Religious Education and Practices in Romania," (Bucharest: Ministry of Cults, 1990), p. 4.

munities is presented in a fair and objective way, although the need for this was recognized in a dialogue between the deans of the Baptist and the Orthodox Theological Institutes at the University of Bucharest.[11] The religious communities have made substantial progress together in the development of the new legislation on religious freedom but a final draft has yet to reach the Parliament for its consideration.

While the Reformation Protestant Churches have engaged in two new ecumenical ventures which involved the Romanian Orthodox Church and a wing of the Roman Catholic Church, the evangelical communities have largely reconciled their differences and have been involved in a literal explosion of religious activities. Immediately after the overthrow of Ceauşescu, the evangelicals held consultations with one another and formed an Evangelical Alliance. They agreed on a constitution and a common statement of faith closely related to that of American evangelicalism.[12] The Alliance is a complex religious movement which represents the most significant attempt in Romanian history to unite the evangelical groups. Commissions were established on: (1) evangelism and mission, (2) the publication of Christian literature, (3) radio and television, (4) education, (5) organizations for children, young people, and women, (6) social work, and (7) religious freedom and the relationships between church and state.[13]

The Evangelical Alliance, especially through its Baptist leadership, has been engaged in ways to preserve and extend its new religious freedom, challenging whatever efforts it may perceive as restrictive or subversive of its rights. The Baptists sent appeals to the US Congress to grant the Most Favored Nation (MFN) status to Romania. They emphasized the freedom that they enjoyed in their evangelism, teaching, and social work and stressed that the MFN relationship would be well received at a time when Romania was developing its democratic infrastructures. The Baptist Church stated that it wanted to serve as "a bridge of trust and an instrument of strengthening the relationship between the USA and Romania."[14] The missionary zeal of the evangelicals, however, has caused considerable apprehension among the leadership of the Orthodox Church. It is clear that they planned to become politically active on matters of religious freedom and issues related to

[11]"Romania: Orthodox and Baptists Seek Common Witness," *EPS*, June 15, 1994.

[12]"Crezul Evanghelic" (Bucharest: Evangelical Alliance, March 1990).

[13]"Statutul Alianţei Evanghelice din România" (Bucharest: March, 1990).

[14]"Romania: Baptists Appeal to U.S. for Most Favored Nation Status," *EPS*, June 21-30, 1991.

their convictions. Unquestionably they have become an important Romanian religious movement within what was once an Orthodox world.

In 1990 there were some strong differences of opinion between the SSRA and a number of the religious communities regarding the parameters of the newly found freedom until new religious legislation was to be developed to replace the odious 1948 Law of Cults. The SSRA was considered to have made decisions which were regarded as subversive of authentic religious freedom; furthermore, references made to the possibility of new legislation based on the 1928 Law of Cults only intensified the tensions because this Law was regarded as discriminatory by some of the churches.[15] To avoid further conflicts, Nicolae Stoicescu, the first head of the SSRA, established a committee that spring with representatives chosen by the fifteen religious communities to draft the new religious legislation which would then be proposed to the country's new parliament for approval. This committee has been at work on this legislation for the past eight years with little prospect of completing the project in the near future. Unfortunately the religious associations, some of which had been ruthlessly suppressed by the communist state, were not represented on this committee. This would cause serious problems for them in the future.

Concurrent with the deliberations by this committee the new Romanian Constitution was formulated, debated, and finalized. It was approved by the Parliament in November 1991 and by popular referendum in December of that year. There were vigorous discussions regarding the clauses on the freedom of conscience and religious belief in Article 29. The final conclusion was that freedom of religious belief could not be restricted in any way and that freedom of conscience was guaranteed, but it must be expressed in a spirit of tolerance and mutual respect. The religious communities were free but all forms of controversy were prohibited. State officials have been deeply concerned because some of the religious communities have had a great deal of difficulty providing positive models for the emerging democratic society. The religions were to be autonomous vis-à-vis the state but they were also to enjoy its support which in time was to involve an extensive financial commitment. Parents had the right to provide religious education for their children.[16] The constitution also stressed that the state

[15]"Evangelical Alliance to Register Despite Minister's Refusal," *KNS*, No. 346 (March 22, 1990), pp. 3-4.

[16]*The Constitution of Romania*, Bucharest, 1991, p. 72.

recognized and guaranteed for the national minorities the right to preserve, develop, and express their ethnic, cultural, linguistic, and religious identity in Article 1 under General Principles.[17] Some of the
minority churches have consistently maintained that this right has not
as yet been fully honored. The constitution also emphasized that the
state would "ensure freedom of religious education in accordance with
the specific requirements of each faith" in Article 32.[18]

The Baptists, in particular, were very attentive to the constitutional discussions and officially presented several amendments of their
own. They proposed that "by the grace of God" be added to the first
article of the constitution which at that time read "Romania is a
national state, sovereign, unitary and indivisible."[19] Their rationale was
that there needed to be a radical break with the official atheism of the
past by including a constitutional acknowledgment of the nation's
dependence on divine providence. They were also uneasy about Article
50, which stated that loyalty to the state is a "sacred duty"[20] and proposed that it be changed to read that loyalty to the state is the "obligation" of every citizen, because in their eyes political loyalty was not the
ultimate loyalty.[21] They were the only religious community to raise
even implicitly the question of the idolatry of nationalism and this proposal was not well received by the ultranationalists. The amendments
do not appear in the final version of the constitution.

The legislation to be formulated by the representatives of the religious communities was to undergird and amplify the constitutional
declarations and to grant the religious communities the fullest self
determination and religious freedom possible as well as to replace the
1948 Law of Cults which had been used by the communist state to
intervene in and to control the churches' internal affairs. The discussions among the representatives of the religious communities at times
proved to be very difficult even though on many issues they shared
similar positions. The proposed legislation by the committee went
through a number of major drafts (1991, 1992, 1993) in which various ministries of the state such as health and education participated,
but always under the careful guidance of Professor Gheorghe

---

[17]Ibid., p. 64.

[18]Ibid., p. 74.

[19]*UBBI* (Buletin de Informare al Uniunii Bisericilor Creştine Baptiste din
România), Anul, nr. 1 (June 1991), p. 8.

[20]*Constitution*, p. 81.

[21]*UBBI, loc. cit.*

Vlăduțescu who succeeded Nicolescu as the head of the SSRA. The final decision on each article was made by the representatives of the religious communities. On October 28, 1993, a 21-page document with 78 articles was reluctantly accepted by the committee with two major reservations after a grueling eight hours of heated discussions; it emphasized the freedom of the churches in a large number of critical areas but did not call for a strict separation of church and state since some of the churches still felt the necessity of the traditional state subsidies.[22]

The new legislation reaffirmed that the Romanian state recognized, respected, and guaranteed the liberty and autonomy of the religious communities. It asserted the obligation of the churches to contribute to the development of the moral and spiritual education of the entire society and to create an atmosphere of understanding and respect among all people. It stressed that the churches had the freedom to organize and conduct spiritual, educational, and charitable activities according to their own statutes and confessions of faith. It emphasized unequivocally that no one would suffer any loss of civil and political rights as the result of his religious faith. It declared that the state would not meddle in any way in the internal life of the religious communities; they would have free access to the public media and have the right to establish their own publishing houses and schools. It stressed that the religious communities were autonomous and equal in their mutual relations. It stated strongly that the ecumenical spirit, tolerance, and mutual respect must be at the basis of the relations among the religious communities.

References to the religious associations were included in the 1991 draft, omitted in 1992, and then included again in the draft of October, 1993.[23] There had obviously been considerable discussion about their freedom and their role in the new Romanian society. They were to be given the opportunity once the law was passed to organize and apply for full constitutional recognition. They could not be in conflict with one of the already legally recognized groups, they must obey the Constitution, uphold good morals, and respect individual rights and the freedom of citizens as stated in the international agreements. The religious associations could be recognized either in relationship to one of the legally recognized entities or on an independent basis. Those which did not apply for or did not receive official constitutional recog-

---

[22]SSRA, "Legea Cultelor" (Bucharest: SSRA, 1993), 21 pp.
[23]Ibid., pp. 18-19.

nition would not be entitled to have their own publications or churches or to receive subsidies for their personnel. There was no provision for them to continue as independent religious associations with full rights to practice their faith without the opportunity to receive state subsidies as many of them would prefer. It is obvious that if some of the representatives of the independent religious associations had been on the committee they could have pointed out the contradictions within the document to authentic religious freedom. It may well be in the not too far distant future that the Romanian state will attempt to gradually phase out the subsidies as has occurred in other countries, but this would arouse a new round of heated controversy.

Professor Vlăduțescu was proud of the early unanimous decision by the committee that there was to be no state church and that all of the religious communities were to be equal before the law and state. There had been vigorous discussions regarding this issue in the constitutional debates, but in the end the implication was clear that all the religious communities were to be treated equally. Vlăduțescu was to recognize too late the serious problems which existed regarding the rights of the religious associations. Unfortunately, none of the representatives of the recognized religious communities appear to have considered their absence on the committee a serious matter in the development of the legislation.

What was hoped to be the final draft of the proposed religious legislation in October, 1993, brought about a serious division among the representatives of the recognized religious communities. The Holy Synod of the Romanian Orthodox Church insisted that the phrase "national church" be added after the listing of the Romanian Orthodox Church in the proposed legislation.[24] This came as a shock to the representatives of the minority churches since this issue had not been raised by the Orthodox representatives on a committee which had been deliberating for more than three years, and the timing was such that there could not be a serious dialogue on the implications of such a proposal before it was submitted to the Parliamentary committees. The first draft of the legislation submitted by the Romanian Orthodox Church before a working common draft was developed did not mention a "national church" and emphasized that the state would assure the

---

[24]Ibid., p. 6.

equality of all of the religious communities before the law.[25] It also did not mention the religious associations.

In an interview on March 2, 1995, Professor Vlăduțescu indicated that his greatest disappointment was that the legislation on which he had worked so hard had ended in controversy and had not at that point been placed on the agenda of the Parliament. He also felt that his greatest achievement was the decision to have the teaching of religion in the state schools.[26] What had been the most significant ecumenical and democratic encounter of the religious communities regarding the rights to which they were all entitled and the freedom which they ought to share ended in a very serious confrontation between the minority churches and the majority church which has yet to be resolved.

The official explanation of the Orthodox leaders was that their church was entitled to this recognition, that this was simply a statement of a historical and cultural fact, and that no legal advantage was intended or desired for their church. The Protestant churches (Reformation and Evangelical alike) were joined by both the Roman and the Greek Catholic churches in radical opposition to this addition and stated this officially in a footnote in the proposed legislation.[27] They were convinced that this addition represented a serious and unacceptable contradiction to Article 4 of their proposal[28] which was an unambiguous declaration of the full equality of all the religious communities before the law and the state. They also felt that it violated the spirit of the Romanian constitution and their proposed legislation regarding ecumenism and mutual respect. They feared that it would reinforce the myth that there was a mystical unity between the Orthodox Church and the soul of the Romanian people and that only Orthodox believers could therefore be trusted as loyal Romanian citizens. They see the Orthodox Church as unequivocally identifying itself as the church of the Romanian people and as the sole vehicle whereby the national and spiritual identity is preserved, thus raising serious questions about its understanding of the importance and enrichment of the religious and

---

[25]Biserica Ortodoxă Română, "Textul Propos: Legea cultelor religioase din România" (Bucharest, 1990), p. 3.

[26]Interview with Gheorghe Vlăduțescu by Earl A. Pope, Bucharest, March 2, 1995.

[27]*Legea, op. cit.*

[28]Ibid., p. 2.

ethnic pluralism within the country and of the true nature of religious freedom and a democracy.

The Romanian Orthodox Church had its own strong reservations regarding the final draft. It opposed state support for private confessional schools other than theological seminaries and institutes presumably because it felt that these schools could become centers for proselytism and that whatever confessional education was organized should be for "the believers of the respective community exclusively."[29] This became an issue of serious concern for the minority religious communities which had a long tradition of sponsoring their own confessional schools as well as for the evangelical communities which were beginning to develop their own educational networks. It is clear that by the end of 1993 the euphoria which some of the religious communities had experienced regarding the development of ecumenism and cooperation in Romania was seriously diminished. The inaugural General Assembly of the Ecumenical Association of Churches in Romania at the Orthodox Theological Institute in Bucharest on November 3, 1993, was sparsely attended, and the festive luncheon room was virtually empty. Bishop Csiha of the Reformed Church, one of the keynote speakers on the occasion along with Patriarch Teoctist, held a press conference in which he strongly criticized the addition of "national church" to the legislation. It was hardly what the organizers of this event had planned.

What had been a very impressive dialogical experience for the churches over more than three years ended in a serious and destructive controversy which brought to the surface a series of tensions which will be all the more difficult to resolve. The religious communities in Romania share important bonds which ought to encourage close cooperation among them: the terrible oppression they have suffered, the hunger for freedom which they experienced, the common message they share, and the overwhelming challenges that they face. There remains, however, an interrelated complex of tensions which have damaged their relationships in the past and in varying degrees continue to trouble them in the post-communist era: cultural, ecclesiastical, ethnic, political, social, psychological, and theological. It is unfortunate that there has never been authentic dialogue as opposed to destructive confrontation between the minority churches and the majority church as to how the national church controversy can be amicably resolved.

---

[29]Ibid., Article 15, p. 4 and Article 45, pp. 11-12.

The Lutheran and the Reformed churches, which had been the primary ecumenical partners with the Orthodox for many years, sharply criticized through their representatives the lack of ecumenism in Romania at a meeting of the Central Committee of the WCC in January of 1994. This "declaration" helped to undermine the hope of the Romanian Orthodox Church that the WCC Assembly of 1998 (its fiftieth anniversary) would be held in Bucharest. The evangelical response to what it perceived to be the real intentions of the Orthodox Church is summarized by Josef Tson, who shocked the communist establishment in the 1970's by his call for a "Christ Revolution"[30] and who now serves as the head of the Emmanuel Bible Institute in Oradea. He was convinced that the "national church" addition was a dangerous threat to the minority religious communities who would then be treated as "foreign intruders" in the life of the nation.[31]

The Romanian Orthodox Church has not wavered in its determination to be legally established as the national church despite the devastating impact that it has had on ecumenism in Romania. In January, 1994, it changed its own constitution to incorporate this concept and it has continually defended its right in this regard even to the point of apparently supporting an amendment to the Romanian constitution. There have been a number of theories as to why the Romanian Orthodox Church would make this last minute intervention which it had to know would be controversial and damaging to Romanian ecumenism. Some of the suggestions made have been the surge of nationalism which reemphasized the unity between Orthodoxy and the soul of the nation, the insecurity of the present leadership of the Orthodox Church in a pluralistic world, and the urgent — indeed desperate — need for additional and extensive state funds to support its priests and hierarchy because of the severe economic crisis.[32] In all likelihood these are at most only partial explanations of a profound and far reaching crisis within the life of the church and its hierarchy which has deep roots in its recent history. There was far more serious damage done to the infrastructure of the Orthodox Church by the communist regime than is

---

[30]Josef Tson, "A Christian Manifesto to a Socialist Society," *RCL* supplementary paper No. 1 (November, 1973), pp. 15-16.

[31]Tson, "A New Law of Religion in Romania," *Romania for Jesus Christ*, Winter, 1993, p. 12.

[32]According to very reliable reports the Romanian Orthodox Church in 1995 had approximately 9,000 priests, more than 12,500 churches, 14 theological faculties with 5,641 students, 28 theological seminaries with an enrollment of 5,524, and 13,367 teachers of Orthodoxy in 11,378 schools throughout the land.

commonly realized and there were serious problems, as ecumenical representatives discovered, in the pre-communist period.

The most significant meeting to publicly discuss the ramifications of the proposed legislation of the religious communities was an international conference on religious freedom held in Bucharest in April, 1994. The conference was sponsored by the International Academy of Religious Freedom and Belief in cooperation with the Romanian branch of the International Religious Liberty Association, the Romanian Institute for Human Rights, and the Institute for Constitutional and Legal Policy. The focus of the conference was on the proposal of the legislation on the freedom of the religious communities, which up to that point had been considered confidential.[33]

The representatives of the IARFB felt that the proposed draft had many positive features but they immediately registered serious concern regarding the Romanian Orthodox being listed as the "national church." They also expressed concerns regarding the distinction between the state recognized religious communities which could claim full religious freedom and the religious associations which had only been approved by the SSRA. Questions were also raised about the right of parents to send their children to confessional schools whether or not they were members of the sponsoring religious community which had been opposed by the majority church. These issues were discussed at considerable length in the various sessions of the conference. The members of the Academy noted that significant progress had been made in Romania regarding religious freedom and the equality of all the religious communities. They felt, however, that these were some of the provisions in the draft that needed to be changed in order to bring the proposed legislation into "full compliance with applicable international norms that are binding on Romania under international law and under the Romanian constitution."[34] The meetings were held at Cercul Militar in the center of Bucharest and were attended by many leaders of the churches including high ranking officials of the Orthodox Church. Professor Vlăduțescu played an active role in the conference and the Patriarch attended the reception. In some of the news media there was a negative reaction to the conference themes and even a call

[33]The author was recommended by Professor Ion Bria, a Romanian Orthodox official at the WCC, to be a consultant to the academy; he provided its members with the 1993 draft, copies of which were then made for the conference.

[34]International Academy for Freedom of Religion and Belief, Press Release, April 5, 1994, Bucharest.

for those who were its Romanian organizers to be disciplined. The determination of the Holy Synod to have its church legally established as the "national church" received extensive national media coverage.

The public activities of the religious associations increasingly became a very sensitive matter, and tensions erupted in July 1996 with the Patriarchal ban on an international congress scheduled by the Jehovah's Witnesses in Bucharest as part of its program of "theocratic education." The Patriarch scolded the state authorities involved in granting the necessary approvals for the conference, including the SSRA and denounced the Witnesses as a "pagan sect" which contributed to the "hatred and violence haunting the world" and which posed a serious threat to "the ancestral faith and national unity."[35] The mass demonstrations against the Witnesses were very alarming to the state authorities. The registration of the Witnesses, however, as an approved religious association was not revoked by the SSRA and it was permitted to hold meetings in other parts of the country.

The Reformation Protestant churches and the evangelical communities continued their concerns and resistance regarding the positions taken by the Orthodox Church in a variety of ways. The Association of Hungarian Churches sent a communication directly to the attention of President Ion Iliescu in June, 1994, calling attention to the violation of their constitutional rights with the denial of the traditional state support for the establishment and operation of their confessional schools in the new law on education passed by the Romanian Parliament on June 23, 1994. They also deplored the fact that their church property "nationalized by the former communist regime" had not as yet been restored.[36] Bishop Csiha of the Reformed Church, a dissident during the communist period and one of the signers of the Iliescu letter, expressed great disappointment that the Orthodox Church failed to support the minority churches in their struggle against the subversion of their rights.[37]

---

[35]"Romanian Church Calls for Ban on Congress for Jehovah's Witnesses," *ENI Bulletin*, XIII (July 9, 1996), pp. 15-16; Carmela Popa and Romulus Cristea, "More than 5000 Orthodox Christians Militated for the Preservation of the Forefathers' Beliefs," *România Liberă*, No. 127 (July 11, 1996), p. 4; Bogdan Ficeac, "Tolerance or Complicity," *R.L.*, No. 127, p. 13; Bogdan Burileanu, "Dangerous Provocations," *R.L.*, No. 127, p. 14.

[36]Letter to President Ion Iliescu from the leaders of the Roman Catholic, Reformed, Evangelical Lutheran, and Unitarian Churches of Transylvania, June 29, 1994.

[37]Bishop Kalman Csiha, Letter to Earl A. Pope, July 18, 1994.

The leaders of the German Lutheran Church obviously were also concerned regarding the positions taken by the Orthodox Church but are now beginning to reexamine their mission in Romania in the light of the unprecedented exodus of most of their members to Germany. Bishop Christoph Klein touched a very sensitive nerve when he stated that the idea of the Lutheran Church as a "folk church" identified with a particular ethnic origin needed to change. The church needed to develop a "new face" dedicated to the service of Jesus Christ rather than to "folk church structures."[38] His deputy bishop, Dr. Hans Klein, has called Sibiu, one of the major centers of Orthodoxy, the greatest mission field in Europe and has stated that his church had reached a point of "creative chaos" and that a new beginning is emerging, inspired by the large numbers of Romanian young people and children who are voluntarily attending the Lutheran churches and confessional schools, thus challenging the claim of the Orthodox that it alone has the right to minister to the Romanian people.[39] This development could bring about a serious conflict situation with the leaders of the Orthodox Church given their version of proselytism. The Transylvanian Saxons, as the German Lutherans are frequently called, have lived on the territory of contemporary Romania for more than 850 years and believe that they have every right to share their faith with their Romanian neighbors, and these neighbors are now flocking to their churches.

The evangelicals felt very deeply that their freedom was being seriously threatened when the "national church" insertion was made in the proposed legislation. The leaders of the Baptist and the Pentecostal churches expressed their concerns very forcefully to the representative of the WCC who had participated in the inaugural meeting of the Association of Churches in Romania in November, 1993. It was evident that they planned to take the offensive in whatever way they felt was appropriate to protect their rights. The Baptist Union of Romania held a Religious Liberties Conference in Bucharest in cooperation with the Southern Baptist Convention in the United States in May 1994, with the theme, "A Free Gospel In a Free Nation."[40] The news release

---

[38]"Romanian Lutherans No longer Able to Pay Pastors," *LWI*, No. 36 (October 4, 1990), p 12.

[39]"Sibiu: Europe's Biggest Mission Station," *LWI*, XVII (September 5, 1996), pp. 11-13; "A New Beginning for Lutheran Church in Romania," *LWI*, XIV (August 27, 1997), pp. 12-13.

[40]Announcement by the Baptist Union of Romania of the Religious Liberties Conference, May 18-20, 1994, Bucharest.

of the Baptists, in which they declared their opposition to the concept of the national church "self conferred" by the Romanian Orthodox Church, brought about a strong response from Metropolitan Daniel of Iași who has been perceived as the leading Orthodox ecumenist in Romania and the successor to the Patriarchal throne. He not only objected to their declaration but also to the efforts of the Christian communities which he maintained had only recently arrived in Romania to evangelize a people who had been Christians for 2000 years. In fact the Baptists had been there for almost 150 years. He reportedly claimed, "The only right way to the truth of God is Orthodoxy and all the other ways chosen by one or another are wrong."[41] Daniel had spent a number of years lecturing at the ecumenical institute sponsored by the WCC in Bossey, Switzerland, and had returned to Romania the year before the revolution. He had a meteoric rise within the Romanian Orthodox hierarchy and was an important member of a committee for the reformation and renewal of his church.[42] He was considered to be the ecumenical leader who would represent his church to the international ecumenical bodies, a role which Metropolitan Antonie of Sibiu had filled during much of the communist era.

The leaders of the Pentecostal Church were also deeply concerned about the Orthodox claim to be the "national church" and maintained that their church also had the right to call itself the national church since it had been growing very rapidly and had Pentecostal communities in almost every village in the country. They also broke their official silence in 1994 of critiques made of their church by Professor Petru David who taught courses in ecumenism at the Orthodox Theological Institute in Bucharest. They took issue with Professor David who they maintained had falsified their history and defamed their church in an article which he wrote in 1992 in *Glasul Bisericii*, one of the Orthodox journals. David charged all of the evangelical communities with proselytism and with being subversive of the nation and the true faith.[43] The Pentecostal leaders emphasized that they were fully exercising their freedom and called upon the Orthodox editors of the journal to publish their response as soon as possible in the most appropriate issue of

---

[41] Corneliu Ciocan, "IPS Daniel, Metropolitan of Moldavia, Firmly Against Baptist Declaration," *Evenimentul Zilei*, May 31, 1994, p. 6.

[42] Alexander Webster, *The Price of Prophecy* (Washington, D.C.: Ethics and Public Policy Center, 1993), pp. 102-104.

[43] Petru I. David, "Misiunea Creștină Astăzi — Neoprotestanți vechi și noi, secte religioase și grupări anarhice," *Glasul Bisercii*, L (January-June, 1992), pp. 52-53, 62-63.

their journal. They also sent a letter to Patriarch Teoctist, whom they called a great spiritual leader animated by genuine ecumenism, protesting the hatred which David had displayed toward their church and calling for the practice of authentic ecumenical principles. These communications were published in their own periodical, *Cuvântul Adevărului*,[44] but there has been no response to these two letters from either the editors of *Glasul Bisericii* or the Patriarch.

The resignation of Professor Vlăduțescu as the head of the SSRA on March 1, 1995, caused considerable concern among the minority religious communities. They had developed great respect for him and felt that he had tried to treat them fairly as the head of a department which had been dominated by the secret police in the communist era and initially presented them with some difficulties after the revolution. Reportedly Vlăduțescu had been asked by President Iliescu to provide special treatment for the Orthodox Church in financial and educational matters. He had refused to approve measures, however, which would increase the financial assistance given to the Orthodox Church at the expense of the other churches, particularly the Roman Catholic, the Reformed, the Lutheran, and the Unitarian. The evangelical churches normally do not accept state subsidies. He resigned from his position shortly after his meeting with Iliescu to return to his philosophy position as the University of Bucharest.

Dr. Ilie Fonta was to head the SSRA for only a short period of time, but he publicly raised very sensitive and important questions on the impact of a decision to have the Orthodox Church legally called "national church," on its divine mission, on the freedom of the minorities which he feared would then be perceived as anti-national, and on the repeated request of the Orthodox Church to receive "full salaries" for all of its priests.[45] He also had serious reservations as to how the Orthodox Church could still claim autonomy if its vast ecclesiastical bureaucracy was fully supported by state funds. He had done extensive research and had written a book on religious freedom and he stated that he knew of no precedent for a religious community which is fully supported by the state to also be fully autonomous. He was impressed by the objectives of the 1996 Black Sea University seminar on *The Role of the Religious Communities as Peacemakers* and expressed disappointment that he had not been invited to be one of the guest lecturers.[46]

---

[44]Emil Bulgar and Trandafir Șandru, "Protestul conducerii Cultului Penticostal," *Cuvântul Adevărului*, V (Mai-Iunie, 1994), p. 26.

[45]Ilie Fonta, interviu acordat *Vestitorului Ortodoxiei*, July 1996, p. 21.

His successor, Dr. Gheorghe Anghelescu, caused a storm of international protest when he sent a circular letter on March 25, 1997, to the municipalities throughout Romania forbidding the religious associations from building churches.[47] This edict later was partially revoked.[48]

When Metropolitan Daniel made a historic ecumenical visit to the Church of England in the fall of 1996, it was inevitable that he would be asked some pointed questions regarding reports of difficulties among the churches in his native land. He eloquently presented the official Orthodox perspective on the religious situation in Romania. He firmly maintained that the Orthodox Church should be defined in the new law as the "national church," but he also denied that this would make it a state church or that it would have privileged treatment. He admitted that his church was dependent on state subsidies for its priests and also for teachers in the state schools, but he stressed that it remained autonomous. He expressed his concern about what he perceived was proselytism in Romania by Adventists, Baptists, and Catholics. He emphasized how cooperation and dialogue with the churches in the West could assist the Romanian Orthodox Church in its mission but apparently failed to mention any significant leadership his church was providing in order that the churches in Romania could cooperate and have dialogue with one another.[49]

It is clear that there is an ecumenical crisis in Romania which has posed serious problems not only for the churches but also for the society for which they had hoped to become positive models of tolerance and ecumenism. Professor Ion Bria, a Romanian Orthodox theologian who spent more than twenty years in various offices at the WCC in Geneva where he also served as the primary consultant on his church until his retirement in 1994, has made a very important analysis of the contemporary situation of the Romanian Orthodox Church which he feels now finds itself in one of the most serious crises in its history.[50]

---

[46]Interview by Earl A. Pope with Ilie Fonta, July 29, 1996; Earl A. Pope and Thomas H. Yorty, "The Role of the Religious Communities as Peacemakers," A Report of the Encounter of Religions in the Black Area, July 14-24, 1996, 6 pp.

[47]Gheorghe Anghelescu, Secretar De Stat Pentru Culte, to "Domnule Prefect," No. C 167 (Bucharest: March 25, 1997), 2 pp.; *Droits de l'Homme Sans Frontieres*, Press Release — Romania, April, 1997, 2 pp.; Earl A. Pope, Letter to President Emil Constantinescu, May 31, 1997, 5 pp.

[48]Willy Fautre, e-mail to Earl A. Pope re: *Religious Freedom in Romania, Human Rights Without Frontiers*, July 10, 1997, 5 pp.

[49]Xenia Dennen, "Interview with Metropolitan Daniel," *Frontier*, November-December 1996, pp. 10-11.

He issues a series of challenges to his church to which he is still deeply committed. He believes that since his church is the church of the majority, it unmistakably has unique responsibility, and he emphasizes that it must learn to live with ethnic and religious pluralism in a creative way. He is disturbed by its lack of ecumenism and stresses that "it must be open to others, willing to understand others and to receive gifts from them, to pray and learn from one another." Bria is alarmed by the "perfidious agnostic indifference" of many Romanians and by the moral and spiritual plight of its young people.[51] Although he is moved by the idea of a mystic unity between Orthodoxy and the soul of the Romanian people and longs for the Orthodox village world, he points to the danger of "nationalistic captivity" and calls for a transformed church which will be fully involved in the burning issues of the day. He is deeply concerned about the lack of leadership to guide the church in a new age. He raises the revealing question as to who the ecclesiastical leaders are who have the right to speak about Orthodoxy as good news for Romania without offering any answers for the contemporary period.[52] Without a profound internal reformation and renewal he warns that there will be empty churches and parallel religious groups.[53]

He unquestionably believes that the Orthodox Church finds itself in the midst of a profound identity crisis and there are moments when he even suggests that his church may be at the point of self-destruction.[54] He finds it very difficult to articulate a significant role that the minorities can have within the Romanian society given the prevailing Orthodox view of the unity of their faith with the soul of the Romanian people. For example, he charges the Lutheran and the Reformed churches as being prompted by "confessionalism and ethnocentrism" of their opposition to the legal recognition of the Orthodox Church as the "national church."[55] This they would unquestionably deny. He fails to recognize that it was the hope of these and the other minority religious communities that there would be a new understanding of the

---

[50]Ion Bria, *Romania: Orthodox Identity at a Crossroads of Europe* (Geneva: WCC Publications, 1995), 54 pp.; Earl A. Pope, "Review of Romania: Orthodox Identity at a Crossroads of Europe," Ion Bria in *Religion in Eastern Europe*, XVII (October, 1997), pp. 38-43.

[51]Ibid., p. 18.

[52]Ibid., p. 53.

[53]Ibid., pp. 47-48.

[54]Ibid., p. 43.

[55]Ibid., p. vii.

churches and their freedom in a democratic Romania. This would enable all of them (majority and minorities alike) to make their maximum contributions to the "soul" of a pluralistic Romania so that they could fully cooperate as equals before the law and the state to bring about the creation of a just, civil, and transfigured society.

Unfortunately, Bria has no word of understanding or reconciliation for the Greek Catholics who underwent tremendous suffering under the communist tyranny and accuses them of proselytism[56] because they are trying to reenter their Transylvanian villages and retrieve their locked churches. The destructive tension between the Greek Catholic and the Orthodox churches has been a source of deep concern for the Romanian state, and this led the Romanian senate recently to vote that in rural areas with several Orthodox churches at least one should be returned to the Greek Catholics, but the Patriarch has charged that this was unacceptable state interference, and the church's monthly periodical maintained that this decision was a form of Catholic proselytism and called upon the House of Deputies to reject it.[57] Actually the Greek Catholic leaders maintain that there are hundreds of former Greek Catholic churches in the rural areas that are under the jurisdiction of the Orthodox church but not even used.

It is readily apparent that the whole concept of proselytism is in need of much greater study and objective analysis than it has received. The majority churches in Eastern Europe make many charges of proselytism and ecumenical agencies frequently agree with them. The question remains, however, as to who will have the courage to tell the majority churches with all their political and social power that they also engage in forms of proselytism by claiming to possess the absolute truth and demeaning other perspectives, by creating and communicating caricatures of other religious communities or demonizing them, by demanding restrictions on the religious freedom of other groups because of their love of power, by instilling false fears regarding the subversion of the nation which they maintain they alone can defend, by encouraging discriminatory actions or even outright violence against those who would challenge their religious monopoly.

---

[56]Ibid., pp. 45-46.

[57]"Quick Resolution Urged to Dispute Over Ownership of Romanian churches" *ENI Bulletin*, No. 16 (August 20, 1997), pp. 18-19; Fautre, e-mail to Earl A. Pope re: "Romanian Parliament To Consider Controversial Law On Church," August 17, 1997, pp. 11-13.

In his conclusion Bria states that there is "no reason for an auto-matic skepticism" because there is "hidden treasure in the Romanian soil and soul." He senses deeply the criticisms that the minority reli-gious communities have made of his church, but he believes that there is "good precedent for hopes that the stone rejected by the builders will some day prove to be the cornerstone of the building."[58] Bria may well see the Romanian Orthodox Church ultimately as the key to the devel-opment of a profound form of ecumenism and religious freedom which can become a model or even a paradigm for the rest of Eastern Christianity. The minority religious communities would be the first to welcome this transformation in their midst. In that event one suspects that the leaders of the Orthodox Church would then find the "national church" mythology a very serious, if not insurmountable obstacle to their true mission and hopefully would unite their forces with the minority religious communities to fully achieve the priorities set forth for the Ecumenical Association of Churches in Romania.

---

[58]Bria, *op. cit.*, p. 54.

Bibliography of Published Works by Radu R. Florescu

A selected listing of publications by Radu R. Florescu

BOOKS

Florescu, Radu R. *In Search of Frankenstein*. New York: Warner Books, 1975.

_____, *The Struggle Against Russia in the Romanian Principalities: A Problem in Anglo-Turkish Diplomacy, 1821-1854*. Iaşi: The Center for Romanian Studies, 1997; reprint, Munich: Societatea Academica Romana, 1962.

_____, ed. *100 Years of American-Romanian Relations*. Roma: Editrice Nagard, 1982.

Florescu, Radu R., Stephen Fischer-Galati and George R. Ursul, eds. *Romania Between East and West: Historical Essays in Memory of Constantin C.Giurescu*. Boulder, Colorado: East European Monographs, 1982.

Florescu, Radu R., and Raymond T. McNally. *Dracula: A Biography of Vlad the Impaler, 1431-1476*. New York: Hawthorn Books, 1973.

_____, and Raymond T. McNally. *Dracula, Prince of Many Faces: His Life and His Times*. Boston: Little, Brown & Company, 1989.

_____, and Raymond. T. McNally. *In Search of Dracula: A True History of Dracula and Vampire Legends*. Greenwich: New York Graphic Society, 1972.

_____, and Raymond T. McNally. *In Search of Dracula: The Enthralling History of Dracula and Vampires*. London: Robson Books, 1995.

_____, and Raymond T. McNally. *The Life and Times of Dracula*. Boston: Houghton Mifflin, 1994.

_____, and Raymond T. McNally. *The Complete Dracula*. Boston: Copley Books, 1985.

_____, and Raymond T. McNally. *The Essential Dracula*. New York: Mayflower Books, 1979.

ARTICLES

Florescu, Radu R. "British Reactions to the Russian Regime in the Danubian Principalities, 1828-1834." *Journal of Central European Affairs* 31(April 1962): 27-42.

_____, "Captain John Smith and Romania," *East European Quarterly* 11, no.4(Winter 1977).

_____, "Chapters on Romanian Intellectual History, Education, the Arts,and Religion," In *Bibliography of South Eastern Europe*. Chicago: Chicago University Press, 1968.

_____, "Comments Concerning the Visit of General Hugh Scott at Jassy in the Summer of the Year 1917," *Anuarul Institutului de Istorie A. D. Xenopol* 32 (1995).

_____, "Contemporary Western Reactions to the Battle of Stalinesti," In *East Central European Society and War in the pre-Revolutionary 18th Century*. New York: Columbia University Press, 1982.

_____, "Cuza, Florescu and Army Reform," In *War and Society in East Central Europe: The Crucial Decade, 1859-1870*. New York: Columbia University Press, 1985.

_____, "Debunking a Myth: The Magyar Romanian National Struggle of 1848-1849," *Austrian Year Book* 12-13, no. 2 (August 1979).

_____, "Decision Making under Cuza: Baligot de Deyne (1820-1884)," *International Journal of Romanian Studies* 6, no. 1 (1984).

_____, "Dracula as a Hero: Apology for a Part-Time Monster," *International History Magazine* 1 (August 1973).

_____, "Dracula in Romanian Literature: From Budai-Deleanu to M. Eminescu." In *Eminescu, the Evening Star of Romanian Poetry*. Ann Arbor: Michigan University Press, 1986.

_____, "Dracula the Hero," *International History Magazine* 8 (August 1973).

_____, "Dumitru Florescu: A Forgotten Pioneer in the History of Romanian Music," *Unirea* 3 (1984).

_____, "Florescu si Reforma Armatei 1859-1866," *Din Istoria Militara a Poporului Roman* 12 (1984).

_____, "From the Memoirs of a Romanian Diplomat during the Roosevelt Era," In *The United States and Romania: American-Romanian Relations in the Twentieth Century*. ed. Paul D. Quinlan. Woodland Hills, California: American-Romanian Academy of Arts and Sciences, 1988.

_____, "General Ion E. Florescu," *Magazin istoric* 27, no. 1 (January 1993): 7-9

_____, "General Ion Emanoil Florescu: Father of the Romanian Army," In *War and Society in East Central Europe: East Central European War Leaders Civilian and Military*. New York: Columbia University Press,1988.

_____, "Hora lui Cuza," *Magazin istoric* 20, no. 1 (January 1986): 17-19.

_____, "Istoria Romanilor in SUA," *Ateneu* 6 (1987).

_____, "King Ferdinand: An Intimate View," *Revue Roumaine d'Histoire 35 (1995)*.

_____, "Lord Strangford and the Problem of the Danubian Principalities, 1821-1824," *Slavonic and East European Review* 34(June 1961): 472-488.

_____, "Magyar Culture in Socialist Romania," *Cross Culture Communications* (1976).

_____, "Myth and Reality: Captain John Smith and Romania," In *100 Years of American-Romanian Relations*. ed. Radu R. Florescu. Roma: Editrice Nagard, 19.

_____, "Nicolae Balcescu: A Forgotten Diplomat," *East European Quarterly* 5, no. 2 (Spring 1973).

_____, "Ottoman Relations with the Balkan Nations: Romania," *Balkanistica: Occasional Papers in Southeast European Studies* (1979).

_____, "Romanian-American Cultural Relations," *Magazin istoric* 16 (1982).

_____, "Romanian Culture in America," *Sinteza* 30 (1978.

_____, "Social Classes and Revolutionary Ferment in Nineteenth Century Bucharest," In *Romania Between East and West: Historical Essays in Memory of Constantin G. Giurescu*. eds. Radu R. Florescu, Stephen Fischer-Galati and George R. Ursul. Boulder, Colorado: East European Monographs, 1982.

_____, "Stratford Canning, Palmerston and the Wallachian Revolution of 1848," *Journal of Modern History* 35, no. 3 (September 1963).

_____, "The Birth of Romania: Fact or Fiction," *History Today* (May 1963).

_____, "The Dracula Image in the Works of the Folklorists Petre Ispirescu and C. Radulescu-Codin," *Cahiers roumains d'etudes litteraires* 3 (1977).

_____, "The Dracula Search in Retrospect," *The New England Social Science Bulletin* 43, no. 1 (Fall 1985-1986).

_____, "The Fanariot Regime in the Danubian Principalities," *Balkan Studies* 9, no. 2 (1968).

_____, "The Impact of the War of Independence on Romania," In *The Tragic Plight of a Border Area*. Los Angeles: American-Romanian Academy of Arts and Sciences, 1983.

_____, "The Influence of Bible Societies in the Development of the Romanian Literary Language," *Revue Roumaine d'Histoire* 31 (January-June 1992).

_____, "The Romanian Impact upon the Ottoman Tanzimat," *Revue Roumaine d'Histoire* 17 (January-March 1978).

_____, "The Romanian Principalities and the Origins of the Crimean War," *Slavonic and East European Review* 43 (December 1964).

_____. "The Russo-Turkish War of 1877-1878: Diplomatic and Military Preparations," In *War and Society in East Central Europe: Insurrections, Wars and the Eastern Crisis in the 1870s*. New York: Columbia University Press, 1985.

_____, "The Sulina Channel Controversy," In *Aspects des Relations Russo-Roumaine*. Paris: Minard, 1967.

_____, "The Uniate Church: Catalyst of Rumanian National Consciousness," *Slavonic and East European Quarterly* 25 (Spring 1991): 91-99.

_____, "The US Press and the Russo-Turkish War of 1877-1878," *Revue d'Histoire Modern* 26 (1979).

_____, "What's in a Name: Dracula or Vlad the Impaler?" *Balkanistica* (1980).

_____, "Vlad II Dracul's and Vlad III Draculea's Military Campaign in Bulgaria 1443-1462," *Romanian Civilization* 6 (Fall 1997): 23-35.